AN EPOCH AND A MAN

KENNIKAT PRESS SCHOLARLY REPRINTS

Dr. Ralph Adams Brown, Senior Editor

Series in

AMERICAN HISTORY AND CULTURE
IN THE NINETEENTH CENTURY

Under the General Editorial Supervision of
Dr. Martin L. Fausold
Professor of History, State University of New York

AN EPOCH AND A MAN
MARTIN VAN BUREN
AND HIS TIMES

DENIS
TILDEN
LYNCH

Volume II

KENNIKAT PRESS
Port Washington, N. Y./London

AN EPOCH AND A MAN

Manufactured by Taylor Publishing Company   Dallas, Texas

KENNIKAT SERIES ON AMERICAN HISTORY AND
CULTURE IN THE NINETEENTH CENTURY

CHAPTER XXXI

Van Buren's return to Albany was followed by a trip to Kinderhook to rest and to get away from politicians and newspapers. It was impossible to pick up a journal and not read of some new demand of the people of this or that State for a canal or highway. And every account, save in the rabid Bucktail press, must refer to Clinton and the Canal, whose final link, from Buffalo to the Great Lakes, would be completed in the fall. Clinton was a national hero. In the spring the citizens of Philadelphia tendered him a banquet at which the Mayor presided. A little later Ohio and Kentucky invited him to visit these States. He accepted; and his journey was made a triumphal tour. The merchants of New York City subscribed $3,500 for a pair of silver vases in recognition of his services to the city.

The spontaneity of these testimonials alarmed the friends of Adams and Jackson. Clinton was outstripping them in popular favor. Jackson, who had again resigned from Congress, was once more proposed by the Tennessee Legislature as a candidate for the Presidency.

Clinton was Jackson's supporter, yet Adams had offered him the first place in his Cabinet and most important diplomatic post at his disposal. Van Buren was Clinton's enemy, yet Adams worked like a Trojan to elevate him to the United States Supreme Court. These strange alliances were passing, and with them the Era of Good Feeling, which produced them. In May of this year, Adams revealed his change of heart toward Van Buren. He confided to Samuel L. Southard, his Secretary of the Navy, "of the transactions and correspondence which preceded the appointment of Smith Thompson as a Judge of the Supreme Court of the United States . . . and the distant and disguised graspings of Van Buren, both at that office and a mission abroad." The foreign mission was the ministry to the Court of St. James's. Adams now bracketed Van Buren with Webster: "a combination of talent, of ambition, of political management, and of heartless injustice."

283

The "heartless injustice" was confined to the realm of partisan or factious politics. Van Buren had also turned against Adams because of his partiality to Clinton. His future lay in opposing Adams. This would probably mean an alliance with Jackson; and in New York, Jackson spelled Clinton, unless Clinton were defeated for reëlection in 1826.

Mutual friends of Clinton and Van Buren arranged a meeting between them; but failed to compose their political differences. Their relations, however, became friendly. In midsummer Van Buren found himself a passenger on the boat for Albany with Clinton. He had a letter from Dr. Cooper—the same Cooper with whom Senator Dickerson had walked to jail upon his conviction under the Alien and Sedition Laws—in which the old Jeffersonian, now head of Columbia College in South Carolina, discussed the possibility of Clinton for President. Cooper admired Clinton; but he believed that Clinton would come under the domination of the clergy. This apprehension was based on Clinton's recent address before the Bible Society. Van Buren handed Clinton the letter, who colored as he read it. As he returned the communication, Clinton smilingly observed that Cooper's fears were groundless.

Then came the second day of November when a cannon thundered its welcome to the waters of the Great Lakes as they flowed into the Canal. Big guns were placed within sound of each other along the entire length of the waterway, and on the banks of the Hudson. Each piece was fired after its fellow to the north was discharged, until the people of New York City were made aware of the union of the waters of the Great Lakes and the Atlantic by the booming of the field piece at the Battery.

Every one of importance in the State, save Van Buren, accompanied Clinton and his party from Buffalo to New York; Van Buren could not, as the State's representative in Congress, avoid joining the party somewhere along the route. This he did at Albany. Clinton remembered, when they reached Manhattan, the stricture of the Bucktails on him and the Canal: "a ditch fit to bury its author in." This was years ago, when he first proposed it. The ditch opened the West to settlers.

It was altogether an eventful month. On the last Monday of November the country had its first taste of opera, when Van

Buren's wine seller presented the famed Garcia family at the
Park Theater in *Il Barbiere di Siviglia.*

The beginning of the next week saw Van Buren in Washington. Until this session his career had been as colorless as that of
the average timeserver. More than once, in statesmanlike speeches,
he displayed a knowledge indicating a life-long study of the
subject in hand. Those who shared his confidence knew that he
was utterly ignorant of many of the questions he discussed so
profoundly until he began his painstaking research of the documents bearing on the matter. This ignorance was a carefully
guarded secret: the first to detect it was Jackson.

Before Van Buren left for Washington he had instructed
his son, John, not yet sixteen years old, to visit their kin and
friends at Kinderhook before spending the Christmas holidays
with the Duers at their home in Greenbush, across the river from
Albany. He wrote reprovingly to the boy, who was studying at
Yale. In this, the first intimate family letter of Van Buren's extant, he bares a grief which we cannot but share; and reveals
how he tried to take a mother's place in the lives of his children.

My dear Son
   I am as you supposed somewhat surprised to hear that you went
direct to Greenbush. I wrote you advising you to go to Kinderhook &
to visit Albany from thence. I know the kindness which induces Mr &
Mrs Duer to wish to have you at their house, & approve your taste
for being pleased with the good society you meet there, but I fear
your Kinderhook friends will think themselves neglected as I think
they well may. You know the pain it gives me [to] express dissatisfaction with your conduct, but I would do injustice to both, were I
not to say that the amount you give me of your expenditures is far
from satisfactory.
   You say you have spent $150 in six weeks, & instead of giving
me an account of it, or even speaking of its absolute necessity, you
tell me of the expenditure of other boys, & the declaration of [Js.
Backner?] as to how much he had spent. You have nothing to do with
the expense of other Boys—when I proposed to make you the depository of your funds, I did so (you know) agt. the opinion & advice of
others—My wish was to excite your ambition to shew that you was
free from the weakness of other boys in this respect, & more deserving
of confidence than they too often are. I endeavored to impress you
sensibly on this point, and assured you solemnly, that the moment I

had reason to apprehend that my confidence was not safely placed, I would withdraw it. I will not judge you definitively until I hear [from] you, but if the amount you give me of your disbursements is not such as it should be, I shall assuredly, promptly, & peremptorily change my course, & leave it to Mr Croswell to advance you from time to time what money you may want—Let me therefore hear from you directly upon this subject.

I sincerely hope you will be able to explain to me this matter fully as I shall be uneasy until you do so—

The money is the least, by far the least, of my concern.

Make my most affectionate regards to Mr & Mrs Duer & all the children.

Your affectionate father

M. V. Buren

Mr John V. Buren

At this early age the habits of this exceptionally brilliant youth were fixed. These traits were to provoke this characterization from Godkin: "aristocratic in his bearing, in his habits, in his training and tone of thought."

On the second day of the session Adams informed Congress that an invitation had been accepted to send ministers to the Congress of American Republics on the Isthmus of Panama to participate in its deliberations "so far as may be compatible with that neutrality from which it is neither our intention, nor the desire of other American States that we should depart."

Back of this movement, as the documents exhibited to the Senate in Executive session disclosed, was the first step toward a close defensive confederacy of the American Republics,—a step further than the Monroe Doctrine contemplated. Under the Senate rules all documents communicated to it by the President shall be kept secret. Van Buren sought to circumvent this by having the Senate adopt an innocent-looking resolution reading:

Resolved, That upon the question whether the United States shall be represented in the Congress of Panama, the Senate ought to act with open doors; unless it shall appear that the publication of documents, necessary to be referred to in debate, will be prejudicial to existing negotiations.

Resolved, That the President be respectfully requested to inform the Senate whether such objection exists to the publication of the documents communicated by the Executive, or any portion of them;

and, if so, to specify the parts, the publication of which would, for that reason, be objectionable.

"Delicate and ensnaring," observed Adams, in noting that "these resolutions are the fruit and ingenuity of Martin Van Buren." And thus he analyzed the design of the resolves: "The limitation was not of papers the publication of which might be injurious, but merely of such as would affect existing negotiations; and this being necessarily a matter of opinion, if I should specify passages in the documents as of such character, any Senator might make it a question for discussion in the Senate, and they might finally publish the whole, under color of entertaining an opinion different from mine on the probable effect of the publication."

In answer to the resolution Adams said:

Believing that the established usage of free confidential communications, between the Executive and the Senate, ought for the public interest, to be preserved unimpaired, I deem it my indispensable duty to leave to the Senate itself the decision of a question, involving a departure, hitherto, so far as I am informed, without example, from that usage, and upon the motives for which, not being informed of them, I do not feel myself competent to decide.

This indirect reflection on the motives of the Senate rankled in the breasts of many. After several days of secret sessions, the Senate adopted a resolution lifting the seal of secrecy from its debates on the propriety of sending envoys to the Congress.

Van Buren appealed to the fears of the Senators supporting the administration—and they were in the majority—by reminding them that supporters of the first Adams had imposed their will upon the early Republicans, and that these triumphs of the Federalists were but forerunners of their self-destruction. And the President they were supporting now, he intimated, had been one of the detested Federalist Party. He denounced the Mission as unconstitutional and violative of Washington's admonition against entangling alliances.

Answering the argument that a confederacy of American Republics was necessary to counter the aggressiveness of the Holy Alliance, Van Buren said:

Wherein consists our objections to the Holy Alliance? Because they confederate to maintain governments similar to their own, by force of arms, instead of the force of reason, and the will of the governed. If we, too, confederate to sustain, by the same means, governments similar to our own, wherein consists the difference, except the superiority of our cause? What is their avowed motive? Self-preservation and the peace of Europe. What would be ours? Self-preservation and the peace of America. . . .

I detest, as much as any man, the principles of the Holy Alliance. I yield to no man in my anxious wishes for the success of the Spanish American States. I will go as far as I think any American citizen ought to go, to secure to them the blessings of free government. I commend the solicitude which has been manifested by our Government upon this subject, and have, of course, no desire to discourage it.

But I am against all alliances, against all armed confederacies, or confederacies of any sort. I care not how specious, or how disguised; come in what shape they may, I oppose them. The States in question have the power and the means, if united and true to their principles, to resist any force that Europe can send against them. It is only by being recreant to the principles upon which their Revolution is founded; by suffering foreign influence to distract and divide them; that their independence can be endangered.

But happen what may, our course should be left to our choice, whenever occasion for acting shall occur. If, in the course of events, designs shall be manifested, or steps taken in this hemisphere by any foreign power, which so far affect our interest or our honor, as to make it necessary that we should arm in their defense, it will be done: there is no room to doubt it.

Van Buren had no more staunch ally than Senator Randolph of Virginia,—John Randolph of Roanoke, as he usually signed himself. Genius had set her chaplet on his brow a bit awry. No one approached him in eloquence in the Senate: Webster was still a member of the House. He had wealth, broad acres, a large stable; he raced his horses and bet on them; he played cards and gambled on them. Clay gambled; Jackson gambled; every one in their class gambled. George Poindexter, Senator from Mississippi, told Jackson and Van Buren of holding an unbeatable hand in a game of brag with Clay. The Secretary of State had lost heavily, and driven desperate by his losses, Clay bet, or bragged, his hotel and lands at Cincinnati against a named sum. Clay would be

MARTHA JEFFERSON RANDOLPH
After an engraving by J. Serz

ruined financially if Poindexter saw his brag. **Poindexter** laid down his invincible hand. Often Clay would remind Poindexter that he once had him in his power—the only man, he would always add.

Randolph had opposed Van Buren's resolution requesting the President to indicate the parts of the documents which could be published without prejudicing the pending negotiations. But after Adams replied, the attitude of the Virginian underwent a violent change.

Randolph of Roanoke had been drinking heavily. Bottled porter was his chief tipple at this session. Under its stimulus his erratic nature was whipped into extremes which knew no curbing. Appeals had been made to Calhoun to call Randolph to order, but he pleaded that he was without power. "This was tolerated by Calhoun," wrote Adams, "because Randolph's ribaldry was all pointed against the Administration, especially against Mr. Clay and me, and because he was afraid of Randolph." Replying to those who wanted him to hold his liquorish tongue in leash, Randolph, in a speech on the Cumberland Road bill, said:

A good deal has been said, sir, about the dignity of this Assembly; about its being improper to talk vernacular English here—we must speak so superfine and mincing that nobody but an accomplished lady from a female seminary can understand us. Is that the case in the House of Commons, or even in the House of Peers? . . . have not assertions, not the most delicate, been made on the floor of both Houses of Parliament, in the House of Peers, with all its robes and wigs, and everything else? Was it not broadly insinuated, over and over again, that there was an adulterous intercourse between the Dowager Princess of Wales and the Earl of Bute, the favorite? Is this very delicate? Is this very sentimental and refined?

Ten days later, on March 30, Randolph, ribald as before, began an oration—drunk or sober he was eloquent—which stands alone in deliberative bodies. Quiet reigned as he rose. Many who blushed at the things he said, remained lest they might miss some phrase worth cherishing.

Before Randolph had proceeded far, it was evident that he intended to make his attack on the Panama Mission a vehicle for personal abuse of the President and the Secretary of State. He said that the proposal was patterned on the abortive attempt by Webster two years earlier to send a mission to Greece, and a resolution offered at the same time by Clay, which asserted that this country would not see, "without serious inquietude, any forcible interposition by the allied powers of Europe to restore the South American Republics to Spain."

In the concomitance of these circumstances on January 20, 1824—a resolution by Webster of Massachusetts, and another by Clay of Kentucky—Randolph saw "an alliance . . . between old Massachusetts and . . . young Kentucky, not so young, however, as not to make a prudent match, and sell her charms for their full value."

Many were hoping that Randolph, who believed the charge of bargain and coalition, would stop here. Randolph then took his audience to England, where he had spent the summer of that year, and returned to Washington in time for the deadlock when —this with fine sarcasm—"the knowing ones [were] . . . intriguing about the Presidency; trying perhaps, to make some dirty bargain about the Presidency, when the question was settled as far back as January, 1824."

Later he referred to "the mover of this resolution . . . about South America [Clay], to whom it does not become me to allude." Followed some prurient allusions, and then:

Sir, in what book is it—you know better than I—in what parliamentary debate was it, that, upon a certain union between Lord Sandwich, one of the most corrupt and profligate of men in all the relations of life, and the sanctimonious, puritanical Lord Mansfield, and the other ministerial leaders—on what occasion was it, that Junius said after Lord Chatham had said it before him that it reminded him of the union between Blifil and Black George?

There was no mistaking that Randolph was comparing the President to Lord Mansfield and to the canting hypocrite in *Tom Jones;* and his Secretary of State to Lord Sandwich and to Fielding's debased character.

Next he drew on *Gil Blas* for invidious comparisons, and then this: "I say I will prove . . . that the President has dropped an extinguisher on himself . . . by the aid of this very new ally. I shall not say which is Blifil and which is Black George."

There were gasps at this. He followed with the charge, which had no other foundation than his copious draughts of porter, that the Spanish documents sent to the Senate by the President, had been forged in the office of the Secretary of State. "My suspicious temper may have carried me too far—if it has, I will beg pardon—but will show enough—not a handkerchief—not to justify the jealousy of Othello—yet I believe that the jealousy might have been pardoned to the noble Moor, certainly by me, had he not been a black man; but the idea to me is so revolting, of that connection, that I can never read that play with any sort of pleasure—see it acted I never could."

Then he bared an old hate for all the Adamses. He began deriding the second Adams as "an apostle of universal liberty," and condemned the first Adams as "an apostle of monarchy." "I was in New York when he [John Adams] took his seat as Vice President," he went on. ". . . I was a schoolboy at the time, attending the lobby of Congress when I ought to have been at school. I remember the manner in which my brother was spurned by the coachman of the then Vice President for coming too near the arms blazoned on the escutcheon of the vice-regal carriage. Perhaps I may have some of the old animosity rankling in my heart, . . . coming from a race who are never known to forsake a friend or forgive a foe."

Having made this avowal and reference to his descent from Pocahontas, Randolph sketched his course against Van Buren in the secret session; and after reading that part of Adams's answer—the dirty lines, he called them—to Van Buren's resolutions which impugned the motives of the Senate, he exclaimed: "The innuendo was that our motives were black and bad. That moment did I put, like Hannibal, my hand on the altar, and swear eternal enmity to him and his, politically." Adverting to the closing hours of the secret session, he said: "After twenty-six hours' exertion, it was time to give in. I was defeated, horse, foot, and dragoons—cut up—and clean broke through—by the coalition, unheard of till then, of the Puritan with the blackleg."

Randolph spoke another quarter of an hour. But no one followed him save the stenographer. It was impossible, because the ears of all were ringing with the phrase: "the coalition, unheard

of till then, of the Puritan with the blackleg." Clay gambled, reck-
lessly as we know; but blackleg—he was not that.

A newspaper account erroneously quoted Randolph as saying that he held himself personally responsible for all that he
had said.

Adams ignored the vilification. Clay, on the assumption that
the newspaper had done justice to Randolph, immediately challenged.

The day following Randolph's speech was Friday. General
T. J. Jesup, bearing Clay's note, was unable to find Randolph at
his lodgings until Saturday. Jesup opened the interview by
announcing the position he occupied, adding that he was aware
that no one had the right to question him outside of the Senate
for anything said on the floor, unless he chose voluntarily to
waive the privilege. Randolph replied that he would never take
advantage of any subterfuge, and proposed that the General take
back his answer. Randolph had forgotten, in his excited state,
the punctilio of the occasion. Jesup recalled it by reminding him
that he should consult with friends before taking so important a
step.

"You are right, sir!" exclaimed Randolph, seizing the hand of
Clay's second. "I thank you for the suggestion. But as you do
not take my note, you must not be impatient if you do not hear
from me to-day. I now think of only two friends; and there are
circumstances connected with one which may deprive me of his
services, and the other is in bad health: he was sick yesterday and
he may not be out to-day."

Jesup assured him that any reasonable time which he found
necessary would be satisfactory.

Randolph had in mind Edward F. Tatnall, a Representative
from Georgia, and Senator Benton. Both were experienced in such
matters. Benton and his younger brother Jesse had exchanged
shots with Jackson and his friend, Colonel Coffee, at Benton's
hotel in Nashville, some thirteen years back. Jackson fell at the
first exchange, his left shoulder shattered. When the pistols were
emptied, dirks were drawn. One of these was wielded by Stokely
Hall, another friend of Old Hickory. Hall had seen Jesse's fire
bring down Jackson. Drawing his sword cane, he lunged, the point

striking a button on Jesse's coat with such force that the blade splintered as though made of glass.

Jesse, who had been recently shot in the buttocks in a duel with William Carroll, another fire-eating friend of Jackson, fell in the onslaught. While on his back he received several gashes on his arms before he was rescued by a peaceable Tennesseean. Coffee and Alexander Donaldson closed in on the elder Benton; their dirks inflicted five flesh wounds before the encounter was ended by several men of peace.

To the elder Benton, whose tirades against Jackson for acting as second to Carroll in the duel with Jesse had led to the affray in Nashville, Randolph repaired after Jesup had left him. Benton knew nothing of the challenge when Randolph entered. Was he a blood-relation of Mrs. Clay? was his visitor's first remark. On learning that he was, Randolph said that that put an end to a request he was about to make. Imposing inviolable secrecy, he confided that it was his intention not to return Clay's fire.

This was in keeping with the tall, gaunt, erratic Virginian. He could not deny Clay satisfaction; but he must not return Clay's fire: to do so would be to concede a point he would not yield, the right of any one to question him on a speech in Congress. ". . . and for any Speech or Debate in either House they shall not be questioned in any other Place." Thus ends Section 6 of Article I of the Constitution. This thought Randolph stressed in the acceptance which reads:

> Mr. Randolph accepts the challenge of Mr. Clay. At the same time he protests against the right of any minister of the Executive Government of the United States to hold him responsible for words spoken in debate, as a senator from Virginia, in crimination of such minister, or the administration under which he shall have taken office. Colonel Tatnall, of Georgia, the bearer of this letter, is authorized to arrange with General Jesup (the bearer of Mr. Clay's challenge) the terms of the meeting to which Mr. Randolph is invited by that note.

The seconds entered into an exchange of letters and interviews which lasted a week, in the hope that Randolph could be induced to offer an explanation that would satisfy Clay. But Randolph proved unyielding. Accordingly, the afternoon of Saturday, April 8, was agreed upon. The field of honor was a bit of Virginia on the right bank of the Potomac above the Little Falls Bridge.

There was a law against dueling in Virginia. Randolph, who was not a lawyer, believed that he would not violate the law by standing, a pistol in hand, to receive Clay's fire! And he had insisted on the interview taking place in Virginia that his State might receive his blood if he fell.

At noon on the day of the duel Benton called at Randolph's lodgings. His seconds were busy making codicils to his will. Benton's errand was to learn if there had been any change in Randolph's sentiments. He could not ask a question which would cast doubt on Randolph's word. But he found a way: he spoke of visiting Clay's home the night before, of seeing Mrs. Clay, tranquil and smiling, and the youngest child of the Clays asleep on a couch, and reflecting, as he viewed the peaceful scene, how different all might be the next night.

"I shall do nothing to disturb the sleep of the child or the repose of the mother," commented Randolph.

At that moment Randolph's servant Johnny entered with the information that officers of the local branch of the United States Bank said they had no gold.

"They are liars!" exclaimed Randolph. "Johnny, bring me my horse."

Benton waited while master and man galloped to the bank, Johnny riding forty paces in the rear, after the manner of the times. Randolph demanded all he had on deposit, and not bills, but money. Some four thousand dollars were to his credit.

"Have you a cart, Mr. Randolph, to put it in?" asked the teller, politely, as he began lifting sacks of silver to the counter.

"That is my business, sir," was the reply.

The cashier, attracted by the scene, learning the cause of Randolph's annoyance, explained that the wrong answer had been given to the servant. This appeased Randolph, who departed with nine gold pieces—his servant's original request—in the left pocket of his breeches. He was now ready to meet Clay.

On his return Randolph handed Benton a slip of paper on which he had written that if he fell, Benton was to take the nine gold pieces from his pocket, keep three, and give the same number to his seconds. He also delivered to Benton a sealed envelope to be returned to him if he survived.

As the hour approached, Randolph and his seconds, Colonel Tatnall and James Hamilton, Jr., a Representative from South Carolina, drove to the dueling ground in a carriage. The faithful Johnny, mounted on one of his master's thoroughbreds, served as outrider. In a second carriage sat Randolph's surgeon. Benton, who had been granted permission to be present, followed on horseback.

Benton was the last to reach the clearing in the forest where the seconds were carefully measuring ten paces. Randolph, who was sitting in his carriage waiting for the summons, called to Benton.

"Colonel," he said, "since I saw you, and since I have been in this carriage, I have heard something which may make me change my determination. Colonel Hamilton will give you a note which will explain it."

Benton needed to hear no more. He understood too clearly. One of his seconds had told Randolph something which might make him change his determination not to shoot at Clay. But the manner in which Randolph had stressed the word *may* indicated that he had not yet made up his mind.

Here a word of explanation is necessary. When the duel had been decided upon, the seconds threw dice for choice of position. Tatnall won. Consequently, this gave to Clay's second the privilege of counting off the time. It was agreed by the seconds that there was to be no practicing by their principals; and in the hope of further reducing the possibility of a tragedy, Jesup assented to giving the word in the quickest possible time.

Early that morning Jesup informed Tatnall that Clay would not consent to the word being given quickly. "If you insist upon it, the time must be prolonged, but I should very much regret it." Clay insisted. This is what Randolph had heard on his drive to the forest clearing. Tatnall cautioned his principal to fire quickly and carefully, and informed him that he would set the trigger on hair. Randolph answered that he did not want this. Tatnall argued, but to no avail. Randolph had not told his seconds of his resolve not to fire at Clay.

Within a few moments after Benton left Randolph the principals were called to the field. As they took their positions, still unarmed, Clay facing the slowly setting sun, they courteously saluted one another.

Presently Hamilton handed Randolph his pistol. Randolph called to Clay's second to repeat the word as he intended giving it when all was ready. This strange duel was opening in a manner characteristic of all things involving Randolph. And Jesup thus complied:

"Fire! One! [There seemed to be an eternity between the two words!] Two! [How long it took him to call it out!] Three! [Why couldn't he count faster?] Stop!"

There was no longer any doubt that Jesup intended giving the word slowly. Ordinarily Randolph would have been satisfied; but this was an unusual moment; so he asked Jesup to give the word again.

Jesup had about completed the request when a deafening explosion silenced his voice. Randolph, in adjusting the pistol butt to the palm of his hand, had accidentally touched the trigger.

Senator Josiah Johnson, of Louisiana, one of Clay's seconds, was carrying a loaded pistol to his principal. He stood stock-still when Randolph's pistol was discharged. Jesup was standing nearer Clay, and Tatnall was occupying the same relative position to Randolph. The surgeons of the two antagonists had assumed their positions, and the servants were partly concealed among the trees. Benton, too, was in the forest.

All turned toward Randolph, whose pistol at the moment of discharge was pointing almost straight downward. The ball had plowed a small furrow near his feet.

"I protested against that hair trigger!" exclaimed Randolph before the others had recovered from their alarm.

Tatnall, who was in duty bound to protect his principal from sacrificing himself, shamefacedly took the blame.

This unusual incident was at once the subject of an inquiry into its cause by Clay's seconds, which Clay ended with:

"It was an accident! I saw it."

The pistol was reloaded. The accidental fire preyed on Randolph's sensitive feelings. The generous remark of Clay only intensified his chagrin. He was fairly beside himself; but outwardly his emotions were under control.

Soon all was ready. The principals and their seconds were at their respective places, and Jesup slowly gave the word. Both men exchanged their fire simultaneously. Randolph, an excellent shot, had fired at Clay! Fortunately the bullet missed Clay's legs. Clay's bullet had torn a hole through the skirt of Randolph's coat.

Benton, who had been invited to the field as a mutual friend, strode quickly to the dueling ground and offered his services as mediator.

"This is child's play!" exclaimed Clay, with an imperious wave of the hand, a gesture to which he was prone. He demanded another fire. Randolph echoed the demand.

While the seconds were reloading, a slow, punctilious process under such conditions, Benton prevailed on Randolph to leave his post, and pressed on him to yield to some accommodation. But Randolph was angry with himself: first for the accidental discharge, which could be interpreted by the world at large to his dishonor; and again, because in the ensuing excitement he had fired at Clay. Randolph had taken deliberate aim at Clay's legs, below the knees, intending merely to foul his aim. He now regretted having done this; for after talking to Benton in his carriage he had renewed his resolution not to shoot. Who would believe this now, save the very few who knew him well? By this really unintentional shot he had violated the law of his State and admitted Clay's right to question him for words said in debate. In his disturbed state he showed impatience at Benton's kindly intentions and returned to his post.

This time the word was given by Tatnall. Clay fired. His bullet passed through Randolph's pantaloons. After receiving Clay's fire, Randolph discharged his pistol in the air, threw it to the ground, and rushed toward Clay, exclaiming:

"I did not fire at you, Mr. Clay."

Clay had followed his example and they shook hands midway on the field.

"You owe me a coat, Mr. Clay," said Randolph, as he laughingly pointed to the rent made by Clay's bullets. He had not noticed the hole in his pantaloons.

"I am glad the debt is no greater," said Clay fervently.

Benton joined the group and unbosomed all that Randolph had confided in him the preceding Saturday. And Randolph added: "I came upon the ground determined not to fire at you, but the accidental discharge of my pistol, with the circumstances attending it, for a moment changed my mind."

That evening Randolph, Benton, Tatnall, and Hamilton regaled themselves at Randolph's lodgings. The sealed envelope was opened: it directed Randolph's interment among his patrimonial oaks. Instructions were also enclosed to have seals made out of the gold coins in Randolph's pocket.

"But Clay's bad shooting shan't rob you of your seals," said Randolph. "I am going to London and have them made for you."

The measure which led to the duel was passed with four votes to spare. The slavery issue was not involved in the Panama Mission. The opposition was predicated almost wholly on factional grounds. Some of the objectors, in the course of the debate, did say that there could be no discussion in any foreign assembly of the country's settled policy of not interchanging diplomats with Haiti, then ruled by blacks. But this was chicane. Nine of the twenty-one Senators from the South who were present when final action was taken, voted for the Mission.

Into the same realm of factious fiction must be consigned the remark attributed to Van Buren after the bill was passed: ". . . if they had only taken the other side and refused the Mission, we should have had them." The secretary of the Mission was William B. Rochester, of New York, whose father had been a business partner of the father-in-law of Clay. Van Buren made a note of this.

But the caution displayed by Van Buren was thrown to the winds by his Regency while the seconds of Clay and Randolph were exchanging notes and interviews. No one in Washington misunderstood Van Buren's intentions toward the administration; yet on April 3, the leading editorial in the Regency's organ, the *Argus*, advocated a non-committal stand with respect to Adams and his program. Edwin Croswell, editor of the paper, advised Van Buren not to be surprised at the tone of the leader, and added: "Whilst there is a great aversion towards Mr. Adams amongst the Republicans of this State, there is a great aversion on their part to any collision with the administration which shall drive them to the support of Mr. Clinton, or that shall force them to encounter the hostility of both. They prefer, for the present at least, to stand in the capacity of lookers on, believing that the natural hostility between A[dams] and C[linton] will be certain of shewing itself, and the sooner if we afford them no other ailment than themselves."

The administration newspapers charged Van Buren with having written or dictated the non-committal editorial. The country rang with the charge, and many stories were invented to build up an image of non-committalism. The word *vanburenish* crept into the jargon of the day. Van Buren, who never took the trouble to deny the accusation, enjoyed some of the vanburenish anecdotes.

One of the stories, at which Van Buren laughed heartily, concerned a wager made by two of his friends that he would not answer any question definitely. Accordingly one asked Van Buren —so the yarn went—if he concurred in the general opinion that the sun rose in the east. Van Buren replied: "I presume the fact is according to the common impression, but as I sleep until after sunrise, I cannot speak from my own knowledge." This passed current for truth among many.

There was nothing more definite than Van Buren's opposition to the measures of the Adams administration, an opposition based almost entirely on partisan grounds. Clay was the great apostle of internal improvements. He was Van Buren's senior by three years. He had entered Congress as a member of the Senate seventeen years before. Van Buren in 1822 and 1823 had voted for toll gates and repairs on the Cumberland Road. But the next year, on the eve of the Presidential election, he introduced an amendment to the Constitution which struck at Clay.

This amendment would empower Congress to make appropriations for internal improvements under restrictions safeguarding the sovereignty of the States. The money from the national Treasury was to be dispensed by the State or States building the road or the canal; but no enterprise could be undertaken without the consent of each commonwealth affected.

In his efforts to injure Clay by holding him up as an anti-State-rights man, Van Buren overlooked that his proposal was in essence a negation of State sovereignty, as the States not benefited by the improvement would have to share the cost.

While opposing the Panama Mission, which was more Clay

than Adams, Van Buren introduced a resolution whose major resolve read: "Resolved, That Congress does not possess the power to make roads and canals within the respective States."

Van Buren's resolution left to a select committee the task of working out an amendment which was to be subjected "to such restrictions as shall effectually protect the sovereignty of the respective States, and secure to them a just distribution of the benefits resulting from all appropriations made for that purpose." There was more of crafty politics than statesmanship in this. The resolution died aborning.

He was consistent in this session. After the Randolph-Clay duel he opposed administration measures providing appropriations for work on the Cumberland Road, surveys for canals and roads, and for subscriptions by the government to two quasi-private canal enterprises. In voicing his objections to the government buying stock, Van Buren reminded the Senate that there was little analogy between this and an investment by an individual.

"Where an individual subscribed for stock," said Van Buren, "he had a personal, a direct interest, which caused him to move with caution, and to see that his interests were properly attended to . . ." He added that where aid was granted in the form proposed, abuses would creep in, and in nine cases out of ten, deception would follow.

While the partisan view of the issue largely governed his attitude, he never resorted to the harsh word. He expressed his guiding principle in debate at the beginning of the speech just quoted from, when he said that he did not wish to entertain feelings of asperity toward those who differed from him.

But he contrived to differ with every measure of moment advocated by the administration. He pictured himself and his followers as the defenders of State rights, and popular government. He made it impossible for any one to take personal umbrage, interspersing his speeches with such professions as: "Different views are taken on this subject by persons who are pure and honest."

Until this year the members of the United States Supreme Court attended circuits, and lived in their respective jurisdictions. The administration proposed to increase the number of circuits— no one could cavil at this—and to constitute the Supreme Court a court of appeals, as it now exists, and relieve the judges of the revisory body of the arduous labors of the circuit.

In arguing against relieving the judges of the Supreme Court from circuit work, he said that "the whole business of the Justices of the Supreme Court will be done here, and sooner or later, they would, in the natural course of things, all move to, and permanently reside at the seat of government." This was the intent of the bill.

Van Buren was for the additional judges, but no more. In this he was sincere: he was fundamentally opposed to centralized government. Had the proposed reform emanated from an administration he was loyally supporting, it would have met with the same vigorous opposition.

In Van Buren's masterful speech against the change, he quoted, without indicating the author, Jefferson's objections to the life tenure of judges, and the strictures uttered by the sage of Monticello on Van Buren's visit, against the impotence of the power of impeachment to remove an unworthy member of the court.

"I know well," said Van Buren, "that the opinion that the tenure of the office of justices of the Supreme Court is the rotten part of the Constitution, is entertained by men who have established for themselves imperishable claims to the character of saviours of their country, and benefactors of the human race."

This was Jefferson; but Van Buren disavowed these as his sentiments, explaining that his early and constant connection with the courts may have biased him. In arguing against the permanent residence in Washington of the members of the Supreme Court, and their separation from their brethren on the circuits, Van Buren made use of Jefferson's belittlement of the impeachment power.

"It is impossible, with the best intention on the part of the Executive branch of the Government, to avoid bad appointments," said Van Buren. "Influence and favoritism sometimes prevail, and to a want of correct information the Government is always exposed. Incompetent men, therefore, will sometimes be appointed."

This incompetency, he reasoned, would be shielded by the capacity and learning of the able men on the Supreme Court bench, but if all had to face the "public ordeal" of holding circuit, bad appointments were less likely to be made. Then he added:

"There is a power in public opinion in this country—and I thank God for it: for it is the most honest and best of all powers—which will not tolerate an incompetent or unworthy man to hold in his weak or wicked hands the lives and fortunes of his fellow-citizens. This power operates alike upon the Government and the incumbent. The former dare not disregard it, and the latter can have no adequate wish that they should, when he once knows the estimation in which he is held. This public ordeal, therefore, is of great value; in my opinion, much more so than what has, with some propriety, been called the scare-crow of the constitution—the power of impeachment."

In mild periphrasis, Van Buren accused the court of encroaching upon the rights of the States under cover of the provision prohibiting the enactment of "any law impairing the obligations of contract." It had been explained that this clause was inserted in the Constitution, he said, to negative the acts adopted between 1783 and 1788 by Virginia, South Carolina, Rhode Island, and New Jersey as reprisals for Great Britain's refusal to comply with the stipulations of the treaty of peace. The measures, although general in scope, were designed to prevent the collection of debts by Britishers.

Van Buren, without vouching for the correctness of the explanation of the origin of the clause, uttered this grain of wisdom: "if it be true that such was its object, . . . it adds another solemn proof to that which all experience has testified, of the danger of adopting general provisions for the redress of particular and partial evils." That Van Buren believed that this was the true explanation is evident from his speech.

Under the broad interpretation of this clause, the court has taken jurisdiction over acts of the State in which contracts are not expressed, "but implied by law, from the nature of the transaction." He continued: "Any one conversant with the usual range of the State legislation will at once see how small a portion of it is exempt, under this provision, from the seven judges of the Supreme Court. The practice under it has been in accordance with what should have been anticipated . . . if the question of conferring it was now presented for the first time, I should unhesitatingly say that the people of the states, might with safety, be left to their own legislatures and to the protection of their own courts."

He observed that it had been said that "there exists not upon the earth, and there never did exist, a judicial tribunal clothed with powers so various and important" as the Supreme Court. It decides whether or no the laws enacted by Congress are "pursuant to the Constitution, and from its judgment there is no appeal." Thus it could veto nine-tenths of the laws passed at each session.

"Although this branch of its jurisdiction is not that which has been most exercised," he continued, "still instances are not wanting in which it has disregarded acts of Congress, in passing upon the rights of others, and in refusing to perform duties required of it by the Legislature, on the ground that the Legislature had no right to impose them."

But his grievance did not lie in this direction, but in the nullification of "statutes of powerful States, which had received the deliberate sanction, not only of their legislatures, but of their highest judicatories, composed of men of venerable years, of unsullied purity, and unrivaled talents . . ."

There was courage in this speech, and Van Buren was not unaware of it. He said: ". . . a sentiment, I had almost said, of idolatry, for the Supreme Court, has grown up, which claims for its members an almost entire exemption from the fallibilities of our nature, and arraigns with unsparing bitterness the motives of all who have the temerity to look with inquisitive eyes into this consecrated sanctuary of the law. So powerful has this sentiment become, such strong hold has it taken of the press of this country, that it requires not a little share of firmness in a public man, however imperious may be his duty, to express sentiments that conflict with it."

He would unqualifiedly concede so much of the "high-wrought eulogies" as credited the members of the court with "talents of the highest order and spotless integrity." And he sincerely believed that "that uncommon man who now presides over the court [John Marshall] is, in all human probability, the ablest judge now sitting upon any judicial bench in the world."

"But to the sentiment which claims for the judges so great a share of exemption from the feelings that govern the conduct of other men, and for the court the character of being the safest depository of political power, I do not subscribe," he continued with feeling. "I have been brought up in an opposite faith, and all my experience has confirmed me in its correctness. . . . I believe that the judges of the Supreme Court, great and good men as I cheerfully concede them to be, are subject to the same infirmities, influenced by the same passions, and operated upon by the same causes that good and great men are in other situations."

Van Buren knew that the majority of the lawyers of the Senate shared these views, and that in his strictures on the bench, mostly by innuendo, he was voicing the sentiments of a goodly number of the Senators who were not of the law. Randolph, the day before his duel with Clay, spent two hours denouncing the court, and on Randolph's return from the field of honor, Senator John Rowan, from Clay's own State, indulged in a savage tirade against the bench.

"The Constitution now exists," said Rowan, mockingly. "The six courts and three judges created by that bill do not now exist. And yet, it will no sooner have passed into a law, than it will be asserted that these six courts and three judges, which will be created by the act, were created by the Constitution. The whole corps will assert it. The Bank of the United States will back the assertion with all its influence—with all its metallic intelligence . . ."

Few dared to talk about the Bank as Rowan did: its tentacles reached into the very halls of Congress, into editorial sanctums, into merchants' counting rooms, and to the hearths of the newest settlers on the nation's frontiers. Mortgages, loans, paid advertisements, retainers, and outright bribes,—these were the sources of its vast influence. It was the savings bank of the poor and the Treasury of the government. It made leaders, and destroyed them. Rowan received his cue from Governor Joseph Desha, who in his message to the Kentucky Legislature, in the preceding November, had denounced the Bank and all banks as hostile to the powers and rights of the States.

In the closing days of the session two select committees, appointed solely to keep alive the old animosities against Adams, and to create new ones, made their reports to the Senate. Benton was chairman of both, and Van Buren their directing genius.

The first report consisted of an amendment to the Constitution, recommended with all solemnity, although few in the entire Congress really believed in it. This provided for the direct election of President and Vice President. The Electoral College would be abolished; but its essential feature was retained by dividing each State into districts coequal with the number of Congressmen from the State. The candidate receiving the largest number of votes in each district would receive the district's vote in the tally made in Congress. A second clause provided that in the remote event of a tie, the two candidates receiving the highest number of district votes would again go before the people at a subsequent election to be held in December; if the seemingly impossible were to happen, and neither received a majority the contest was to go into the House.

Van Buren said that it was too late to act upon the resolution now, but that if he lived, he would press it to a conclusion at the next session; for on no one point were the people more united than "upon the propriety, not to say the indispensable necessity, of keeping the election of the President from the House of Representatives." His sole purpose in advocating the measure was to provide those who had voted for Jackson, Crawford, and Clay with fresh fuel to fire their abating anger.

The second report was accompanied by six bills aimed at an old evil. One deprived the President of designating newspapers for government subsidies in the shape of advertisements and gave the distribution of largesse to the members of Congress. Three others dealt with the country's fighting forces: two transferred the appointment of cadets and midshipmen from the President to the Congressmen; a third prevented a President from dismissing officers of the Army and Navy without just cause.

The remaining two struck at the root of the evil of Federal patronage. One was designed to keep honest collectors and disbursers of revenue in office during their good behavior by mandating the appointing power to inform the Senate of the reasons for removals of men holding places of public trust. The sixth bill provided for Senatorial confirmation of postmasters receiving a salary in excess of a sum to be determined. The attendant publicity, it was believed, would reduce the use of the Post Office Department for political purposes to a negligible factor.

By innuendo Adams was accused of all the wrongs which the measures sought to correct. The report of the select committee, having in view the covert attacks made by Randolph and others on Adams as a monarchist in disguise, said that the names of rulers meant nothing: the first Roman emperor was called the Emperor of the Republic: the late French emperor had a similar title: and if the patronage of the President of the United States was not curbed, and the press freed of the bribery of government advertising, the people might awake some morning to cheer the Emperor of the Republic of the United States.

This report was a fitting prelude to the disgraceful campaign of 1828.

CHAPTER XXXII

VAN BUREN returned to Albany happier than when he had left it in the fall. His plan of attack on Adams had been successful. But it might turn out to be so much labor for Clinton. He had found at Washington considerable sentiment for his old foe, due largely to the completion of the Canal. If Clinton were reëlected Governor, he would be New York's favorite for the Presidency. And Van Buren, more than once, pictured himself managing Clinton's campaign.

The fiftieth anniversary of the birth of the nation was observed July 4. Van Buren retired that night not knowing that the day was made more memorable by the deaths of John Adams and Thomas Jefferson. They had served on the committee of the Continental Congress charged with drafting the immortal document to which Jefferson's name is forever attached; both had directed the nation in its early years. These and like recollections were mentioned reverently at meetings held wherever the Stars and Stripes floated, when the stages brought the tidings. And many saw the interposition of Providence in the singular coincidence.

Toward the end of the month a sudden change came over members of the Regency. During the past winter they had told Clinton that he would not be opposed for reëlection. Van Buren was agreeable to this; but Silas Wright and other aides of Van Buren could not endure Clinton. Van Buren made no effort to stem this sentiment, lest he distract the party. He did not want a conflict, as he did not want to jeopardize his return to the Senate when his term expired on March 3.

On September 21 Clinton was unanimously renominated at Utica. The Regency was for naming William Paulding of Westchester County, and called a convention for this purpose at Herkimer on October 4. Two or three days before the meeting Van Buren summoned Wright and other aides to a conference in Albany and told them that deep as was his respect for Paulding he had strong objections to running him against Clinton. One was that Paulding and most of his county had been opposed to the construction of the Erie Canal; another was that their choice had a monomania regarding his physical perfections, believing himself strong as Hercules and handsome as Adonis. Van Buren recalled that this vanity of Paulding was common gossip in the State, and reminded his hearers of Clinton's powers of ridicule, and pictured Paulding laughed out of the campaign by Clinton's sallies.

Van Buren revealed a plan which amazed even these intimates, who knew him as a master unapproachable in the realm of intrigue. He sketched the history of the last election, when the coalition of the Clinton-Jackson faction with the friends of Adams and Clay had contributed heavily to the overthrow of the Regency. He reminded them that it was public property that Adams had privately offered the first post in his Cabinet to Clinton, and upon his declension had appointed Clay; and it was a matter of record that Adams had tendered the highest diplomatic honor to Clinton. Consequently, Adams, Clay, and Clinton were one in the public mind, and the supporters of the Administration would vote for Clinton unless the Regency named a man closely identified with Adams and Clay, and thereby gave his nomination the appearance of being dictated by Washington.

Van Buren had the man: William B. Rochester, Secretary to the Panama Mission, and, as we also know, son of a business partner of Clay's father-in-law.

Rochester was nominated, and the Regency spread the report that the National Administration had forced his nomination. No denial of this fiction came from Washington, and the deceit worked as Van Buren anticipated. Tens of thousands of votes which would have gone to Clinton were cast for Rochester. Enough Van Burenites were elected to the Legislature to return him to the Senate. The vote for Governor was close, but every indication pointed to the defeat of Clinton. For four days after the polls closed the result was still in doubt.

Clinton and his wife were members of the Presbyterian Church. Van Buren sometimes attended Clinton's church, a habit he had acquired through his wife, who in her closing days embraced its teachings. Marcy visited Van Buren on the Sunday following Election Day. Both were discussing the belated returns when the siren announced the arrival of the steamboat from New York.

A minute later a friend of Clinton ran past Van Buren's window in the direction of the Governor's residence. No one but the bearer of good news would be in such haste, observed Van Buren to Marcy as he pointed out the messenger. Marcy suggested that his friend was needlessly alarmed.

On their way to church Van Buren predicted that the mystery would be solved when the Clintons came to service: if the messenger brought word of victory, the Governor and his wife would be late, as they would entertain the visitor; if bad news, they would hasten to church. Never was Van Buren more distracted at his devotions. He was noted for his vigorous voice during the congregational singing, but his thoughts were not upon hymns now. His attention was on the pew reserved for the Governor, which remained unoccupied until the services were well under way. Van Buren and Marcy were seated across the aisle. As Mrs. Clinton settled herself in her seat she glanced triumphantly at her husband's enemies.

"The election is indeed lost," Marcy whispered mournfully to Van Buren as the Governor's wife turned her gaze from them.

Clinton had won by the narrow margin of three thousand, six hundred and fifty; Henry Huntington, nominee for Lieutenant Governor, was defeated by Nathaniel Pitcher, the Regency candidate.

The election was a distinct shock to the Regency. All had expected Clinton's defeat by at least ten thousand. Van Buren, anxious to make up his losses on his bets in the election of two years before, had wagered heavily, and on the very eve of the balloting he wrote to Churchill C. Cambreleng, one of New York City's Congressional delegation: ". . . Dont forget my bets. I cannot think of letting this election go by without making up for most losses. If you cant bet on ten thousand you may on nine or a suit of clothes or 8. thousand."

The Regency reluctantly agreed that Clinton could not be ignored as a Presidential possibility. Not a word passed between Clinton and Van Buren; but after the latter left for Washington, the Governor learned from one of the Regents—Knower, Marcy's

father-in-law, maintained friendly relations with the Governor—
that Van Buren "would place him on an equal footing with his
compeers in the Presidential canvass." Marcy sent Van Buren a
summary of political happenings in which he noted: "Gov Clinton
has said that Gen Jackson's popularity is on the decline and that
you would be convinced of it when you got to Washington. Is
that so?" The reply is missing, but several incidents indicate that
Clinton thought Van Buren was with him; for in the Legislature
Clinton's friends voted for Van Buren's reëlection.

But Van Buren had made up his mind in favor of Jackson
at least three days before he was reëlected to the Senate as evi-
denced by a letter introducing to Jesse Hoyt a subscription
solicitor of the *Telegraph*, recently established at Washington
in the interests of Jackson. "Any assistance you can give him in
promoting his object will be gratefully remembered by the editor
and oblige your friend," wrote Van Buren.

Jackson's popularity was not declining. Aiding Van Buren
in directing the canvass for Old Hickory were Edward Livingston, New York's quondam Mayor, and now, after five years of
service in the House, a member of the Senate from Louisiana;
Jackson's old foe—and older friend, Senator Benton; the unscrupulous Samuel Swartwout; Duff Green, editor of the *Telegraph;* and William B. Lewis, husband of a niece of Mrs.
Jackson.

After Congress adjourned on March 3, Van Buren, accompanied by Cambreleng, made a short political tour of the South
on behalf of Jackson. At a dinner given at Raleigh to his
colleague, Senator Robert Y. Hayne, of South Carolina, he spoke
on State rights. He visited Crawford at his home in Georgia, to
obtain first hand—his enemies later charged—the whispered
story that Calhoun, while Secretary of War under Monroe, had
proposed at a Cabinet meeting that Jackson be punished for his
high-handed acts in the Seminole War.

On May 12 Van Buren paid Adams a morning call; and the
President entered in his diary: "Van Buren is now the great
electioneering manager for General Jackson, as he was before
the last election for Mr. Crawford. . . . His discourse with me
this day was upon the late Mr. Rufus King, his history and

character, and upon Mr. Monroe and his affairs; also upon the Petersburg horse-races, which he has been attending."

The next day, Sunday, Van Buren started homeward with Cambreleng. It was generally reported that Jackson, if elected, would make Van Buren his Secretary of State, would support him for President at the end of his term. The campaign of 1832 was already well under way.

An editor supporting Adams applied to James Barbour, the Secretary of War, for a copy of the order of execution of the six militiamen which Jackson had signed. Adams told Barbour that compliance would be considered a measure of hostility to Jackson, and suggested a refusal. When a Jackson editorial supporter joined in the request the next week, Barbour thought it would now be proper to make public the documents; but Adams remained of the same mind: he did not want a second term through unfair means.

Jackson was campaigning with a reckless zest. On June 5, nearly two years after the Bargain and Corruption calumny had been refuted, Jackson revived it. He wrote to Carter Beverly of North Carolina that "a distinguished member of Congress" had proposed, in the name of friends of Clay, to vote for him in the House if he would declare that Adams would not be continued as Secretary of State; and that he had replied that before he would sit in the President's chair through bargain and corruption "he would see the earth open and swallow both Mr. Clay and his friends and himself with them!"

This was not a difficult thing for Jackson to fancy, believing, as he always did, that he had been robbed of the Presidency by Clay and Adams. In this letter Jackson insinuated that the proposition had been made to him at the instance of Clay, and added that immediately after he had refused to bargain, Clay came out for Adams.

Jackson's word was challenged. He replied that the "distinguished member of Congress" was James Buchanan, then in his third term in the House of Representatives. The future President of the United States, an ardent supporter of Jackson, failed to sustain the General's charge. He said that he had gone to Jackson as his friend, and not as the agent of Clay or any one else;

and that he did not believe or suspect that Jackson thought otherwise until he saw the revival of the charge in print.

As the summer waned, and after Clinton was nominated for President by meetings in Virginia, Ohio, and elsewhere, an article appeared in the *Evening Post*, declaring that Clinton was not a candidate for this high office, and that his choice was Jackson. Clinton realized that the best he could hope for was second place, as Jackson's nomination had long ceased to be in doubt.

Although the election was a year and some months away, the partisans of Jackson and Adams were canvassing with an intensity usually reserved to the last weeks of the most stubbornly contested struggles. It was a campaign of scurrilisms of which the least vile was Jackson's revival of the Bargain and Corruption calumny. The supporters of Adams replied with more of the coffin broadsides and attacks on the good name of Mrs. Jackson. The General's friends published a defense written by Judge John Overton, who knew all the circumstances of Jackson's courtship of Rachel Donelson Robards. Quickly followed attacks on the honor of Adams, which plumbed the depths of the original mud when it was said that he had surrendered an American servant girl to Czar Alexander, "*e più volte carnalmente la cognobbe.*" Charges of wasting public funds, and of defrauding the Government while Minister to the Russian Court, which could have been disproved by citing the record, Adams treated with the same contemptuous silence.

Van Buren was of Adams's mind on this. On September 14 he wrote to Nashville advising the General to refrain from issuing any more defensive publications. He began by saying that Jackson's election could be prevented only "by some indiscretion of our own." Then he struck at Clinton with: "For four-fifths of the time since 1800 the old Republican Party has possessed the power of this state. It does ⁻ɔ now to a greater extent (the Gov. alone excepted) than it has done for many years." Then followed the advice:

One word more & excuse me for the liberty I take in referring to it. I can well appreciate your feelings under the torrents of malignant vituperation to which you have been exposed, & I am sensible of the difficulty of avoiding replies to direct applications which are (sometimes with the best intention but not unfrequently from mere vanity on the part of their authors) made to you from different parts of the Union. But I think I hazard nothing in saying that for the future the case must be an extreme one that can make full explanation from you personally necessary. The obvious design to bear you down by calumny has produced a great reaction, & I am quite certain that they have so much overacted their parts as to render their past as well as future vituperation entirely harmless. Our people do not like to see publications from candidates. It is a singular fact that in almost every case in which they have (with us) been attempted on the eve of an election they have operated agt. the cause they were intended to serve.

Knowing how peppery Jackson was, Van Buren added: "Do not infer from this that it is my intention to complain of the past. On the contrary I am clearly of [the] opinion that all that has been done was not only proper but unavoidable and has been useful." Van Buren's advice was followed.

Van Buren believed in campaign literature—of the right sort. He directed the preparation of numerous pamphlets and like contributions. Hamilton—Alexander's son, James A.—also penned at least one laudatory tribute to Jackson's personal character. These effusions, before being given to the public, were gone over carefully by Van Buren and his "board of censors"— as he described his Regents in a letter to Cambreleng.

A word on one of the calumnies of this campaign. The most baseless of all is still repeated. The day Van Buren called on Adams after his Southern electioneering trip, Adams entered in his diary: "He [Van Buren] is now acting over the part in the affairs of the Union which Aaron Burr performed in 1799 and 1800; and there is much resemblance of character, manners, and even person, between the two men." Adams is occasionally periphrastic.

Van Buren resembled Burr in manner as did any other courtly citizen of the day. The chief characteristic of Burr's private life—his affairs with women—was absolutely lacking in Van Buren. They were adepts in the art of political intrigue, and great lawyers; but Van Buren was Burr's master in each field. In person they were alike in one respect only: their smallness of stature. Here all physical comparisons cease. Burr, stood five feet six, and was a little taller than Van Buren. Van Buren had yellow hair; Burr's was brown; Burr had dark hazel eyes; Van Buren's were blue; Van Buren had a Roman nose; Burr's was pronouncedly retroussé.

In Parton's *Recollections of Winfield Scott* occurs: "Speaking of Martin Van Buren, for whom General Scott had a great regard, he alluded to the popular tradition that the ex-President was the son of Aaron Burr. He gave a decided denial to the scandal, and adduced convincing reasons for rejecting it."

With more plausibility the pothouse politicians might have said that Van Buren was the son of Napoleon; for there was an undeniable kinship in noses.

During the summer and early fall, Van Buren remained most of the time in Albany, receiving county leaders, and directing affairs outside the State by post. Hamilton was enlisting old Federalists of substance in Jackson's cause. Before this missionary work began, which was mainly carried on by letter, Van Buren wrote to Hamilton: "Does the old gentleman have prayers in his house? If so, mention it modestly." Van Buren kept a check on the newspapers, and when the Jacksonian press blundered, he hastened to correct the error, as is instanced by the following to Cambreleng:

> I am sorry to see that a paper of so much real promise as the Courier should fall into so great a mistake as to speak lightly of the Morgan affair. Depend upon it that this course may do us much injury. There never was in any part of the world a more deep & general solicitude upon any like subject than now pervades the western counties in relation to the fate of Morgan. You will see by the Argus of today that last week there was a meeting of 3000 persons in one County. The editors are also mistaken as to the fact. There is no rational doubt that Morgan is dead & has perished by violence. Speak to them. . . .

The Morgan affair was then in its infancy. William Morgan had been dead for about a year. There was a hidden drama in his death which fired the imagination; and none, save his slayers, knew how he died, or how they had disposed of his body. And no one knew who had killed him, save his executioners, and they were not talking. Clinton, as Governor, had offered a reward of $2,000 —a princely sum in those days—for the apprehension of the guilty, and appointed a special prosecutor.

All that is definitely known is that on September 11 Morgan was seized at his home in Batavia, in the western part of the State, and taken by a company of men to Canandaigua on a petty criminal charge. He was acquitted of the count and immediately rearrested on a civil process for a small debt. Upon judgment being obtained he was committed to prison. The following night the debt was paid and he was taken from the prison by those who had obtained his release and thrust into a carriage and taken to Fort Niagara, where he was imprisoned in the magazine.

What happened after is not a matter of record: that he was slain is beyond question.

Before Morgan's abduction his neighbors knew that he was engaged in publishing a book purporting to reveal secrets of the first degrees of Free Masonry. Local Masons were accused of having abducted Morgan, and subsequent investigation revealed that the disappearance of Morgan was not known to any man, Mason or non-Mason, outside of the two western counties of Genesee and Monroe, until after search of him had been instituted.

When Van Buren wrote to Cambreleng, the affair was being capitalized by petty politicians who raised the cry that the entire Masonic fraternity was behind Morgan's abduction, and that Governor Clinton, as Grand High Priest of the Grand Chapter of Royal Arch Masons, had ordered the execution of Morgan! Van Buren was not concerned in Clinton, but he was in Jackson, who was also a prominent Mason, and whose name was being linked up in the mysterious disappearance of Morgan.

Van Buren realized that the Jacksonian press, in view of the General's lifelong affiliation with the order, must not deny the known facts. In the western part of the State, many who were not Masons, were demanding proscription of all Masons. A candidate for State Senator in the Western District was rejected because he was a Mason, and T. H. Porter, a non-Mason, nominated in his stead. In this obscure convention was the germ of an organization which was to introduce bigotry into American politics on a national scale.

Early in October Van Buren, whose moods are often reflected in his letters, asked Cambreleng to collect a debt from an unnamed Colonel. "You have really disappointed me in getting the money

from the Col. so soon," wrote Van Buren on October 22. "If you
will come & live with me I will make you my Collector General."
Then he added, with his usual disregard for punctuation: "Why
dont I get the wine. Let me have it before Thursday at least the
dozen that has been drawn of[f] on that [day] I give a dinner
to all the young Jackson Blood in the city." That he practiced
the rigorous economy he preached to his son is evident from the
following: "I wish to stay at your house but I cannot afford to
pay $2 a day for a room nor will it do for me to be stuck up in a
garret." He was not seeking luxurious couches as his next line
indicated: "When I was there in the Summer I had N°. one with
a cot in [it] & was comfortable. . . ."

On Thursday, November 25, Van Buren complimented John
on his progress at Yale, and urged his son to take his fair prospects as a stimulus to continued and renewed exertions. "I leave
here on Tuesday for Washington in indifferent health but good
spirits," he wrote John. His good spirits were due not only to the
reports of John's improvement in his studies, which tended to
belie the reports he had heard of John's fondness for the tavern,
but to the progress of the campaign. The Jacksonians had
elected a majority to the Legislature; gains were reported in
other States.

CHAPTER XXXIII

No happier man than Van Buren answered the opening roll call of the first session of the Twentieth Congress. Another fifteen or eighteen months and the Senate would know him no more. John would have his degree by then. They would practice law together. But Fate had planned otherwise. Van Buren was soon to plead his last cause in court, and his Congressional career was to end with the present term.

For the first two months Van Buren paid more heed to the campaign than to legislation. His first speech of any length was on January 28 on the bill giving half pay to officers of the Revolution. But not until the debate on the vain efforts to clothe the Vice President with power to call a Senator to order did Van Buren take a stand on any controversial question. In leading the opposition Van Buren characterized the proposal as violative of the Constitution and referred to the Bank of the United States as "the first of Constitutional encroachments."

This speech was delivered on February 11. That day Clinton had been at his office in New York's Capitol, and read his mail, heavy with letters praising him for the reference in his annual message to the wanton attacks on Mrs. Jackson. After dinner that evening, while seated in the library talking to his two sons, his head fell forward in eternal sleep. Within the week the news reached Washington. Clinton was not quite fifty-nine years old.

Two days passed. On the evening of the 18th, Representative Thomas J. Oakley, who succeeded Van Buren as State Attorney General, wrote to Van Buren that there would be a memorial meeting of the New York delegation in the Capitol the following morning. Oakley said that Nathaniel Sanford— shelved to make way for Van Buren—who had been elected to fill King's seat, would be present, and added: "I suggest, whether, under existing circumstances, *you* ought not to take the lead in this business—with some appropriate resolutions and remarks— Such a step will be well received in our State."

Van Buren's speech that morning showed that the death of the Governor had dazed him. He said little. He referred to Clinton's talents; to the Canal—"the greatest public improvement of the age"; and then: "For myself, sir, it gives me a deep-felt, though melancholy satisfaction to know, and more so to be conscious that the deceased also felt and acknowledged, that our political differences have been wholly free from that most venomous and corroding of all poisons—personal hatred." This might have better been left unsaid. But we must remember that he was speaking extemporaneously and under intense emotion.

"In other respects," he continued, "it is now immaterial what was the character of those collisions. They have been turned to nothing, and less than nothing, by the event we deplore." His heart now began to speak, and after a few words more he said:

"I, who whilst living, never,—no never, envied him anything, now that he is fallen, am greatly tempted to envy him his grave with its honors."

When Jefferson died, debts swallowed his estate. Clinton, too, died penniless; and while the people mourned, the sheriff sold the roof over the heads of Clinton's widow and children.

Van Buren was now without a rival in New York.

As the session progressed it was apparent that Van Buren was determined not to alienate votes from Jackson by speeches on doubtful subjects. Another Cumberland Road appropriation gave him an opportunity to declaim on State rights. But this and his reference to the Bank were his only ventures into the realm of the controversial.

The debate on the most important economic measure introduced in Congress since its beginning, started May 5. This was Clay's "American System" with a list of imposts objectionable to the South. The Southern Senators sought to destroy the bill by adding oppressively high duties, so that the bill became known as the "tariff of abominations." Early in the year the New York Legislature had instructed its Senators to vote for a duty on wool. Van Buren, who before long was to espouse free trade, interpreted the instructions with extreme liberality and voted for the entire tariff. During the entire three weeks of debate he uttered not a single word, save to announce his vote.

This silence, in view of Van Buren's acknowledged leadership of his party in both houses, was unprecedented and remains unparalleled. Two years earlier he had voted against the repeal of the impost on salt. Local motives then governed, as New York taxed its own salt production to pay for the Canal. At the same session he also voted to reduce the duties on wines, teas, and coffees. The division on the "tariff of abominations" was sectional. Sixteen of the seventeen Southern votes were cast against the bill. The only other opposition came from five New England Senators. The entire delegations from the Middle Atlantic and Western States with six New England Senators and one from Louisiana supported the tariff. It was this division, together with the rôle he played as campaign manager for Jackson, which dictated the silence of Van Buren.

When the debate was at its height Van Buren was made downcast by reports from Yale. Briefly he wrote his son: "It has given me great pain to receive a letter from the President of the College informing me that he was instructed by the faculty to inform me that your conduct in not attending at the chapel in the morning was cause of dissatisfaction & that it would be necessary *to increase* your exertions greatly to enable you to succeed with any thing like credit at the examination in July. I hope it can only be necessary to inform you of the circumstances to secure your prompt and indefatigable exertions." A month earlier, he had written to the youth: "I send you a check for the $200 but am bound to say that taken in connexion with the amount previously advanced your expenses for the last six months are unreasonably high. Send me the items that I may not suspect you of the folly of extravagance."

On his return to Albany Van Buren made his last appearance as a lawyer. This was in the case of Varick *vs.* Jackson before the Court for the Correction of Errors. When Van Buren finished, the court turned to Burr, the senior counsel. Burr announced he could add nothing to what his assistant had said.

Had Clinton lived, he would have been renominated for Governor, and the union of the Clintonians and the followers of Van Buren would have meant a clean sweep in the State for the Jackson electors. Most of the Clintonians joined the Adams following. The Bucktails must nominate their most outstanding man for Governor; they had agreed to retire Nathaniel Pitcher,

Governor since the death of Clinton, because he had not shown sufficient subserviency to the Regency. Late in the spring Van Buren decided to make the race himself.

This was political expediency at its worst. If Jackson were elected, Van Buren would be Secretary of State, so that he could not serve as Governor more than two months and three days: his running mate, Enos T. Throop, would serve the remainder of the term as Governor.

The Anti-Masonic party was extending itself, and nominated Francis Granger for Governor, and John Crary for Lieutenant Governor. This party of proscription was against Jackson because Jackson was a Mason.

The Adams convention in New York nominated Smith Thompson for Governor. This was the first time that a member of the United States Supreme Court permitted his name to be dragged through the mire of a State campaign; for he did not resign from the bench. There was a working arrangement between the Adams delegates and some of the leaders of the Anti-Masonic party, and Granger was named for Lieutenant Governor. The leaders of these two anti-Jackson groups hoped to unite forces, carry the State for Adams, and defeat Van Buren and Throop.

Crary agreed to decline the Anti-Masonic nomination for Lieutenant Governor after Granger tendered his declension of the major nomination. Crary, for a reason never explained, failed to live up to his part of the agreement. In vain it was urged upon him that an Anti-Masonic ticket would only divide the Adams vote for Governor and would result in the probable election of Van Buren and Throop. Then the real character of the backers of the movement was revealed when the corrupt Solomon Southwick was named for Governor in Granger's stead.

Thompson was made the target of the Jackson party, who recalled that the people in ratifying the State constitution, had declared that a judge holding office during his good behavior ought not to be a candidate for elective office. This legally only applied to the State judiciary; but, morally, it applied with even greater force to the highest court in the land.

Van Buren was elected as a result of the division created in the ranks of the opposition by the Anti-Masonic party. He polled 136,783 votes, three thousand less than the combined votes of

Thompson and Southwick, who received 106,415, and 33,335, respectively. Jackson carried eighteen of the thirty-four Congressional districts, which assured him twenty from New York in the Electoral College, as the majority would choose the Electors-at-Large.

In this campaign the Adams men called themselves National Republicans; the Jacksonians styled themselves the Democratic-Republican party.

The Friday following election Van Buren wrote to Hoyt: ". . . We shall . . . have enough votes to put Jackson's election out of all question, and what is over is only important on the score of bets." The next week he went to New York to collect his winnings. While in the city he wrote to the President-elect —whom he addressed as "My dear General": ". . . We lost two or three Districts by the disgraceful direction given to the excitement growing out of the Morgan affair. But we have enough and to spare. I will not harass you by a description of the virulence that has characterized the contest in this State."

One of the canards which waddled through New York's campaign was a droll bird. It was said that Van Buren sprayed his side whiskers with *eau de Cologne* and gave up part of each morning and evening to posing before his mirror.

While working on his message to the Legislature, a bit of gossip concerning himself gave him much amusement. Suspecting Cambreleng, he wrote him: "You rogue you—you have put me in a peck of trouble—Throughout *my* dominions—The story is that I am to be married to M^{rs}. O. S. in a few weeks & all upon your authority— . . . If Gen. Jackson has any regard for me I hope he will let me try and execute you under the seccond [*sic!*] section & I shall ask no farther favour from him. . . . & if you speedily give me a detailed account of all the sayings & doings of Washington as well in the female as political departments I may forgive you for bringing all the young & old & middle aged women in the State upon my back. . . ." This is the only reference we have seen to the mysterious Mrs. O. S.

Van Buren was inaugurated Governor on January 1, 1829. In his few weeks he accomplished more than many executives who served their full terms. In his annual message he recommended several noteworthy reforms. He urged the choice of Presidential

Electors by general ticket, instead of districts; he advocated a law limiting the use of money in elections to printing. This was also enacted into law; but was permitted to remain a dead letter. A third recommendation urged the separation of State and National elections. This desirable reform was opposed by his Regents. He did not press it.

Another admirable proposal, which was almost immediately carried into effect, protected the public from wildcat banks. There were forty banks in the State, with aggregate deposits of $30,000,000, and a paid-in capital of half that amount. This financial reform created a "safety fund"—hence the name given to the innovation—to be maintained by contributions from the banks not to exceed more than half of one per cent annually on their capital. This fund, designed to redeem dishonored notes of member banks, was guaranteed by the State, so that henceforth the scrip of a defaulting institution would be taken up by the commonwealth. The idea of the "safety fund" was suggested by Joshua L. Forman, of Syracuse, but perfected by Van Buren and two friends. In his message, while disclaiming authorship, he proudly proclaimed himself its sponsor.

He paid a gracious compliment to the achievements of Clinton; he reviewed the accounts of the State's finances, its public works, its institutions of learning and benevolence; and philosophically adverted to the lamentable virulence of the campaign: "These excesses are the price we pay for the full enjoyment of the right of opinion, which is emphatically the birthright of the American citizen."

There were clamorous demands for more canals. Impressive petitions had been submitted to Van Buren by the advocates of these projects. He could not, without hurting his party in the State, avoid mention of these applications in his message. He talked at length about them, but the nearest to a recommendation was his declaration that the State ought to apply such portion of its means as could be spared from other necessary objects on works on internal improvements. But he did not say when, nor did he commit himself one way or the other on the merits of any of the various proposed canals. "Non-committalism," commented his adversaries.

On January 15, Charles E. Dudley, of Albany, was elected

Van Buren's successor in the United States Senate. A less competent man would have been hard to find. Dudley's qualification, which he displayed as a member of the State Senate, was his absolute subserviency to the Regency. He could not make a speech, and was so shy that he could converse only with difficulty.

Marcy was broke. He needed a well-paying job badly. Van Buren appointed him to the Supreme Court and made Silas Wright State Comptroller.

The cries of the faithful for patronage were heeded with few exceptions. Behind one of his refusals is the Van Buren of private life. Tammany demanded all the places in the State Health Department's Quarantine Station on Staten Island. Why they did not get one place is explained by Van Buren in the following apologetic message to Hoyt: "I cannot dismiss Dr. [Joseph R.] Manley. His extraordinary capacity is universally admitted; and his poverty, and misfortune in regard to the new Medical College which he brought into existence but failed to get a place in it, has excited a sympathy for him with medical men in all parts of the State of unprecedented extent. Mr. Clinton was so sensible of it that he once actually nominated him for health officer, and was upon the point of doing it again the very week when he died. His removal if made could only be placed on political grounds." Hoyt was the New York representative of New York's spoils system, now on the eve of being made a national institution.

The formal tender of the first place in the Cabinet was made on February 15. On its receipt five days later, Van Buren accepted. Not until March 12 did he resign as Governor. His followers in both houses immediately adopted resolutions approving his acceptance of the place in Jackson's Cabinet. Senator William H. Maynard protested, saying that the resolves could not be adopted with propriety, as Van Buren, in consenting to be a candidate for Governor, gave an implied pledge that if elected, he would serve the full term of two years,

CHAPTER XXXIV

It was dark when Van Buren reached Washington. On alighting from the stagecoach he was followed into his hotel by a swarm of office seekers. He was weak from illness and the fatigue of his trip. He showed it. But that did not deter the office-hungry horde from trooping after him into his room, grouping themselves round him when he threw himself upon a sofa. He listened to their pleas for an hour, committing himself to nothing. Then he excused himself—as he had apprised them he would—to pay his respects to the President.

As the door of the White House opened, Van Buren found himself in a vestibule lighted by a solitary camphine lamp. In his weak condition his first impression was one of gloom. In the President's office he again saw a single light, a glimmering candle on the desk. His morbid feelings vanished in the warmth of Jackson's greeting; and then he noticed the glowing logs in the fireplace.

Jackson's health was also low. He still grieved over the loss of his wife. He believed that her death in the previous December was hastened by the shameful attacks upon her in the campaign. Discovering that his visitor was in no shape for a protracted interview, Jackson told him to return to his lodgings and rest, and come back on the morrow.

Van Buren's political pamphleteer of the recent campaign, James A. Hamilton, had been Acting Secretary of State since March 4. Van Buren quickly picked up the threads of the office. From Hamilton and other friends he heard the gossip which had not found its way into the newspapers. All the New York delegation was talking of the visit to the White House of Solomon Van Rensselaer, who knew that Chauncey Humphry and at least three other Van Burenites were trying to displace him. After a cordial greeting by the President, the Albany postmaster, instead of making his exit through the East Room, seated himself on one of the sofas. Here Jackson saw him when the rest of his visitors had departed, and was about to engage him in conversation when Van Rensselaer blurted out:

"General Jackson, I have come here to talk to you about my office. The politicians want to take it from me, and they know I have nothing else to live upon."

Before Jackson could reply, the old soldier excitedly began to remove his coat.

"In heaven's name what are you going to do?" asked Jackson. "Why do you take off your coat in this public place?"

"Well, sir, I am going to show you my wounds which I received in fighting for my country."

Van Rensselaer's coat was now off.

"Put it on at once, sir!" commanded Jackson. Remembering the older man's years, and his excitement, he added softly: "I am surprised that a man of your age should make such an exhibition of himself."

Jackson averted his head as he said good-by to the old man, whose first commission, "Captain in Squadron of Light Dragoons," bore Washington's signature. Jackson's eyes were suffused with tears. Van Rensselaer did not lose his place while Jackson was President.

There was another side of Jackson. When Joseph L. White, delegate from the Florida Territory, inquired why twelve officials in Florida had been displaced by men "most of whom could be shown fitter candidates for the treadmill than public office," Jackson passionately replied he had been abused from Dan to Beersheba for the removals, but that not a single man had been removed except for oppression or defalcation. White repeated Jackson's remark to Van Buren and demanded that he particularize the acts of oppression or defalcation. "The President's recollection must be at fault," replied Van Buren. "We give no reasons for our removals." And he wrote in similar tone to a clerk in his own department.

Van Buren's hand is evident in the case of John McLean, a Methodist minister, who had served as Postmaster General under Monroe and Adams. When McLean refused to be party to the removal of postmasters solely on political grounds, Jackson got rid of him by appointing him to the United States Supreme Court. William T. Barry of Kentucky was then placed at the head of this department, the principal source of the spoilsman. Barry did what was expected of him.

Van Buren early saw the possibility of building up a political machine with the aid of the Post Office Department. We have seen him trying his hand at it in 1822, when he wrote to Knower, Marcy's father-in-law, that the Post Office Department was "one of the most interesting departments of the government, and instead of spending our time in small matters, I am for taking the bull by the horns at once . . ." He explained that he hoped to induce President Monroe, with the aid of Vice President Tompkins, to convert the department, in so far as it affected New York, into a spoils machine. There was no Monroe to hinder him now.

The evidence, documentary and otherwise, all points to Van Buren as the originator of the extension of the New York spoils system to our national government. Before he left Albany for Washington the removals were under way: but he had written to Hamilton: "If the General makes one removal at this moment he must go on. Would it not be better to get the streets of Washington clear of office holders first in the way I proposed? . . ." When Van Buren attempted to enlist the entire Monroe administration in his fight against Clinton nearly ten years before, we recall that he wrote to Rufus King: ". . . he [Clinton] has collected around him a set of desperadoes, who, instigated by the hope of official plunder, will never be content to limit their depredation to the boundaries of this State, but would if successful here, without doubt, extend their incursions abroad . . ."

Clinton was dead; the set of desperadoes that existed then only in Van Buren's fancy were now alive in the flesh, and conducting their incursions with a cruelty and thoroughness that shocked and astonished the country, which remembered that Adams had removed only two men, and both for cause. And it was plunder—to use Swartwout's word—that many of them were after. Samuel Swartwout, Jackson's political majordomo in New Jersey, wrote to Jesse Hoyt while Van Buren was en route to Washington: ". . . I hold to your doctrine fully that no damned rascal who made use of his office or its profits for the purpose of keeping Mr. Adams in, and Gen. Jackson out of power, is entitled to the least lenity or mercy, save that of hanging. So we think both alike on that head. Whether or not I shall get any thing in the general scramble for plunder remains to be proven; but I rather guess I shall."

Swartwout was seeking the biggest plum at the disposal of the administration, that of Collector of the Port of New York, with its revenues of $10,000,000, and perquisites sufficient to enrich a man in four years. He was not a resident of the State, but was well known to the politicians, and his reputation was very unsavory.

Van Buren had his allies throw several obstacles in Swartwout's path. Samuel D. Ingham, of Pennsylvania, Secretary of the Treasury, also opposed Swartwout. In April Van Buren wrote to Cambreleng: ". . . Mr Ingham has advised me to request you to get some fifteen or twenty of our strongest men to write to the President directly setting forth (mildly and kindly of course) but firmly and distinctly the objections to Swartwout's appointment. . . . Neither my name or [sic!] Mr. Ingham's must under any circumstances be mentioned in this matter except to Mr Walter Bowne [Mayor of New York City]. . . ." In this same letter Van Buren avowed his intentions to continue the proscription of Clinton's friends. The factional war had extended beyond the grave.

Swartwout was appointed because he was one of Jackson's "original friends"—to use Van Buren's phrase. Whereupon Cambreleng wrote Van Buren: ". . . if our collector is not a defaulter in four years I'll swallow the Treasury if it was all coined in coppers." Swartwout stole $1,222,705.69 from the Custom House receipts and fled to Europe with the plunder. He was indicted. When most of his money was gone a friend of his happier days met him in a drinking place in Algiers. Presently Swartwout burst into tears and sobbed that he could never return to his native land.

High and low felt the axe of the spoilsman. The hundreds of clerks in Washington, old men many of them, some carrying the honorable scars received in battle, suddenly found themselves without the jobs they had worked at for years. These, for the most part, were the shabby genteel of the land: There was the graybeard who had seen better days; the superannuated teacher or preacher distinguished by the worn coat, threadbare pantaloons and the immaculate white stock; the paterfamilias from the coun-

try, lured by the glamour of the Capital and the better schools
the vicinity afforded; the typical clerk, happy in his work, and
asking only to be let alone. These, or their types, had been here
since the seat of Government was moved from Philadelphia. Administrations came and went, but these humble ones were undis-
turbed till now.

"I turned out six clerks on Saturday," wrote Amos Kendall
in a letter to his wife. Kendall had just been made an auditor
in the Treasury Department. "Several of them have families and
are poor. It was the most painful thing I ever did. . . . Among
them is an old man with a young wife and several children. I
shall help to raise a contribution to get him back to Ohio."

There was a veritable Reign of Terror in the various departmental offices. Spies abounded who repeated anything said
in the least critical of the administration. The identity of the
members of the espionage corps was jealously guarded; consequently everybody suspected everybody else. Men who had been
longest in these small jobs dreaded their loss the most. They had
become accustomed to their groove. They could not move outside
of it. In Van Buren's own department a clerk went crazy at the
thought that he might be removed from his accustomed rut. In
the War Department, another unfortunate, similarly obsessed,
concealed his madness until he had slashed his throat from ear
to ear.

The case of Elbridge Gerry, son and namesake of the Signer
and Vice President, showed that the spoilsmen drew no distinctions. He was well on in years. The family fortunes were low.
His mother and four unmarried sisters lived with him. All were
dependent on his income as Surveyor of the Port of Boston. It was
not much, but it enabled them to keep up appearances. The Gerrys
and Adamses were friends for generations; naturally he supported
Adams in the campaign. Pocketing his pride he confessed to Jackson his political offense and his need of a job. Jackson promised
to keep him. Nine months later he heard that he was to be removed. He arrived in Washington as Jackson sent the name of
his successor to the Senate. Jackson flew into a rage when reminded of his promise. He denied making it, and ordered Gerry
from the White House for circulating a report that he had.

This is not the only instance of Jackson's broken promises

during the degrading orgy of removals and replacements. But he was distracted by intrigues, within and without his official family. No administration was so beset by storms. Jackson bore the brunt of them.

An occasional Adams supporter was temporarily continued in office. One of these was Van Buren's friend, John Duer. A few others equally well-connected in New York were also permitted to remain. Jesse Hoyt wrote to Van Buren a few days after the latter's arrival in Washington that he had found him a valet, who had previously been in the employ of William B. Astor, son of John Jacob Astor.

Hoyt was in a violent mood when he penned this letter. The heads of Duer and all others who had supported Adams must drop into the basket. Hoyt, who was seeking Duer's place, was offered the office of District Attorney of New York County through Van Buren's influence. This he spurned, and in his protest to Van Buren said: "I will hold no office from any political party that will keep Mr. Duer in his present station." Hoyt gave Van Buren a week in which to remove Duer from the office of United States Attorney of the New York district. If this were not done Hoyt said he would write a pamphlet on *The Life and Adventures of John Duer* "to hand in person to every member of the Cabinet." And Hoyt hurled covert abuse at Van Buren, as he had in an earlier letter.

"I never expected," answered Van Buren, "to see the day when I should be constrained, as I now am, to address you in the language of complaint. Nothing but my strong conviction of the extent and sincerity of your friendship could sustain me in resisting the belief that you have a settled purpose to quarrel with me. Here I am engaged in the most intricate and important affairs, which are new to me, and upon the successful conduct of which my reputation as well as the interests of the country depend, and which keep me occupied from early in the morning until late at night, and can you think it just to harass me under such circumstances with letters, which no ordinary man of common sensibility can read without pain? Your letter to me at New York contained many truths, for which I was thankful, and reflections which I thought just, but the whole were expressed in terms so harsh, not to say rude, as to distress me exceedingly. I have

scarcely recovered from the effect of so great an error in judgment, to say nothing else, when I am favored with another which
transcends its predecessor in its most objectionable features. I
must be plain with you. I have all my life (at least since I have
known you) cherished the kindest solicitude for your welfare, and
have manifested at least my good will towards you, and should
be extremely sorry to have occasion to change those feelings, but
it is due us both that I should say, that the terms upon which you
have seen fit to place our intercourse are inadmissable. . . ."

The salt was washed out of the wound with the subscription:
"Your friend and humble servant in extreme haste, M. V. Buren."
But Hoyt was not to be appeased with words. He reminded Van
Buren that he had labored twelve years in the city of New York
"to advance your reputation as a man, and your integrity as a
politician" and not without success. And he had no intention
of changing his sentiments, expressed in his letters or elsewhere.
He softened all he said by signing himself: "Yet, as I ever have
been, your friend, J. Hoyt."

Van Buren never let a friendship of long standing be sun-
dered by a display of ill temper. Hoyt was unscrupulous,—and
serviceable. There was a phrase in the last letter which characterized him far more than volumes could. He was hurt by Van
Buren's charge of rudeness, and rudeness, he observed, "always
detracts from the gentlemanly deportment I am most anxious to
preserve." Van Buren had unintentionally torn through the
veneer. Hoyt was mollified later when Duer was supplanted by
James A. Hamilton.

In the midst of these scrambles for office Van Buren found
himself thrown into intrigues unlike anything he had before en-
countered. One was his undoubted duty to solve. This was the
dread of Jackson which had been assiduously nurtured by the
Bank of the United States, both here and in England where a large
part of its stock was owned by the aristocracy. Jackson's election was regarded as ominous of war by the people of England,
whose leaders, inspired by the holders of Bank shares, went to
King William with their alarms.

Van Buren ended these apprehensions by inviting Sir Charles
R. Vaughan, the British Ambassador, to become well-acquainted
with Jackson as the surest way of assuring himself of the utter

falsity of this prevalent opinion. Vaughan was soon convinced of his error. Jackson, in his first message to Congress, changed the tone of England by observing that "with Great Britain, alike distinguished in peace and in war, we may look forward to years of peaceful, honorable, and elevated competition . . ." And to preserve these "cordial relations" was his avowed purpose.

Van Buren extended similar invitations to the rest of the diplomatic corps. The tact Van Buren had displayed in the political squabbles in New York, he was now successfully applying to world affairs.

There was one member of the diplomatic corps who was not a foreigner—to Van Buren. This was the Chevalier A. de Bangeman Huygens, Minister from the Netherlands. Van Buren would go, uninvited, to the home of the Huygenses to forget the cares of state in the charming company of the Chevalier and his lovely wife. Here he would gladly forego his customary glass of wine for Schiedam, which he sipped as he puffed away at a long clay pipe. Tender memories of the little tavern at Kinderhook were revived as they talked in the language that, as a lad, he knew better than English. He always greeted Huygens as "my Dutch brother."

In sharp distinction were his relations with his fellow Cabinet members. Although all were personally pleasant toward him, he was looked down upon because he had come into Jackson's camp in the eleventh hour. They felt the superior talents of Van Buren, a feeling which always rankles small minds. Save Van Buren, Jackson had selected mediocrities to head his departments.

Besides Barry and Ingham, Van Buren's colleagues were: John M. Berrien, of Georgia, Attorney General; John Branch, of North Carolina, Secretary of the Navy; and John H. Eaton, of Tennessee, Secretary of War. They were sycophants all. Jackson, although he arrived in Washington nearly three weeks before his inaugural, did not pay his respects to Adams, who retaliated by leaving only a servant to welcome Jackson to the White House. Jackson's conduct was inspired by his belief that Adams was behind the scurrilous attacks on Mrs. Jackson. Eaton, Branch, Ingham, and Barry felt that they must also snub Adams.

Van Buren had been in Washington a few days when he called on Adams, who noted in his diary: "Of the new Administration he is the only person who has shown me this mark of common civil-

ity. . . . All the members of his [Jackson's] Administration have
been with me upon terms of friendly acquaintance, and have repeatedly shared the hospitality of my house. I never was indebted
for a cup of water to any of them, nor have I given one of
them the slightest cause of offence. . . . Ingham is among the
basest of my slanderers, Branch and Berrien have been among
the meanest of my persecutors in the Senate. Among them all
there is not a man capable of a generous or liberal sentiment towards an adversary, excepting Eaton; and he is a man of inde-
cently licentious life."

The Eaton imbroglio had its beginning three months before
Van Buren arrived in Washington. Eaton, then a member of the
Senate, married the beautiful Margaret O'Neale Timberlake.
Peggy O'Neale, as she was then familiarly known, had been the
wife of Purser J. B. Timberlake, U.S.N., until the preceding
summer, when he made her a widow by taking his own life. The
accepted reason for Timberlake's act was his jealousy of Eaton,
who lived at the tavern which Peggy's father kept, and where
his daughter tended bar. It was a popular inn, and here, too, in
his brief Senate career, Jackson lived. Two other reasons were
advanced for the suicide: his fear of a drunkard's grave, and the
shortage in his accounts. Eaton was now oftener in Peggy's company; gossip grew louder; and before his appointment, Eaton
discussed the scandal with Jackson, who agreed with him that
marriage would silence the talk.

When Van Buren reached Washington the members of the
Cabinet and their wives, with the exception of Barry and Mrs.
Barry, were holding aloof from Mrs. Eaton. The appointment
of her husband as Secretary of War brought Mrs. Eaton a new
name—an allowable pun—Bellona. A detractor, with a knowledge
of Italian, prefixed the bellicose soubriquet with the definite article, ordinarily applied to a singer or a strumpet. La Bellona
did not sing. Besides Barry, La Bellona had a stout friend in
Jackson, who went far afield in his efforts to induce his official
family to accept Mrs. Eaton.

On his arrival in Washington Van Buren's mind was made
up: he would treat all members of the Cabinet and their families
on equal terms,—an easy solution for a widower. This further
endeared him to Jackson, who packed off his private secretary,

A. F. Donelson, and Mrs. Donelson, who was Mrs. Jackson's niece, when the latter refused to visit La Bellona.

The first snub given to La Bellona by the wife of a member of the Administration came from Mrs. Calhoun, the wife of the Vice President. And it also happened that before Van Buren was in Washington a month the movement to make Calhoun Jackson's successor had spread to New York. Calhoun was in Van Buren's way as Mrs. Calhoun was in La Bellona's way. Jackson was perhaps the only person in Washington who believed that an open rupture with his Cabinet could be avoided. Van Buren saw the hopelessness of it when he failed to persuade Mrs. Donelson to change her course, if for no other reason than the President's sake. Mrs. Donelson presided over the domestic circle of the White House. Her husband was working secretly for the political advancement of Calhoun.

The genius of Van Buren could not have invented an intrigue to approach in excellence the one he found ready made. Only a master would have remained unappalled in contemplating the situation or dared to give it direction. Van Buren was capable of both.

Jackson found recreation in the saddle. His companion on these rides was Van Buren. On these excursions into the neighboring countryside the two talked of everything in the world save the Eaton imbroglio—until a pleasant November afternoon. It was eight months since his administration began, and he had not as yet given the traditional Cabinet dinner. Jackson confided that he was fearful of declensions from all save Barry. When the ride was over Jackson had thrown off his fears. The invitations went out and all the Cabinet members and their wives attended, and no one snubbed La Bellona. It was obvious, however, that only the presence of Jackson himself prevented some untoward scenes; for the conversation at the table was rigidly formal, and the party broke up at a very early hour.

Van Buren now assumed direction of this unique affair. Many feared it would not end before some one was sent to join the unfortunate Timberlake. The President having shown the way, Van Buren, as the ranking member of the Cabinet, issued cards for a Cabinet dinner. As Van Buren lived alone, and the Secretary of the Treasury was the next ranking officer of the Cabinet, it

would not do to let this avowed enemy of La Bellona preside at
the table. Van Buren's ingenuity found a way out: he gave the
dinner jointly in honor of his Cabinet and Mrs. Thomas Mann
Randolph. Every one in Washington reverenced this sole sur-
viving daughter of Jefferson, now a widow. No one dared protest:
further, there was no occasion for objection. Mrs. Randolph and
all the members of her family had been fond of Van Buren from
the early days of their acquaintance. Van Buren had made her
son-in-law, Nicholas P. Trist, Jackson's private secretary. Mrs.
Randolph readily entered into Van Buren's plans, impelled by
those all-controlling qualities, ever present in woman, the love of
adventure and intrigue. She was curious to meet La Bellona, who
could crush an adversary with a toss of her Botticelli head, or
an almost imperceptible movement of the lips.

Ingham and Branch accepted for themselves, the latter coldly
informing Van Buren that "he is requested to say on behalf of
Mrs. Branch and the young ladies [their daughters] that circumstances unnecessary to detail deprived them of the pleasure
of dining with him." Berrien and Ingham sent excuses for their
wives. In declining on his own behalf, Berrien pleaded the traditional prior engagement. Barry and Eaton attended, but La
Bellona and Mrs. Barry remained away, taking refuge behind
suddenly acquired poor health.

This dinner was a choice morsel of gossip in the homes and
in the anti-Administration press throughout the country. But
still choicer morsels were in the making. Van Buren's intimate,
Sir Charles Vaughan, also a bachelor, gave a reception and ball
which La Bellona attended. Then Van Buren gave a second party,
and invited most of official Washington. Van Buren's cards were
hardly out before an article appeared in a local journal accusing
Van Buren and Sir Charles of intriguing to force La Bellona
on Washington society. The writer, who masked his identity behind Tarquin—the circumstances lent an unpleasant connota-
tion to the pseudonym—urged the ostracism of Van Buren for
his championship of La Bellona.

When the dancing commenced, Van Buren took advantage
of the distraction as his guests filed into the ballroom to snatch
a few minutes' repose on the lower floor. By so doing he missed
seeing an exciting encounter between La Bellona and the wife of

Major General Alexander Macomb, Commander-in-Chief of the United States Army. They had accidentally brushed one another with the elbows, whereupon each accused the other of willful assault, and displayed resentment in other ways.

The party was followed by one given by Baron Krudener, the Russian Ambassador. He, too, was a bachelor, and did not hesitate to invite La Bellona. And Van Buren was accused of having inspired the invitation which gave offense to so many. Mrs. Ingham, of course, absented herself, making the wife of the Secretary of War the ranking American woman present. Baron Krudener gave his arm to La Bellona, and together they led the guests—save two—into the dining room with its famous gold service. The exceptions were the Huygenses. The Baron, aware of the determination of the wife of the Dutch Ambassador not to break bread with La Bellona, had tried to persuade her to relent. But she remained obdurate, and departed with her husband.

With the coming of the New Year, gossip had it that Madame Huygens had consulted with the wives of the Cabinet members who would not associate with La Bellona, and that all four would give receptions from which the wife of the Secretary of War would be excluded. On January 6 the home of the Dutch Ambassador opened its doors to all official Washington save the proscribed lady. And rapidly followed similar parties at the homes of the Secretary of the Treasury, the Secretary of the Navy, and the Attorney General. Jackson, who had earlier doubted the reports, now believed that Madame Huygens and Mistresses Ingham, Branch, and Berrien had conspired to drive the Eatons out of Washington society and Eaton from the Cabinet.

In the last days of January Jackson sent for Van Buren. They talked over the events of which La Bellona was the pivot. Jackson did most of the talking. He was for dismissing the offending members of his Cabinet after he had sent Chevalier Huygens his passports. Jackson must first obtain proof of the conspiracy, which he reduced to an attempt to punish him for appointing Eaton.

Van Buren on returning to his office sent a note to his Dutch brother saying that he desired to see him on business, but as it would also be necessary to communicate with Madame Huygens, he would call at their house at their convenience. There was the usual affectionate greeting when Van Buren called, and he was at once invited to a pipe and Schiedam.

The Huygenses knew the object of the call, but being diplomats both, waited for their friend to speak his piece. Van Buren stated that the President disclaimed any intent or right to meddle with their social relations, and had no concern in whom they invited to their home; and then he repeated the gossip of the conspiracy. Madame Huygens declared she had been too long in diplomatic life to lend herself to such an enterprise. Van Buren waited only long enough to hear her disclaimer, as he was anxious to make a written report to Jackson, who replied: ". . . I am happy Madame H. has stated they are not true as far as she is concerned. . . ." This was dated the same evening as Van Buren's note, January 24, 1830.

This, of course, prevented Jackson's dismissing the Calhoun members of his Cabinet. They had never been other than mere departmental heads to Jackson. From the beginning of his administration he had depended on the advice of a group consisting of Amos Kendall and two other editors, Duff Green and Isaac Hill, and Jackson's artful neighbor, Major Lewis. They were all secondary to Van Buren. This was the Kitchen Cabinet.

Lewis alone approached Van Buren in guile; and long before the Eaton imbroglio was under way he had set out to destroy Calhoun. But it was not until January, 1828, when Van Buren dispatched his aide, James A. Hamilton, on an electioneering tour, that the dream began to materialize. Save for the presence of the son of Alexander Hamilton in this intrigue, the hand of Van Buren is nowhere visible. Hamilton's intimacy with Van Buren, in itself, is sufficient warrant for assuming that the master himself at least knew all that was going on. Lewis instructed Hamilton to see Crawford and what to say to him. Hamilton, failing to see Crawford, entrusted the mission to Forsyth, who under date of February 8 wrote to him that Calhoun had tried to have Jackson censured for his conduct in the Seminole War. Jackson had lured two Indian chiefs to an American ship flying the British flag, and hanged them. Equally reprehensible was his hanging of the aged Alexander Arbuthnot, a British subject who had spent many years trading with the Seminoles, and Robert Ambrister, a former lieutenant in the Royal Marines. To cap all this he took

ANDREW JACKSON
After an engraving by H. B. Hall

possession of Florida, then the territory of Spain, with which we were at peace. These highly censurable acts occurred three years after the Battle of New Orleans, and when Calhoun and Crawford were members of Monroe's Cabinet.

All this was kept dark by Hamilton, Forsyth, and Lewis until November, 1829, when the Eaton imbroglio was given momentum by Jackson's Cabinet dinner. A banquet to ex-President Monroe at the White House afforded the plotters the opportunity they had been seeking since the early fall when the Kitchen Cabinet decided that Jackson must run again in order to solidify the party. Eaton was now dragged into the conspiracy against Calhoun. After the coffee had been served, Lewis and Eaton discussed the letter from Forsyth to Hamilton so near to Jackson that the President overheard. Jackson asked questions.

Calhoun was doomed that night. He always distrusted Van Buren, and had appealed to Jackson not to appoint him to the Cabinet. After Jackson was satisfied that Calhoun had attempted to tarnish his military record, a story, inspired by Jackson, appeared in Van Buren's New York City organ, the *Courier and Enquirer*, advocating Van Buren for President if Jackson did not run again. The *United States Telegraph* replied that such talk was premature. Duff Green, Calhoun's sole ally in the Kitchen Cabinet, edited the *Telegraph*.

On December 31, twelve days after the *Courier and Enquirer* opened the war between the Van Buren and Calhoun editors, Jackson wrote Judge Overton lauding Van Buren as worthy not only of his confidence, but of that of the nation. "Van Buren was not an intriguer, but frank, open, candid, and manly; an able and prudent counselor, pleasant, and well qualified to fill the highest office in the gift of the people, who in him will find a true friend and a safe depository of their rights and liberty." And then this Jacksonian thrust at Van Buren's adversaries: "I wish I could say as much for Mr. Calhoun and some of his friends."

This letter was suggested by Lewis, who wanted Jackson's indorsement of Van Buren on paper, lest Jackson die suddenly: his health had been poor for months.

Jackson determined to destroy the "monster"—the Bank of the United States. Calhoun was silent on this. Jackson was for enforcing the tariff which South Carolina was opposing. Calhoun had encouraged the resolutions which the Legislature of his State had adopted: he had not yet propounded his defense of nullification, the right of a State to oppose by force of arms any act of the Union infringing upon her sovereignty.

During the first days of 1830 Van Buren directed his Regents to have the Jacksonians in the Legislature adopt resolutions urging Jackson to be a candidate for renomination. On February 13 his wishes were carried out. The following month Lewis had the Pennsylvania Legislature appeal to the President to serve his country another four years. He enclosed the appeal he wanted signed, and counseled his correspondent to secrecy, observing that it would not help to have it known that Jackson's friends in Washington were behind the movement.

Then came the first Jackson Day banquet. This was Calhoun's idea. On Monday, April 12, the day before the celebration, Van Buren visited Jackson, as he believed Calhoun and his supporters intended to conduct the proceedings at the dinner in a manner "portentous of danger to the Union." There had been gossip that nullification would be thrust to the fore, and Van Buren's recollections of his conversations with Calhoun during the enactment of the "tariff of abominations" lent credence to the reports. He was apprehensive that Calhoun's stand would make him the outstanding defender of the ultimate of State rights. Perhaps he might follow the example of the Governor of South Carolina and give for his toast: "The right to fight!" Van Buren and Jackson planned to stop Calhoun before he got started. For some time they worked on their toasts; and they parted confident of nullifying anything the great nullificationist might say.

On the following evening the first volunteer toast called for was the President's. A tense silence pervaded the assemblage as Jackson arose. Van Buren, who was at the second table, stood on his chair so that he might see over the heads of those in front. Jackson, in copying the toast he and Van Buren had agreed upon, omitted one word, so that when he read it, the diners heard:

"Our Union—it must be preserved."

Robert Y. Hayne, one of South Carolina's Senators, rushed to the President and requested him to insert the word *Federal*. This was the word Jackson had omitted. He assented, and the toast as published, reads:

"Our Federal Union—it must be preserved."

There was no intent on Jackson's part to wound any one's feelings wantonly, ready though he was, as he implied in his toast, to put all the forces of government behind the tariff which South Carolina opposed.

The Vice President was next called upon. Calhoun's great weakness was an incapacity to confess error, a common complaint of public men. Instead of bowing to the inevitable he gave as his toast:

"The Union—next to our liberty the most dear; may we all remember that it can only be preserved by respecting the rights of the States and distributing equally the benefit and burden of the Union."

Then came Van Buren with: "Mutual forbearance and reciprocal concessions; thro' their agency the Union was established —the patriotic spirit from which they emanated will forever sustain it."

This was the prologue to the epic drama on which the curtain was rung down at Appomattox.

The last week in June Van Buren wrote to his son John, now practicing law in Albany, warning him against drink. "What you may regard as an innocent & harmless indulgence will take you years to overcome in the public estimation. . . . The light & vain feeling of desiring to be regarded as a dashing fellow is surely gratified at too great an expense in this way. Washington is full of reports at your expense. It was no longer ago than last evening that I was informed by a friend—well meaning but fond of gossip —that Major Fane should have said here that you had been twice carried drunk from the race course. I knew of course that this was untrue."

A few days later Van Buren returned to New York for the first time since he had resigned the Governorship. Jackson had also left Washington for a rest. On July 12, from the Hermitage, he made veiled reference to the new slanders which were being circulated about him: now it is that he has more than a fatherly interest in La Bellona. ". . . I cannot speak with certainty," he wrote Van Buren, "but do suppose during next winter will live quite a batchellors [*sic!*] life, would to God I had commenced it with my administration, it would have prevented me from much humiliation

& pain that I have experienced, and have prevented much injury
to the innocent, by the secrete [*sic!*] slanders circulated here &
fed from the city—time will unfold the authors."

Van Buren's vacation ended early in September. The last
week or so was spent in New York. On Thursday, September 2,
his son John, evidently on his way back to Albany, bade his father
farewell. Van Buren did not sleep that night. In a letter to John,
written the following evening, he gave the reason: ". . . I only
regret that I must always part with you with mortification, but
[it] seems to be unavoidable. My reflections on the course of life
which you appear to have marked out for yourself, & in which
eating, and drinking, & dressing appear to be most important, not
to say least exceptionable of your persuits [*sic!*], have given me
a feverish & sleepless night. . . ."

The sorrow that was gnawing at his heart was softened as
he resumed his labors and his rides over the Georgetown hills
with Jackson. On one of these Old Hickory advanced the most
audacious proposal of its kind in our history. The President,
some six or seven months earlier, had convinced himself that
Calhoun had proposed his arrest or reprimand for his high-
handed acts in the Seminole War. Although the public was not
aware of it, Jackson had severed all relations with Calhoun.
Jackson led up to his daring plan without intimating its nature.
He spoke of his resolution not to serve more than one term. Of
course that resolve had been undone by circumstances. But Jackson had thought of a middle course. He would run again; and
Van Buren must be the candidate for Vice President. Both would
be elected. Jackson's years and health dictated his retirement. He
would resign as President after serving a year, or two at the
most, and Van Buren would automatically carry on his work.

Van Buren was pleased beyond measure at this evidence of
Jackson's faith in him. But he was dumbfounded by the child-
ishness of the proposal. He must check this madness before it went
further, but without wounding Jackson's sensibilities. Van Buren
began with voluble thanks, and confessed his ambition to be President some day. He dwelt on the purity of Jackson's motives, but
reminded him how his enemies would blacken them. They would
say that Jackson had smuggled Van Buren into the Presidency

to gratify his resentments against Calhoun and his friends.

Van Buren thought that he had won Jackson from his idea, which probably had its genesis in 1828 when Van Buren smuggled Throop into the Governorship of New York. But a year later, as we shall see, Jackson, in two letters to Van Buren, revealed that he had not abandoned his wild idea.

In October word came that Louis McLane, now Ambassador to the Court of St. James's, had successfully paved the way for reopening to American shipping British ports in the West Indies which had been closed since December 1, 1826, by an Order in Council. This was the culmination of eleven years of retaliatory measures by both countries. Gallatin had vainly tried to break the diplomatic deadlock in 1827.

Van Buren instructed McLane to open his negotiations with the British by stressing that the election of Jackson was a rebuke by the people to the Adams administration, whose attitude resulted in the deadlock, and that the United States was ready to comply with the Act of Parliament of 1825, which established the terms on which nations might trade with her colonies. After the Adams administration blunderingly ignored the Act, Clay sent Gallatin to England to concede "that the President acquiesced on the decision taken by the British Government that the Colonial trade shall be regulated by law." The British ministry, resentful at what they regarded as contumacy, declined to negotiate.

In the spring, Congress, anticipating a settlement of the question, had empowered the President to declare the retaliatory measures repealed when England treated American shipping in West Indian ports on the same terms as her own. In November the war of discriminatory duties and other reprisals ended.

This was the crowning act of Van Buren's settled plan to effect harmony between England and America. The merchants and shippers, especially of New England and the Middle Atlantic States, hailed the recovery of the profitable trade with the West Indies as a triumph of Jackson, and the administration press reëchoed their praises. The few who made a study of our foreign relations, knew that the credit belonged to the Secretary of State. In December the first non-political honor conferred on Van Buren was awarded him by the New York Alpha Chapter—

Union College—of Phi Beta Kappa, which elected him an honorary member.

Congress was in session now and it was whispered that a row was impending between Jackson and Calhoun; but it was not until February that Calhoun published his pamphlet exhibiting the correspondence between him and the President over the Seminole War controversy. Calhoun followed this with a communication to Duff Green, who published it in his paper, charging Hamilton with acting dishonorably in the affair. The joint purpose of the letter and pamphlet was to fasten the plot on Van Buren. Calhoun, while not naming Van Buren, was sufficiently pointed in all he said to indicate him. Van Buren publicly denied in the Calhoun organ that he had sought "to prejudice the Vice-President in the good opinion of General Jackson." In the same issue Duff Green gave the lie direct to Van Buren. Whereupon Van Buren returned to his old policy of silence. Green next charged Van Buren with having directed the Eaton imbroglio as part of the conspiracy to destroy Calhoun. The anti-Jacksonian press repeated it. Van Buren remained silent.

Van Buren became the country-wide medium through which the Calhoun forces attacked Jackson. New names were hurled at him. He was no longer the spoilsman, the political juggler, the manager; they now called him the great magician, the red fox of Kinderhook, and the Flying Dutchman.

The problem was unique. Its solution called for a factor, novel and unprecedented. Van Buren had it. He would resign. He confided this to his eldest son, Abraham, who had been living with him since he won his epaulettes at West Point. He would submit his resignation to Jackson on one of their rides. It was early spring. One day when overtaken by a heavy thunderstorm they sought shelter in a tavern. Jackson suddenly became unusually serious. Van Buren left him to his thoughts, and conversed with a farmer who had also found shelter at the inn. When the rain ceased Jackson and Van Buren spurred their horses to a brisk canter, as the skies were still threatening. Without warning Jackson's horse slipped. Van Buren seized the bridle and prevented a spill. "You have possibly saved my life, sir!" exclaimed Jackson. Van Buren responded that he did not regard the danger so gravely, but congratulated himself on having been of the slightest service. Jackson half muttered that he was not certain that his escape from death, if it was one, was worthy of congratulation under existing circumstances.

Van Buren had started on this ride determined to tender his resignation as Secretary of State. But this accident upset his plans. On their next ride, Jackson, in a happier frame of mind, epitomized his hopes for an end of the internal strife with: "We shall soon have peace in Israel." Van Buren took this as his cue. "No, General, there is but one thing can give you peace." "What is that, sir?" "My resignation."

Earnestly Jackson looked at Van Buren as he said with impressive solemnity: "Never, sir! Even you know little of Andrew Jackson if you suppose him capable of such a humiliation of his friend by his enemies."

The two continued their ride. A quarter of a century later Van Buren resumed the story thus: "I thought I could satisfy him that the course I had pointed to was perhaps the only safe one open to us. He agreed to hear me but in a manner and terms affording small encouragement as to the success of my argument. I proceeded for four hours, giving place only to brief interrogations from him, to present in detail, the reasons upon which my suggestion was founded, extending to a careful and, as far as I was able, a clear review of the public interests and of our own duties and feelings involved in the matter." Jackson inquired what he intended to do if he accepted his resignation, and Van Buren replied he would return to the law. Jackson then suggested the English mission, having in mind his intention to have Van Buren run for Vice President the following year.

We can only conjecture what arguments Van Buren used, as he is silent regarding them. Van Buren was attracting assaults on the Administration because he was known as Jackson's successor; the friends of Calhoun and other rivals for the Presidency formed a combination and had already rejected some of Jackson's appointments and were menacing his legislative program; his resignation would end the hostility, and thus pave the way for the enactment of laws in the interest of the public. These arguments we can read into the maze of ambiguities which Van Buren subsequently published; and these are undoubtedly the propositions he advanced to Jackson.

He did not mention that his resignation would inevitably force Eaton to resign. These two resignations would leave Barry and the three friends of Calhoun in the Cabinet. Jackson would not long endure such a situation. But Van Buren was not the first Secretary of State who had Presidential ambitions.

The attacks on Van Buren were directed at him largely because he was the champion of La Bellona and the head of the conspiracy against Calhoun. And Van Buren, in not making these things clear to Jackson, imposed upon the guilelessness of the President.

Van Buren relates that the discussion was resumed the following morning at the White House, and continued in the afternoon while they were horseback-riding. That night Jackson consulted Barry, Eaton, and Lewis. All were in agreement with Van Buren. The following afternoon all five foregathered at the President's office; subsequently Eaton, Lewis, and Barry repaired to Van Buren's house for supper. As they entered, Eaton exclaimed: "Why should you resign? I am the man about whom all the trouble has been made." Three or four days later Jackson had Van Buren's and Eaton's resignations in his hands, Eaton's being dated prior to Van Buren's, as agreed.

The resignations of Berrien, Branch, and Ingham were demanded; but two months elapsed before the Cabinet was dissolved. Barry alone remained. Butler was informed of the circumstance confidentially, and under date of April 22 he answered Van Buren: ". . . I see no objection to your being brought forward for the V. Presidency . . . and *you* with your present reputation would again make that office what the older Adams & Jefferson found it—the nearest & most direct avenue to the higher station. . . ."

Noah had broken with Van Buren because he did not get the job he was after, and he editorialized: "Well indeed may Mr. Van Buren be called the great magician for he raises his wand and the whole Cabinet vanishes."

Van Buren left Washington before Eaton sought to meet Berrien, Branch, and Ingham on the dueling field. He was succeeded by Edward Livingston, now an idol of the world of learning. New York's former Mayor was sixty-seven years old, and as he countersigned Van Buren's commission as minister to England, he musingly recalled the days when his brother, the Chancellor, had filled the same post: then it went by the name of Department of Foreign Relations.

CHAPTER XXXV

VAN BUREN remained in New York two months before sailing for England. The dissolution of the Cabinet created a greater storm than he had anticipated. Much was made of the charge of Ingham, the ousted Attorney General, that Richard M. Johnson, United States Senator from Kentucky, had said to him "that the President had finally determined on our removal from office unless we agreed at once that our families should visit Mrs. Eaton, and invite her to their large parties." Many circumstances supported Ingham's story, although Johnson denied that he had used the threatening language. In Pendleton, South Carolina, at a dinner to Calhoun, the toast to the President was omitted. Several reflecting on Van Buren, in which his name was not mentioned, were given, but before the dinner ended, this one was drunk:

"Martin Van Buren—
  'Ah! that deceit should steal such gentle shape,
  And with a virtuous visor hide deep vice.' "

On August 16 Van Buren sailed on the packet ship *President*, accompanied by his son John, an attaché of the Legation. They were met in London by Washington Irving, who had been appointed Secretary of the Legation by Van Buren two years earlier at the behest of Captain John B. Nicolson, U.S.N., a common friend. After his formal presentation to King William, Van Buren was a guest at the palace, and on one occasion the King had a heart-to-heart talk about Jackson. He described the extent of the alarm created among "all classes of his subjects" by Jackson's election. "But I kept myself free from those alarms," confided the King; "for I have made it a rule through life never to condemn an untried man; and in respect to other matters, I regarded Mr. Jackson as placed in that position. I said to those who addressed to me their apprehensions: 'I will judge Mr. Jackson by his acts.' I have done so, and I am satisfied that we shall have no reason to complain of injustice at his hands."

Irving had resigned before Van Buren's arrival, but instantly formed a warm attachment to the new Minister, and agreed to serve under him. They became fast and lifelong friends, and this is Irving's measure of the man: "The more I see of Mr. Van Buren, the more I am confirmed in a strong personal regard for him. He is one of the gentlest and most amiable men I have ever met with; with an affectionate disposition that attaches itself to those around him and wins their kindness in return."

The author lived with Van Buren, who leased a large house on Stratford Place, a quiet street in a fashionable part of town. This cost him $2,500. His servants and their keep took $2,600 out of his pocket, and he lavished $1,550 on the latest in coaches, although he had taken his own carriage with him. Irving, who knew England well—and he was not a stranger to Kinderhook, having found the originals of Ichabod Crane and other characters there while tutoring the children of Van Buren's old preceptor, the late William P. Van Ness, dead now some five years—played guide to Van Buren in a tour of old castles, ancient abbeys; they ate boar's head "crowned with holly" and drank wassail in the Yule log's warmth in quaint taverns of hallowed memory; and watched mummers, morris dancers, and listened to glee singers.

On his return to London from this holiday jaunt Van Buren found that politics had not changed in the States since he had left them. Cambreleng was sending the gossip, and Van Buren was ever begging for more. ". . . Your last," he wrote to the faithful correspondent, "was written with the freedom, and in the spirit I desire. It was committed to the flames, as I shall do all that speak in the same way of men and things, for it is useless to keep them on file. Therefore speak on. . . ."

The fanatical Anti-Masonic party had met in national convention in Baltimore and nominated William Wirt, of Maryland, for President and Amos Ellmaker, of Pennsylvania, for Vice President. They stole a march on the old parties by innovating the representative method of naming national candidates. Jackson on December 6 wrote: "Everything is going on well at present. Nullification and antimasonry are both declining fast, & will ere long be *buried in oblivion*, doing no harm, but carrying with it the promoters, exciters, and supporters." Calhoun is "an ambitious demagogue." The new Cabinet is harmonious, but he misses

Eaton and Van Buren "very much." In this same letter Jackson referred to the proposal he made during one of their rides together: that Van Buren run on the same ticket with him, and after serving a year, he would resign and make Van Buren President. "I do hope," wrote Jackson, "that in the *selection of a vice president*, I may be placed in such a situation at the time I have heretofore sugested [*sic!*] to you to withdraw to the peaceful shades of the Hermitage, from the busy scenes of public life—on this subject, I will write you fully in a few months."

Jackson was still in feeble health: hence his wish to surrender the office to Van Buren. He felt, as did all his advisers, that he must run again to keep the opposition down. In an earlier letter, dated September 18, Jackson begins with his usual complaints of the abuse and slanders which are being heaped upon him daily, and reverts to his intention to resign in Van Buren's favor: "How disgusting this is to a virtuous mind, & how I long for retirement to the peaceful shades of the Hermitage, for I assure you the depravity of human nature which is daily unfolding itself, by the slanders of the wicked part of the opposition have truly disgusted me. I therefore wish how soon I may be able, with honor to resign the trust committed to me to another & a better hand." Thirteen days earlier, Jackson ends a seven-page letter with: "I cannot close without again repeating that I hope circumstances will occur to enable me to return to the Hermitage in due season and set an example worthy to be followed and give an evidence to my country that I never had any other ambition than that of serving my country when she required it, and, when I know it could be better served by others, to open the door to their enjoyment; *you will understand me.*"

While Van Buren was enjoying the glamorous life of London, Calhoun, Clay, and Webster were concocting a scheme for his destruction. As Van Buren's had been a recess appointment, Jackson, on December 7, sent his name to the Senate. Rumors reached Jackson that the opposition was considering rejecting Van Buren. On December 12, the National Republicans, after the example set by the Anti-Masons, met in national convention in Baltimore, and nominated Clay for President, and John Sergeant, of Pennsylvania, for Vice President. Five days later Jackson told Van Buren of the nominations and of Calhoun's attack on Van Buren for his success in his negotiations over the Northeast boundary and fugitive slave questions. Next he referred to the plot: "The opposition would, if they durst, try to reject your nomination as Minister, but they dare not,—they begin to know if they did that the people in mass would take you up and elect you Vice President without a nomination. Was it not for this, it is said, Clay, Calhoun & Co. would try it."

On January 13, three days after Senator Littleton W. Tazewell, of Virginia, for the Committee on Foreign Relations, favorably reported Van Buren's nomination, Senator John Holmes, of Maine, moved to investigate the causes leading to the dissolution of the Cabinet "and also, whether the said Martin Van Buren, then Secretary of State, participated in any practices disreputable to the national character, which were designed to operate on the mind of the President of the United States, and calculated to smooth the way to his appointment to the high office to which he has been nominated." This motion was tabled. When the nomination was called up the vote was a tie; and Calhoun left the Vice President's chair and by his casting vote tabled the nomination. The junior Senator from New York was William L. Marcy. On January 24 Marcy moved that the Senate resume consideration of Van Buren's appointment. The next day, again by the casting vote of Calhoun, the way was paved for an indictment of Van Buren on the following counts:

1. The instructions drawn up and signed by Mr. Van Buren as Secretary of State, under the direction of the President, and furnished to Mr. McLane, for his guidance in endeavoring to reopen the negotiation for the West India trade.

2. Making a breach of friendship between the first and second officers of the Government—President Jackson and Vice-President Calhoun—for the purpose of thwarting the latter, and helping himself to the Presidency.

3. Breaking up the Cabinet for the same purpose.

4. Introducing the system of "proscription" (removal from office for opinion's sake), for the same purpose.

A *prima facie* case, at least, could have been made out against Van Buren on the second and third counts. He was unquestionably guilty of the fourth. But the first charge in the indictment was puerile. Yet it was on this that the opposition, led by Webster and Clay, made its principal attack. The hollowness of this charge, which they hoped would rouse the country, lay in the fact that Van Buren's instructions to McLane had been before the Senate for more than a year, and no one questioned them during the months Congress was in session; and all these nine months Van Buren was serving as Secretary of State.

In instructing McLane to remind the British that there was a new administration in power, Van Buren wrote: "I will add nothing to the impropriety of any feelings that find their origin in the past pretensions of this Government to have an adverse influence upon the present conduct of Great Britain." Webster, as he quoted this, and more of the same tenor preceding it, exclaimed, tongue in cheek: "Sir, I would forgive mistakes; I would pardon the want of information; I would pardon almost any thing, where I saw true patriotism and sound American feeling; but I cannot forgive the sacrifice of this feeling to mere Party. I cannot concur in sending abroad a public agent who has not conceptions so large and liberal, as to feel, that in the presence of foreign Courts, amidst the Monarchs of Europe, he is to stand up for his country, and his whole country; that no jot and tittle of her honor is to come to harm in his hands; that he is not to suffer others to reproach either his Government or his Country, and far less is he to reproach either; that he is to have no objects in his eye but American objects, and no heart in his bosom but an American heart; and that he is to forget self, to forget party, and to forget every sinister and narrow feeling, in his proud and lofty attachment to the Republic whose commission he bears."

Clay made a speech also fit for the hustings, from which we quote: "On our side, according to Mr. Van Buren, all was wrong; on the British side, all was right. We brought forward nothing but claims and pretensions; the British Government asserted, on the other hand, a clear and incontestable right. We erred in too tenaciously and too long insisting upon our pretensions, and not yielding at once to the force of their just demands. And Mr. McLane was commanded to avail himself of all the circumstances in his power to mitigate our offense, and to dissuade the British Government from allowing their feelings justly incurred by the past conduct of the party driven from power, to have an adverse influence towards the American party now in power. Sir, was this becoming language from one independent nation to another? Was it proper in the mouth of an American Minister? Was it in conformity with the high, unsullied, and dignified character of our previous diplomacy? Was it not, on the contrary, the language of a humble vassal to a proud and haughty lord? Was it not prostrating and degrading the American Eagle before the British Lion?"

Calhoun spoke through Hayne who said: "From facts and circumstances which have fallen under my own observation, many of them notorious to the whole country, as well as from information derived from sources on which I implicitly rely, I have arrived at the following conclusion; that when Mr. Van Buren came into the Cabinet, he found a state of circumstances here that opened a door to the establishment of an influence favorable to his personal views; that, instead of exerting himself to remove the causes of discord and dissention by which the executive was unhappily surrounded, he dexterously. availed himself of them, and wielded them for the promotion of his own personal and political interests, and for the advancement of his friends and supporters to office, to the exclusion of almost all others."

One phrase born in this bitter debate has become almost a household saying. During Marcy's denial of the charge of intrigue against his chief, and his plea of guilty to the last count in the indictment, he said: "It may be, sir, that the politicians of New York are not so fastidious as some gentlemen are as to disclosing the principles on which they act. They boldly preach what they practice. When they are contending for victory they avow their intention of enjoying the fruits of it. If they are defeated, they expect to retire from office; if they are successful, they claim, as a matter of right, the advantages of success. They see nothing wrong in the rule that to the victor belongs the spoils of the enemy."

Marcy's rendering of the Brennic "Woe to the conquered!" grated harshly on the ears of his confrères. The spoilsman was caught unawares. In the excitement of the occasion he had forgotten that Jackson had attempted a defense of the wholesale removals in a message to Congress with a more palatable phrase: "rotation in office."

This debate lasted two days. A dozen set speeches against Van Buren were matched with impromptu rejoinders by Marcy, Forsyth, Bedford Brown, of North Carolina, and Samuel Smith, of Maryland. These were Van Buren's only defenders. Even Benton, his friend, companion, and political bedfellow, was silent. He probably thought he would profit by what might happen. Jackson was not mute. Through Smith he told the Senate that Van Buren's instructions to McLane were his own.

On January 26, by Calhoun's casting vote, Van Buren was rejected as Minister to the Court of St. James's. Some friends of the South Carolinian doubted the wisdom of rejecting Van Buren. But the Vice President silenced their doubts with: "It will kill him, sir, kill him dead. He will never kick, sir, never kick." But he lacked the profundity of Van Buren, who had said to Judge Skinner: "There is such a thing in politics as killing a man too dead."

Marcy divided the enemies of Van Buren into two groups: the friends of the Adams administration who voted to reject him because he "denounced the government to a foreign power and invoked favors upon party considerations"; and the friends of Calhoun. Of them he wrote to the recalled Minister: "Calhoun and his little band . . . came to the aid of Webster and Clay but the grounds were very different. You had seduced they represented—not a woman—but the President—made a breach between him and our worthy presiding officer—you were a great intreguer [*sic!*]—the author of sundry plotts [*sic!*]—&c &c."

Marcy also informed Van Buren that he would be made the candidate for Vice President. "Gen. J[ackson] is advanced in life & to be frank with you is in feeble health. I must say, however I may wish otherwise, that I think the chances are against his lasting five years longer. With the best of those now spoken of for Vice Prest. at our head as chief Magistrate we should be in a miserable situation. This consideration has had great influence with our wisest friends in bringing them to the conclusion that you should in all events be a candidate for V. P."

Immediately the Regency had the New York Legislature address a memorial to Jackson protesting against the indignity to her favorite son. Jackson replied in like spirit, and repeated what Smith had said in his behalf to the Senate; professed his

EDWARD LIVINGSTON
After a drawing by J. B. Longacre

incapacity to tarnish the pride or dignity of that country whose glory it had been his object to elevate; denied that Van Buren had been party to the rupture between him and Calhoun; asserted that he had asked Van Buren to serve as Secretary of State to meet the general wish and expectation of the Republican party and because of his own respect for Van Buren's great private and public worth and integrity.

Van Buren was too far away to be more than a pawn in the game which he could play so well. But the players were not amateurs: Marcy, Lewis and Cambreleng were making the moves. Meetings of protest were held in Tammany Hall in the last two days of January, and these were followed by like gatherings in villages and cities up-State.

Van Buren was ill in bed when the news reached him. An unusually large batch of letters was brought to him with his breakfast. He sifted them until he recognized an envelope in the familiar manuscript of Cambreleng. "I most sincerely congratulate you on your rejection by the Senate—23 to 23 and by the casting vote of the Vice President," Cambreleng's letter began. ". . . Poor Hayne has laid himself on the grave of Calhoun—and Webster & Clay die in each other's arms. . . . you will be made V. P. in spite of yourself—and you will ride over your adversaries, or rather drag them after you *à l'Achille.* Come back as quick as you can—we have not triumphal arches as in ancient Rome, but we'll give you as warm a reception as ever Conqueror had."

This letter effected a complete recovery: he had planned to stay in bed all day. He dressed hurriedly, but with his usual care, went downstairs, and surprised Washington Irving at the breakfast table. He handed the author Cambreleng's communication, which cheered Irving; for he had just read the meager news in the *Times.*

Van Buren told Irving that he regarded his presence at the Queen's Drawing Room imperative in view of his rejection. Irving agreed, provided it did not involve too great a sacrifice of feeling. Van Buren was not concerned over that. When he reached the Palace, Lord Palmerston took him aside and said that he had received an intimate picture of what had happened from the British Chargé at Washington, and had transmitted it to the

King. Early in the morning the King had sent for him and commanded him to assure Van Buren that His Majesty was satisfied the rejection had been inspired by partisan consideration, and while it was far from the King's habit or inclination to meddle in the purely domestic affairs of other governments, he felt it due to the President and Van Buren to say that his respect for him was unimpaired. And there were more gracious and considerate sentiments expressed by the King. As the company, preceded by the diplomatic corps, passed through the Throne Room, the King halted the procession to express his regrets personally to Van Buren.

Van Buren waited until another mail arrived before making any move. Cambreleng again advised him: "I think on reflection that I would endeavor to arrive in this Country about the 11ʰ of May about 2 or 3 weeks before the meeting at Baltº." Lewis was for an even longer stay: he recommended his entry after the Baltimore convention. Jackson, knowing the difference in opinion among his political managers at home, told Van Buren to use his own discretion. Van Buren decided that it would look better if he did not return until after he had been nominated, and made his plans accordingly.

Late in March he was received by the King and Queen at Windsor, and the beginning of the second week of April found him in Paris. He made a trip to Germany, where his stay was equally brief; but he spent nearly a month in the land of his ancestors. He was received by the King of the Netherlands, William I, who suggested that they were distantly related, saying that his title of Count Buren came from an ancestor who married the Countess of Buren, then head of an ancient family, now no more, whose castle was in the old town of Buren. Van Buren replied that all he knew of his family was that the first American ancestor "came over in 1633." Van Buren, as we know, was in error by two years, as he was in believing that the family name was Buren. But there was no Holland Society in those days, and no one was especially concerned over the old Dutch records in and around Albany.

Early in June Van Buren and his son sailed for home. On July 5 they landed at New York, where Van Buren learned, as he had anticipated, that the Democratic-Republican National

Convention had nominated him on May 21. Jackson was not nominated at the convention; this had been already done by the State Legislatures; the convention merely indorsed Jackson's nomination.

A periodic visitation of the cholera was raging in New York when Van Buren arrived. Demonstrations had been planned in his honor, but he declined to attend them. His enemies charged him with cowardice. As usual, he made no explanation; but one is found in a letter from Jackson, which was directed to him at the ship, requesting him to come immediately to Washington.

To understand the dramatic scene awaiting Van Buren at the White House, a word of explanation is in order. The renewal of the Charter of the Bank of the United States was the dominant issue before the people. Although its grant would not expire until 1836, the question had been before Congress for more than a year. The convention which nominated Clay had declared in favor of a renewal. The delegates who nominated Jackson and Van Buren had been silent on this and all other questions. They were content to adopt a brief resolution praising Jackson. And on Jackson's desk, at the time Van Buren reached Washington was the bill extending the life of "the monster."

The letter which Jackson had sent to meet Van Buren's ship was written three days after the bill had passed the Senate, and while it was still before the House. It was a pitiful cry for help from a very sick man. We quote from it: ". . . The coalition are determined to press upon me at this session the Bank, and a few more internal improvement bills—I am prepared to meet them as I ought—but I want your aid—The able heads of Departments, except Woodbury and the Attorney General, are all in favor of the Bank—Let me see you as early as you can."

On arriving at the White House Van Buren was shown to Jackson's bedroom. The President was emaciated and pale, reminding Van Buren of a specter. But there was an unquenchable fire in his blue eyes. He took Van Buren's hand, wearily ran his free hand through his white locks, and in an even voice, utterly devoid of passion, said: "The Bank, Mr. Van Buren, is trying to kill me; but I will kill it."

Jackson vetoed the bill July 10. In the remaining few days of Congress, Webster, Clay, and other friends of the Bank tried to muster the necessary two-thirds to override the President's veto. But Van Buren was flitting around the corridors of the Capitol to prevent them. Clay met him, and in ending a speech, informed the Senate that he had just shaken hands "with our late Minister to England, Mr. Van Buren, and was gratified to find him in excellent health and appearing to great advantage in his English dress."

Clay did not know, or he would also have made a point of it, that Van Buren brought more than clothes from England; his ultra-modish English coach came on the same ship with him.

CHAPTER XXXVI

THE type of campaign waged against Jackson and Van Buren is illustrated by a broadside issued by the Massachusetts National Republicans pretending to be an order for a procession and dinner at Haverhill, and signed: "Per order of the Kitchen Cabinet, Van Buren, Auctioneer." One of the toasts read: "By an incipient Tory: 'The Greatest and Best.' The *greatest* robber, the *best* distributor of the spoils. Overture to the Forty Thieves." Jackson, of course, was the Tory. Another ran: "By Black Hawk: '*Mrs. Eaton.* Handsome Squaw, big petticoat cover up all old man's sins. Tune *An Old Man Went a Wooing.*'" The *Old Man* was Jackson also. There was a thrust at Jackson's ancestry in this: "Gentlemen who take part in the procession may be assured that the Irishmen and members of *Infant Schools* will be removed so that nothing shall remain to annoy the senses of the most fastidious Tory."

But the writers of broadsides and pamphlets, with their allies on the venal journals, had overdone their tasks in the campaign of 1828. They made little impression, one way or another. And the espousal of the Bank by the opposition, with the suspicion—well founded—that some of the supporters of Clay were in the Bank's pay, outweighed the talk of spoils and Mrs. Eaton and the Kitchen Cabinet. Francis P. Blair, who supplanted Duff Green as chief of the Jackson editorial corps after the Calhoun scissure, wrote to Van Buren: "The Bank cannot buy the majority of the nation." Webster had obtained $32,000 from the Bank in "loans." One was a sum of $10,000, surreptitiously paid by the President of the Bank, Nicholas Biddle, the Monday following Webster's speech against Jackson's veto message on the Bank's charter. The speech was worth it. Congress, in March, knew that Webster was $22,000 "in debt" to the bank, and that other members of Congress were also in its clutches. The list of these Congressional beneficiaries of the Bank was embodied in a minority report of the Clayton Committee, which had investigated the corrupt acts of the Bank. The report was sent to the Government printer, who, for a reason never explained, suppressed it. "Czar Nicholas," as Biddle was known, only partly complied with the demand of Congress to enumerate "the loans made by the Bank and its branches to members of Congress, editors of newspapers, or persons holding office under the general government." In *The Globe* of August 23, Blair charged Webster with corruption in his relations with the Bank; but Webster and Biddle remained silent to the end of their lives. The Bank, at its expense, circulated Webster's $10,000 speech as a Clay campaign document.

After leaving Washington Van Buren journeyed through New York, visiting leaders on both sides of the river on his way to Albany. The State seemed safe enough, but he did not want to leave anything to chance. When he reached Kinderhook the birds were singing counter to the melancholic monody of the katydids, whose first notes are still regarded by the inhabitants of the Dutch counties as an unfailing sign that frost will be with them six weeks later to a day. The early asters were beginning to blossom along the roadsides, another indication that summer was on the wane. He had been in the village little more than a day when he thought it was time to call on Peter Van Schaack. Ever since he had become a power in the State Van Buren had never returned to Kinderhook without calling on him. Van Buren had tramped that part of London where Van Schaack had lived during his banishment, noting every change in the neighborhood. All this had been for the delectation of the man who had challenged him at the polls when about to cast his first vote. That was well-nigh a generation ago.

As Van Buren was about to start, young Van Schaack called and said that his father was waiting for him as it might be their last time together. When Van Buren entered the library the dying Tory raised himself on the bed and extended his hand. He was happy to hear Van Buren's voice again; he knew his tread; he had learned to recognize the footsteps of his friends during the past twenty years: he had been blind that long. Van Buren was saddened to see his bed moved into the library, as it was Van Schaack's wish—all his friends knew it—to die amidst his books. After the exchange of greetings, Van Schaack volunteered that he was going through the last change. Van Buren was voicing the hope that such might not be the case when the old man cut him short with a vigorous "No!" He calmly added that death was inevitable, and a part of life; he had lived the full measure of his days—eighty-five years in all—and was thankful to God that his mental faculties remained unimpaired to the end. Blindness was nothing. Van Buren let him finish and then talked of Van Schaack's retreat in London, and of the changes there. And then they gossiped of the village, of their friends, and of the law-suits they had tried together.

It was now growing late. The sun had dropped behind the Catskills. A servant lighted the candles. It was time to depart. Van Schaack held Van Buren's hand in their last good-by. "I am happy, sir, to think," said the old man slowly, "that we have always been——" No! that was not so; he had been Van Buren's enemy once: he could not say they had always been friends. He had never been guilty of duplicity; he had suffered for opinion's sake; he could not, even unintentionally, begin now. Through his mind surged recollections of bitter party strife, beginning with that Election Day twenty-nine years earlier, when he challenged Van Buren's vote. He still held Van Buren's hand, as lawyer-like he rephrased his utterance: "I am happy, sir, to think that you always came to see me when you visited Kinderhook." This was Van Schaack; and he inclined his head graciously as Van Buren bowed and said farewell.

The survey of the State, and the work done by Van Buren, left no doubt as to the outcome. The western counties, where Anti-Masonry had its birth, were overwhelmingly against him and Jackson. There were reports of money being used by the Bank throughout the country. Subsequently it was proven that the Bank spent $80,000 in pamphleteering alone: how much was used in bribery and vote buying is a matter of speculation. Isaac Hill wrote from New Hampshire: ". . . we may be relied upon giving a decisive majority for Andrew Jackson. Yet the Bank is scattering its thousands here to affect us." Aaron Ward, Van Buren's lieutenant in Westchester County, wrote: "I fear the Bank influence more than anything else. I have no doubt that the Bank managers will expend a large sum of money in this county." Blair wrote to Van Buren: "We cannot & ought not to employ money to bribe voters. . . . The Bank cannot buy the majority of the Nation. . . ."

In spite of the Bank the election of Jackson and Van Buren was foreshadowed long before Election Day. The Hickory Clubs were more potent than the Bank and its branches. Jackson, under date of August 30, wrote from the Hermitage that he was about to return to Washington, and asked Van Buren for advice on his message to Congress. "I wish your views not only that my course may be consistent, but that if any accident should befall me, that the Government may continue to be administered as we have commenced it, and the Government brought back & administered agreeable to the true reading of the constitution." This letter also revealed that Jackson was inclining from the tariff.

On October 4, replying to an inquiry from a meeting at Shocco Springs, North Carolina, Van Buren set forth his views on the tariff. Explicit was Van Buren's characterization of his sentiments to his interrogators; but a vaguer letter Van Buren never penned. On the same day that Jackson had written him, J. Grant, Jr., of Raleigh, North Carolina, had warned him to be wary of the seemingly friendly address from Shocco Springs. Van Buren did not need the warning: he replied he was for a more equitable adjustment of the tariff; that he was opposed to oppressive inequality or imposts designed to benefit one section of the country to the disadvantage of another; that he favored a reduction of the revenue to the wants of the government; and expressed a preference for encouraging manufactures essential to the national defense, and extending protection to industries adapted to our country and of which the raw material was produced by ourselves. These "explicit" views stamped him as either an ultra-protectionist, or a tariff reformer: you could take your choice. But there was nothing equivocal in his attitude on the Bank, internal improvements, and nullification: he was against all three.

In another public letter written in the close of the campaign, Van Buren spoke of the unceasing hatred and contumely that had been visited upon him by his political enemies since his entrance into public life. Other men in official life had been attacked, but they had had respite, while he had never known a moment's peace. He consoled himself by observing that there had been scarcely a man who had been the victim of unwarrantable obloquy who had not risen in public estimation in exact proportion to the intensity and duration of the abuse.

The victory for Jackson and Van Buren was more decisive than it had been for Jackson and Calhoun four years earlier. Jacksonian Governors and Jacksonian Legislatures were elected in most of the States. In New York, Marcy was chosen Governor by 13,000 majority; his seat in the Senate was later filled by Silas Wright. Twenty-three of the States had adopted the system of choosing Presidential Electors by popular vote; South Carolina alone clung to the undemocratic method of leaving this privilege to the Legislature, a practice maintained until 1860. South Carolina was going it alone, in more ways than one: it nominated John Floyd, of Virginia, for President, and Henry Lee, of Massachusetts, for Vice President, and gave them its eleven Electoral votes. Pennsylvania had nominated a Jackson ticket, but in obedience to the Bank, had chosen Electors pledged to William Wilkins, of Pennsylvania, for Vice President. Vermont went Anti-Masonic. Jackson received 219 of the 286 votes in the Electoral College, and Clay 49; Van Buren 189; the difference represented Pennsylvania's vote for Wilkins.

Van Buren on arriving in New York to collect his election bets found himself a social lion. Hone recorded, after meeting him at several parties: "Mr. Van Buren . . . is all the fashion at present. . . . he must be more or less than a man if he can avoid exultation when he assumes the Vice-President's chair, vacated by the man who gave the casting vote in the Senate which recalled him from his honorable station abroad."

He was more sought after than Signora Edelaide Pedrotti— he always heard her called La Pedrotti—the prima donna of the Italian opera company, which opened the season at the old Richmond Hill Theater in the last week of September. Of all the socially prominent families, the Hones alone failed to invite the soprano to their home. Hone made her acquaintance at the John Delafields', on Park Place, the night following his dinner with Van Buren at the Marches. She had sung that evening the title rôle in Mercadante's *Elisa e Claudio*. She was very tired. She had responded with generous encores to the enthusiastic bravas and the cries of *"Bis! Bis!"* All begged her to sing just a little bit. She curtseyed her thanks in declining. Still the Delafields and their guests were hopeful. "And she refused to sing, too, after Mrs. [Henry] Parish and Helen McEvers had kindly set the example," observed the incensed Hone. "If she did not sing, why was she there? And then the elegant amateurs of Italian music pretend to compare this woman to Fanny Kemble; nay, pretend to say that, independently of her singing, she plays better and has more grace!" Thenceforward La Pedrotti's glorious eyes, as dark and mysterious as night, were "staring"; her Venus-like figure was "immense" and "vulgar"; her modest dress "tawdry."

There was some truth in Hone's criticism of the admirers of La Pedrotti: New York's society found more witchery in her than in "the greatest Juliet of her day" because she was from the Continent: Fanny Kemble could only boast England as her birthplace. Everything European was worshiped and imitated by the *élite* of the Metropolis. Even Hone went into ecstasies when his set began giving elaborate luncheons and called them by the French equivalent for a substantial breakfast. "A *dèjeuner à la fourchette* is something of a novelty in this country, and the last imitation of European refinement," wrote Hone. "This series of breakfasts given by Mr. William Douglas at his fine mansion, corner of Park Place and Church Street, can hardly be called an *imitation;* for in taste, elegance, and good management it goes beyond most things of the kind in Europe. . . . The company assembles at about one o'clock, and remains until four. Breakfast is served at two o'clock, and consists of coffee and chocolate, light dishes of meat, ice-cream and confectionery, with lemonade and French and German wines. The first two floors, elegantly furnished, of this spacious house, are thrown open; the dining room opens into a beautiful conservatory, in which, amongst other pleasant objects, is an aviary of singing-birds, the delicate notes of the canary mingling sweetly with the shrill pipe of the foreign bullfinch, and the whole concert regulated and stimulated by the great leader of the feathered orchestra, our own native mocking-bird. A band, also, of a more commercial nature, plays at the head of the stairs during the whole time of the entertainment, and after the young folk have partaken of their breakfast-dinner, cotillions and waltzes are danced until the hour of reluctant departure. . . ."

La Pedrotti, in declining to entertain the Delafields and their guests, was not following custom. When the wine had mellowed all, those with accomplishments the least out of the ordinary, contributed to the entertainment of the occasion. It was a rare gathering which did not number a celebrity. Charles Kemble, who played Mercutio before the public, at these dinner and supper parties would frequently play Romeo to his daughter's Juliet. And their own Edwin Forrest seldom needed a bidding to declaim his favorite passages from Lear, Othello, Macbeth, and other dramas which made him wealthy and famous. Irving, who was of their own circle, never failed them for a story. Domenick Lynch needed no importuning to sing the latest French or Italian air. But the favorite was Charles Matthews, the comedian, who always played to crowded houses on his visits to this country. His days were numbered; but he concealed his doom from his audiences. In private homes he sang and recited, and told stories of Daniel O'Connell "and other eloquent Irishmen in order to illustrate the different kinds of Irish brogue." And when he died in England in the early 30's, Hone said: "Few men of the present age have contributed so much to the amusement of others. . . . I have seen him at my own table delighting and surprising the company with stories, songs, and imitations, himself the only person whose heart was not light and joyous by the merriment he caused."

No entertainment was complete without dancing and wine. Hone had two wine closets to supplement his cellar. And when, toward the end of Van Buren's term as Vice President, he sold his house at Park Place and Broadway, and moved almost a mile to the north—to Broadway and Bond street—he inventoried 2,180 quart bottles and 254 gallon bottles of Madeira and sherry. Hone's cellar was modest, as the cellars of Gotham's fashionables went.

Van Buren's social graces astonished those who met him for the first time. They had expected to find a typical farmer's son: they had forgotten that Albany, too, boasted a society of which the Patroon was the acknowledged leader, and that while the ballrooms were few in the seat of Knickerbocker New York, dancing masters made annual visits even to the smallest villages of the Dutch counties. They saw that Van Buren not only danced the plain waltz and the hop waltz, but was as lively as the next in the spirited gallopade, and could lead a cotillion. But he was deficient in two of the accomplishments of the dandies of the day: he played neither the flute nor the guitar; and he was a stranger to the pianoforte.

Van Buren's round of entertainments ended Monday, November 26, when Tammany observed the anniversary of the evacuation of the city by the British. It was only fitting that the venerable and beloved Morgan Lewis, one of the few heroes of the Revolution left, should preside. Lewis, before leaving to meet his old enemy in the War of 1812, informed his many tenant-farmers that those who took up arms or sent a son to the war need not worry about any rent then due or which might be due in the future: instantly Lewis's income from his tenants was reduced to almost nothing. In introducing Tammany's guest, the son of the Signer recalled his words to Van Buren in the spring of 1814 when Van Buren was finishing his second year in the State Senate: "Being a much older man than yourself, you will excuse me for saying it to you, that should you retain your talents and integrity, the first honors of your country will await you." And Van Buren had lost neither his integrity nor his talents; and part of Lewis's prediction was fulfilled.

There was more cheering when Van Buren rose to speak; and after he finished he gave the scheduled toasts. The first was to the memory of the Signers. The glasses were emptied while the orchestra played "Oft in the Stilly Night." As they drank to the memory of Washington, the musicians sounded the noble and elegiac strains of Pleyel's Hymn. Lewis had selected this number. Its significance was not lost on the Masons present. In the preceding year Lewis had been elected Grand Master of the Craft.

From his seat on the dais Van Buren had an excellent view of the hundreds who were crowded into the Long Room of the Wigwam. All were well dressed; but there were many who were obviously out of place. These were the keepers of pot-houses and waterfront grog shops. They were beginning to make themselves felt in the two political organizations of New York. They controlled the votes of fellows more debased than themselves. But no one imagined that within a decade they were to be entrenched in the political councils of New York and other large cities. They fattened on misery in the mass. A few weeks back, while Van Buren was in the midst of the campaign, newspapers told of the alarm felt by officials of Canada and the United States over the unprecedented emigration of the poor from the British Isles. This great flow was caused by "the distress of the lower classes in England and Ireland." In the five months following the opening of navigation of the St. Lawrence in the spring, 49,569 debarked at Quebec alone. "A large proportion find their way into the United States destitute and friendless." There were countless hundreds entering daily the ports of Boston, New York, and Philadelphia. Most of them remained in these congested centers, and there was no organized effort to relieve their distress. Thousands had already gravitated into the network of crooked streets immediately to the north of where Van Buren was being entertained by Tammany. Here lived the very poor, in wretched hovels. Whole families, native born and foreign stock, lived in the cellars of these rude shacks unfit for cattle. In the mornings the little children of these unfortunates came out into the fresh air. Some —many of them little girls of eight and nine years—carried brooms. With these they swept the crossings on Broadway and other main streets. The less ambitious begged for pennies. Other little ones sought refuge from hunger in crime. Their elders— when they had the price—purchased momentary forgetfulness in the grog shops, whose keepers, on Election Day, dictated their votes at the polls. Before many years had passed, these harpies of politics were to occupy the seats of honor now occupied by Van Buren, Lewis, and their kind.

In returning to Albany Van Buren passed many farms, and envied the peace of those who tilled them. He was looking forward to the day when he would cast the cares of office and return to the quiet of a farm in Kinderhook. The village had none of the city's splendor; and it had its poverty, too, as he himself could bear witness; but no one went hungry, and squalor was unknown.

Calhoun did not serve out his term; for his State at a popular convention, presided over by Governor Hamilton—Randolph's second in the duel with Clay—declared the tariff laws passed by Congress in 1828, and in July of the current year, null and void. Secession was one step removed. Jackson answered immediately by ordering two war vessels to Charleston, and troops within striking distance of South Carolina's border. The newspapers of December 12 published Jackson's proclamation to the people of South Carolina. There was fatherly advice in it, and this: "I consider the power to annul a law of the United States, assumed by one State, incompatible with the existence of the Union, contradicted expressly by the letter of the Constitution, unauthorized by its spirit, inconsistent with every principle on which it was founded, and destructive of thr great object for which it was formed."

These sentiments shocked all State-rights theorists. Nathaniel Macon, in honorable retirement after a lifetime of service in Congress, wrote to Van Buren that a State had the right to secede. All knew that the proclamation was beyond the power of Jackson, and Hone wrote: "Whoever shall prove to be the author has raised himself to imperishable glory." One of Hone's predecessors in New York's City Hall, the framer of the Louisiana Code, had written it. Three days after Christmas Calhoun resigned the Vice Presidency, and was elected to the Senate to succeed Hayne; and from the floor of Congress disavowed any hostility toward the Union. Calhoun personally feared Jackson, who had threatened to hang the nullifiers; and in letters to Van Buren Jackson expressed the wish to lead a *posse comitatus* into South Carolina and arrest Calhoun and his immediate lieutenants.

Van Buren remained in Albany during the first two months of the legislative session. There were two United States Senators to be chosen; one to fill the unexpired term of Governor Marcy, and another to succeed Dudley, whose tenure of office ended March 3. Silas Wright was chosen without opposition for the first place. The Regency was divided on a successor to Dudley, some demanding Jacob Sutherland, a Supreme Court Justice, who had married a Livingston, and others, led by Knower, advocating Nathaniel P. Tallmadge, of Poughkeepsie, a State Senator, and an avowed protectionist.

Wright was elected on January 4. Van Buren sent him posthaste to Washington with a letter commending him to Jackson. And Jackson waited for another communication from Van Buren. In his annual message to Congress, which was read in both houses on a month to a day before Wright's election to the Senate, Jackson had informed Congress of the situation in South Carolina, of his views on the tariff and the Bank. Legislatures in other States had commended him for his stand, but New York remained silent. Then came Jackson's special message on South Carolina's bellicose acts "which manifest a determination to render inevitable a resort to those measures of self-defense which the paramount duty of the Federal government requires . . ." Congress heard it on January 16. Jackson waited nine days longer to hear New York's Legislature approve his attitude, and growing impatient, wrote to Van Buren: ". . . whispers and innuendoes . . . are circulated, to injure you, carrying out the idea, that you wield the Legislature & thro fear of results are silent. Friendship dictates that I should let you know that such is the course of your enemies—and the silence of the Legislature gives a colouring to these false suggestions."

Van Buren did fear the results. He wanted to avoid taking a stand, if possible. He did not agree with the negation of State rights involved in the doctrine pronounced by Jackson, originally voiced by the Federalists. The survivors of this party, led by Webster and Harrison Gray Otis, had been foremost in organizing meetings to approve Jackson's course. The erratic John Randolph of Roanoke was tearing up and down Virginia shouting —ardent Jacksonian though he was—that Jackson "had disavowed the principles to which he owed his elevation to the Chief Magistracy . . . and transferred his real friends and supporters, bound hand and foot, to his and their bitterest enemies, the ultra Federalists, ultra tariffites, ultra internal improvement and Hartford Convention men—the habitual scoffers at State rights, and to their instrument, the venal and prostituted press."

The exaggerated language of Randolph voiced the sentiments of the extreme State-rights theorists. It would not do for Van Buren to slight them; and he could not ignore Jackson. Consequently he wrote a report to please both. He catered to the State-rights men with: ". . . the states must be regarded as parties to the compact . . . it is a Constitution established by 'the people of the United States,' not as one consolidated body, but as members of separate and independent communities, each acting for itself, and without regard to their comparative numbers." He praised Jackson for his stand on the Bank, on the tariff, and spoke on nullification in a way to avoid offense to either side: "It is a thorough conviction, that anarchy, degradation, and interminable distress will be, must be, the unavoidable results of a dissolution of the union of these States. . . . We may differ as to the time, the manner, or the extent of the measures to be employed, whether of conciliation or coercion. . . . If every man looks only to his own interest, or every State to its own favorite policy, and insists upon them, this Union cannot be preserved." And there was more praise for Jackson and more conciliatory talk; but no specific mention of South Carolina. This report was adopted in the Legislature Thursday, January 31.

Conciliation was also practiced by Van Buren in the election of Dudley's successor. His choice was his old law partner, Benjamin F. Butler; but the majority of the Regency were for Tallmadge. He had his way in the matter of Marcy's successor. Van Buren was living at Congress Hall, where Tallmadge also resided during the session. They visited each other in their rooms; but Van Buren never broached the Senatorship. Tallmadge gathered courage to say that his name had been mentioned as a successor to Dudley. Van Buren resorted to his favorite artifice of turning the conversation and inquired if Tallmadge had read George Canning's recently published work. Hearing a negative, Van Buren said he would send him the volumes, and left the room. The books were faithfully delivered, but Tallmadge had little heart for reading until the pressure of the Regents forced their Director to give his assent to Tallmadge's election.

Van Buren reached Washington on the last Tuesday in February. The following Monday he was inaugurated Vice President, the oath being administered by Chief Justice Marshall, who a few moments before had sworn in Jackson. Congress having adjourned the preceding Saturday, Van Buren had no work to do as Vice President until the Senate convened the following December. His stay at the White House was far from pleasant. Blair and Kendall had won over Jackson to their scheme of removing the Government funds from the Bank. When Kendall broached the subject to him, Van Buren heatedly said that the resolution adopted on March 2 in the House of Representatives declaring the deposits safe in Biddle's institution should have ended the agitation. Kendall answered that the recharter of the Bank before the next Presidential election was certain unless it was crippled by this blow. The Government's deposits exceeded those of all private depositors; and Kendall argued that the Bank would use the power that went with the deposits to corrupt Congress, and once rechartered, the opposition, aided by the Bank, would elect the next President of the United States. "I can live under a corrupt despotism as well as any other man by keeping out of its way, which I shall do," said Kendall, who threatened to lay down his pen if the deposits were not removed. But before leaving Washington Van Buren told him: "I had never thought seriously upon the deposit question until after my conversation with you; I am now satisfied that you were right and I was wrong."

Jackson and his intimate advisers had believed that Biddle, through his Bank, was aiming at control of the government. The record revealed Biddle as a petty pattern of Louis XVI, against whom, during his trial before the National Convention, was hurled: "All kinds of corruption were employed by you: you paid the expenses of publishing libels, pamphlets, and journals, which tended to pervert the public opinion . . ."

James Gordon Bennett was having a hard time this spring keeping the *Pennsylvanian* alive. He sent five begging letters to Hoyt in an effort to induce Van Buren to advance him money. First he suggested $10,000, then dropped to $2,500. When he obtained nothing he talked of the ten years he had worked "day and night for the cause of Mr. Van Buren and his friends," and of his hopes that he could find a friend "somewhere between heaven and earth" to enable him to carry out his "fixed purpose in favor of Van Buren and his friends." His failure to find this angel he blamed on "the Vice President himself." Bennett then indulged in a little polite blackmail: "I am beset on all sides with importunities to cut him [Van Buren]—to abandon him—what can I do? By a word to any of his friends in Albany he could do the friendship I want as easily as drink a glass of Saratoga water at the Springs. What shall I do? I know not. . . . I do not know whether it is worth while to write to Van Buren or not —nor do I care if you were to send him this letter."

He followed this with an appeal to Van Buren; but Van Buren declined to submit to blackmail. He informed Hoyt from his retreat at Saratoga Springs: ". . . I cannot directly or indirectly afford pecuniary aid to his [Bennett's] press . . . If he cannot continue friendly to me on public grounds and with perfect independence, I can only regret it, but I desire no other support. Whatever course he pursues, as long as it is an honest one, I shall wish him well." A month after this incident, Jackson, under date of September 19, said that "the Bank had bought up Bennett."

All through the summer Van Buren and Jackson corresponded on the Bank question. McLane, because he opposed the removals, had been transferred from the Treasury to the Department of State, vacant through the appointment of Livingston as Minister to France. William J. Duane, of Pennsylvania, son of the noted editor of the *Aurora*, was given McLane's place in expectation that he would give the orders for depositing the government moneys in the various banks, chartered by the States. Roger B. Taney, Attorney General, prepared a paper advocating the removals because of the Bank's duplicity in its dealings with the Government, its political activity, and its unconstitutionality. This was read by Jackson to his Cabinet on September 18. He disavowed any attempt to dictate to the Secretary, who was charged by law with control of the deposits, but assumed the responsibility of deciding that no more public money should be placed in the Bank and the Government's funds therein drawn out and deposited in State banks. Duane refused to sign the order and was dismissed. Taney succeeded him; and the removals commenced. Van Buren had his old law partner made Attorney General; but Butler, who knew he could make more money in private practice, took the post reluctantly.

All of Jackson's Cabinet, with the exception of Taney, were opposed to the removals, at least during the recess of Congress. This was Van Buren's attitude. Once Jackson had determined on his tempestuous course—wholly justified by the acts of aggression of the Bank—Van Buren was for the measure. This violent blow at the Bank's credit could only have been given by one of Jackson's mold, just as it took the cautious and calculating mind of Van Buren to find not only a substitute, insofar as the Government's needs were concerned, but a preventive against the revival of the Bank. This he was to accomplish a few years later. Historians have assumed, on the basis of erroneous conclusions of contemporaries of Jackson and Van Buren, that there was a temporary break between them over the removal of the deposits, and that Taney for a time was Jackson's closest adviser. Van Buren remained in New York until the middle of October, when the heavy assaults on the Bank had been under way for a fortnight. This and information gleaned from a fragmentary part of the correspondence between Jackson and Van Buren would tend to support these false assumptions. But the complete exchange of letters between Jackson and Van Buren shows that the friendship —there has been nothing like it in our political history; for Jackson loved Van Buren as a father does a son—continued unbroken, and that had Van Buren held out against a removal of the deposits during the recess of Congress, Jackson would have implicitly followed his advice.

Jackson was pitiably sick this summer. Only the excitement kept him up. On July 29, before leaving Washington for the Rips Raps, he penned, with obvious bodily pain, a four-page letter to Van Buren, wherein he recounted the reasons why the deposits should be removed. And he added this qualification: "Still as my health is feeble, & life uncertain, and the administration of the Government on my death must devolve on you, I would not wish to do an act of such importance, without having your full views upon this subject." Two days before the removals began Jackson wrote Van Buren: ". . . my duty to my country, & the perpetuity of our happy republican government dictated the course which I have adopted & if the people do not sustain me, then indeed a private station is the part of honor."

These removals were followed by many abuses. Three New York banks had been selected, and two of them Jackson described as the Macanics [Mechanics] and the M Hattan [Manhattan]. Taney, said Jackson, wanted Van Buren to name the fourth. Van Buren knew that any one who meddled in the selection of these banks stood a chance of being tarred. He resolved to keep clean in this, as he had done throughout his career in all matters involving money. "I have no choice," Van Buren answered. He said that he had "mentioned Mr. Taney's wish in respect to the additional bank to Mr. Cambreleng & requested him to confer with his associates in Congress from this city." The selections of the State banks to act as Government depositaries were made on recommendation of the politically powerful; hence their name— pet banks.

Meanwhile the Bank mustered all its forces for the fight, which was waged with renewed and desperate vigor in the press; and anticipating the convening of Congress on December 2, sought "to force a restoration of the deposits, and . . . extort a renewal of its charter" by trying to create a financial panic, as Jackson charged in his annual message. "It must now be determined whether the Bank is to have its candidates for all offices in the country, from the highest to the lowest, or whether candidates on both sides of political questions are to be brought forward, as heretofore, and supported by the usual means," Jackson said to Congress.

Van Buren arrived in Washington toward the end of the second week of the session, it being traditional for the Vice President to absent himself until the Senate committees had been appointed. On taking the chair on Monday, December 16, he made his first public utterance as the second officer of the land. It was short and one such as others before and after him have made; totally devoid of significance. It provoked no comment; but the coach he had brought over from England did. The adverse journals described it as an English coach of state—"a very splendid carriage, drawn by two beautiful blood-horses, their heads and tails full of a great deal more of intellect, passion, feeling, and sublimity than their owner. . . . It is of a dark-olive hue, with ornaments elegantly disposed, shining as bright as burnished gold," and "far more superb than the equipages of royalty."

Scarcely a day passed without Clay, Webster, or some of the lesser lights of the Senate presenting a memorial from some city telling of the distress of the people, and protesting against the removal of the deposits. These memorials were written by the same hand, or from a pattern supplied by agents of the Bank. Some of these meetings were undoubtedly of spontaneous origin; but their direction was singularly the same. In 1811, when the Bank attempted to extort a recharter from another unwilling Congress, it had resorted to similar means. Then it lost by the casting vote of Vice President Clinton.

On March 7, after Webster had presented a memorial from a meeting of building mechanics in Philadelphia, and moved its publication, Clay, rising to second, appealed to Jackson's supporters in the chamber to urge the President to retrace his steps, and abandon his fatal experiment. And then apostrophizing Van Buren, Clay said: "No one, sir, can perform that duty better than yourself. You can, if you will, induce him to change his course. . . . Go to him and tell him, without exaggeration, but in the language of truth and sincerity, the actual condition of his bleeding country. Tell him it is nearly ruined and undone by the measures which he has been induced to put in operation. . . . Depict to him, if you can find language to portray, the heart-rending wretchedness of thousands of the working classes cast out of employment. Tell him of the tears of helpless widows, no longer able to earn their bread, and of unclad and unfed orphans who have been driven, by his policy, out of the busy pursuits in which but yesterday they were gaining an honest livelihood. . . . Tell him of the ardent attachment, the unbounded devotion, the enthusiastic gratitude, towards him, so often signally manifested by the American people, and that they deserve, at his hands, better treatment. Tell him to guard himself against the possibility of an odious comparison with that worst of the Roman emperors, who, contemplating with indifference the conflagration of the mistress of the world, regaled himself during the terrific scene in the throng of his dancing courtiers. If you desire to secure for yourself the reputation of a public benefactor, describe to him truly the universal distress already produced, and the certain ruin which must ensue from perseverance in his measures. Tell him that he has been abused, deceived, betrayed, by the wicked counsels of unprincipled men around him. . . . Entreat him to pause and to reflect that there is a point beyond which human endurance cannot go; and let him not drive this brave, generous, and patriotic people to madness and despair."

Van Buren drank in every word of Clay's appeal. Long before he entered Congress he had read every speech of the Kentucky statesman he could lay his hands on. To him, Clay's oratory was matchless. He never took his eyes off the face of his foe during the delivery of this splendid specimen of histrionics. When Clay took his seat Van Buren surrendered his chair to a Senator, and with all eyes focused on him, he stalked slowly over to Clay's seat and whispered. Clay, somewhat astonished, complied with the request by offering Van Buren his snuff-box. Van Buren took a pinch of the rose-scented snuff—Clay always used the finest maccaboy Martinique produced—and walked away.

Clay's purpose was to cast part of the odium of the panic and its consequences on Van Buren. And the Bank agents arranged a meeting in Philadelphia at which resolutions were adopted asserting "that Martin Van Buren deserves, and will receive, the execrations of all good men, should he shrink from the responsibility of conveying to Andrew Jackson the message sent by the honorable Henry Clay, when the builders' memorial was presented to the Senate. . . ."

Three weeks later Clay introduced a resolution censuring Jackson for removing the deposits, holding that he had "assumed upon himself authority and power not conferred by the Constitution and laws, but in derogation of both." The resolution was adopted by a vote of 26 to 20. Benton at once served notice that he would move to expunge the resolution of censure from the Senate journal, which he did at the next session.

These attacks were having their effect. In New York City, Jackson's greatest stronghold in the north, the opposition, now calling themselves Whigs, carried a majority of the Common Council in the April elections. Cornelius Van Wyck Lawrence, the Jackson candidate for Mayor, was elected by the slim margin of one hundred and seventy-nine votes. The Jacksonians resorted to violence in their efforts to carry the city, as they were apprehensive of its effect on the gubernatorial election in the fall. Preserved Fish, Abraham LeRoy, and George D. Strong, and other blue bloods in Tammany incited the Irish to drive the Whigs from the polls. Not much persuasion was required, as the opposition to Jackson had cried down his Irish ancestry. On the third and last day of the election, Thursday, April 10, pitched battles occurred in the streets. Stones, cudgels, and dirks were freely used. When Gideon Lee, the Mayor, led a large body of watchmen to quell the rioting, the warring partisans turned on the police and routed them, injuring many; eight policemen were taken to the hospital. Then the battle between the Americans and the Irish—as the anti-Jacksonian press always designated the factions—was resumed, lasting until word reached them that a troop of cavalry and a regiment of infantry were on the way.

Although the Jacksonians elected their Mayor, the New

York election was distinctly a Whig triumph, as all the officials received their appointments from the Council. The following Tuesday the Whigs celebrated at Castle Garden, consuming 1,512 quarts of wine, and 40 barrels of beer. Food was also served. The victory in New York was the excuse for Whig jubilations elsewhere. These were jointly promoted by Whig leaders and agents of the Bank. A week after the Castle Garden meeting, a multitude was feasted on the outskirts of Philadelphia. Tens of thousands came from adjacent States. "The whole number congregated was supposed not to be less than fifty thousand. . . . Many cattle and other animals had been roasted whole, and there were 200 great rounds of beef, 400 hams, as many beeves' tongues, &c., and 15,000 loaves of bread, with crackers and cheese, &c., and equal supplies of wine, beer, and cider. . . . Strong bands of music played at intervals, and several salutes were fired from the miniature frigate, which were returned by heavy artillery provided for the purpose."

At these meetings Van Buren received "the execrations of all good men," and the comminations were continued in the Senate. Congress sat until the end of June. On the 23d of the month the Senate rejected the nomination of Andrew Stevenson, seven years Speaker of the House of Representatives, as Minister to England to succeed Van Buren. Jackson decided to help them in their efforts to make themselves ridiculous by letting it be known that he would not send in another name for this most important post. As both Jackson and Van Buren were avowed friends of England, this could be done without offense. It was not until the close of Jackson's term in 1836 that the Senate gave its assent. This affront to the President was followed by another: the rejection of Taney as Secretary of the Treasury.

With the view of hurting Van Buren in the South it was said that he favored freeing the slaves by act of Congress. In a letter to Stephen Gwin, of Clinton, Mississippi, a fortnight after the adjournment of Congress, Van Buren not only nailed this lie but proclaimed himself a staunch advocate of the slave-owning States. ". . . The subject is, in my judgment, exclusively under the control of the State Governments; and I am not apprised, nor do I believe, that a contrary opinion, to any extent deserving consideration, is entertained in any part of the United States.

. . . I do not see on what authority the General Government could interfere, without a change of the Constitution, even at the instance of either or of all the slaveholding States."

The deadliness of this falsehood lay in the fresh impetus given to the manumission movement by the Act of Parliament in the preceding year freeing some 800,000 blacks in the British West Indies. William Lloyd Garrison, who had been firing the North for the past four years with his uncompromising demand for immediate emancipation without compensation to the slave-owners —England indemnified the former owners of slaves—had become a living nightmare to the South. His *Liberator* was proscribed below the Mason and Dixon Line: the Legislature of Georgia offered $5,000 reward for the arrest of any one circulating it.

At the beginning of 1834, the little band of fanatics which gathered round Garrison when he began his labors in Boston, had swelled to considerable proportions. In New York the Abolitionists held several meetings, some in churches where the pastors and congregations went bodily into the movement. These gatherings had been attended throughout by considerable turbulence. On July 11 the anti-Abolitionists went to the homes of Lewis Tappan and his brother Arthur, two of the wealthiest and most conspicuous Abolitionists in the metropolis, broke the doors and windows, destroyed the small pieces of furniture, and hurled the large pieces to the street and made a bonfire of them. Then they marched through the city, attacking several churches, and were finally driven off by a regiment of infantry. John Quincy Adams —now in his third year as a member of the House of Representatives—and other conservative antislavery men, looked upon Garrison and the Abolitionists as incendiaries, and equally dangerous to the peace of the Union with Calhoun and his nullifiers.

The following month several hundred men, dressed as for a masquerade ball, assembled in the shadow of the unfinished Bunker Hill Monument. The hour was midnight. Many carried torches, others axes, and a few shouldered muskets. They marched in orderly ranks to their objective. The most dispassionate description of what happened thereafter, and its cause is found in Hone: "A most disgraceful riot occurred on the night of Monday, August 11, at Charlestown, near Boston. The populace having been deceived by ill-designed persons into an erroneous belief that a young lady was confined against her will in the Ursuline Convent, a highly respectable seminary under the charge of the Roman Catholics, made an attack upon the convent, a noble edifice, and the other buildings belonging to the sisterhood, and burned them to the ground with all the valuable furniture, desecrated the cemetery, and committed every species of outrage." There were about sixty young women in the convent when the mob, crying "No Popery!" gave the nuns a scant few minutes to leave the building with their charges. The firemen were driven off by the mob. At a meeting in Faneuil Hall, Harrison Gray Otis, Josiah Quincy, and others denounced the outrage. A committee of investigation appointed at this meeting disclosed the facts. The ringleaders were arrested; all save a youth were acquitted, and he was pardoned by the Governor of Massachusetts. The temper of the State was reflected in the refusal of the Legislature to indemnify the sisterhood for its loss.

Bigotry had been taught the generation by the politicians during the Anti-Masonic excitement.

Mobs next arose in Philadelphia, sacking and burning the homes of the freed blacks, destroying thirty buildings including two churches during the three nights of rioting. A negro asleep in his home was thrown through the window to the street below.

The State campaigns were waged on national issues. It was the prelude to the Presidential campaign of 1836. Van Buren wrote the address to the people of the Democratic-Republicans of New York State; he supervised the preparations of pamphlets, the speeches on the hustings, urging especially that ridicule be heaped on the Whigs, who were to be asked by what name they would be known in another year. The Whigs had made the spoils system and the Bank the dominant issues. The Van Burenites ignored the first, but answered the second with "Down with the Aristocracy!" and "The Rich Against the Poor!"

A new member was added to the Regency at the beginning of the campaign. Although only twenty-four years of age, he was regarded by Van Buren as possessed of more ability and undeveloped capacity than any other member of the Regency. The latest acquisition was his son John. He had sown the wildest of his wild oats; he still drank, but not more than the average youth in his set. He was an inveterate gambler, and, like his associates, given to profanity. His chief task was tabulating the predictions made by the various subordinate leaders in the machine, State and national.

John had lost heavily in stocks following the transfer of deposits: he had guessed the stock market the wrong way. He called on Washington Irving with a long face in the spring and bemoaned his losses. All his earnings from his law practice were wiped out. He vainly tried to borrow $1,000 from his father, but was able to raise funds somewhere to stay in the market. Most of his trading was done through Jesse Hoyt. When John gave him an order to buy and enclosed none of the wherewithal, Hoyt wrote back for money, provoking this response from John: "Why G—d d—n you Jesse! buy my stock and draw upon me at sight. You must be poor bitches down there, if you cannot raise this two penny sum. If the stock has gone up, let it go to Hell. The Bank will come against the Safety Fund Banks, and depress stocks—the Governor's message will eventually relieve the country."

The reason for John's anger was Hoyt's failure to understand that when he gave him the original order on Friday, March 22, 1834, he had information that Marcy would send a message to the Legislature recommending that the State extend its credit to the Safety Fund Banks to the extent of five to six million dollars. In his letter asking Hoyt to buy he wrote: "I fear stocks will rise after Monday. . . . There will be something done here [Albany] Monday. . . ." It was not until Tuesday that John heard from Hoyt. Marcy's message was then twenty-four hours old, and the necessary legislation to enable the State banks to continue specie payments, and extend their loans, was being drafted. Hoyt bought the stock on receipt of the second letter, but at the beginning of the fall campaign John was again in poor straits as the opening sentence of a letter to Hoyt revealed: "For God's sake send me my over coat—my underclothes are all worn out, and I'm a beggar."

Toward the close of the State election, in which John recouped most of his stock losses, Van Buren went to Kinderhook where the Whigs were making a desperate struggle so that their organs might publish: "Van Buren Defeated in His Native Village." From here, when confident of victory, Van Buren wrote to Hoyt: "I almost begin to pity the poor Whigs. Their next cognomen will be *Democrats*—mark what I say." The winnings of John totaled more than $9,000 in cash through Hoyt. Early in September he began placing wagers on Marcy's majority, on the fate of various candidates for Congress, and on the results in Ohio, Maine, and Pennsylvania. He could not lose, and knew it. "If you can," he wrote Hoyt three weeks before election, "get me an even bet against Marcy to any amount less than Five Thousand Dollars. . . . I consider Marcy's election, by from 7,500 to 15,000, as sure as God." Marcy defeated William H. Seward, "the young man with the sandy hair," by 11,000. In addition to cash Hoyt collected wagers consisting of fire-wood, wheat, hams, barrels of apples, bales of cotton, a $7 pair of boots, a $10 hat, and cases of champagne. John Duer lost a suit of clothes costing $50; Alexander Hamilton, Jr., $250 cash; John A. King, $100; Charles L. Livingston, $100; John Hone, the diarist's brother, $150. How much Van Buren himself won on the election is not disclosed.

Van Buren resumed the Vice President's chair with the opening of Congress. His opponents, disappointed over the results of the State elections, were downcast. They had used the very arguments they were counting on to win the next Presidential election, and had failed to impress the nation. Some were despondent; others desperate. The extreme of their desperation was revealed after Benton had made public his letter to Wiley Davis, of Mississippi, declining the nomination for President by its State convention, and citing the reasons why Van Buren should be nominated. Benton's colleague, Poindexter, who had voted for the resolution censuring Jackson, now became embittered toward Van Buren. The brilliancy of Poindexter's intellect was dulling under the effects of drink, dissipation and domestic embroilments. He was reckless in conversation and debate. Men feared to cross him. Within a few days of the publication of Benton's letter Van Buren learned that Poindexter intended to quarrel with him over some official trifle, and shape therefrom a situation which would lead to a duel or a beating, and thereby render Van Buren an object of scorn. Doubts as to the accuracy of his information vanished after the New Year when he received the prelude to a challenge. Poindexter's carefully phrased letter read in part:

The unusual punctuality, with which you attended, as the Presiding officer of the Senate at the commencement of the present session of Congress, has been attributed by certain newspapers edited by your friends and supporters, to considerations having a direct personal relation to myself. . . . I refer especially to an article in the Newburg Telegraph, which has been copied into other kindred prints, and cannot have escaped your observation:

The President of the Senate was in his chair at the opening of the session and thus preserved it from being disgraced by "that bloated mass of corruption—Poindexter."

. . . I will not permit myself to believe that in taking your seat at the opening of the session, you were actuated by the unworthy motives, which your friends have so indiscreetly attributed to you, until you manifest a disposition to place yourself in that attitude. I should much prefer for your own sake, and that of the august body over whose deliberations you have been called to preside, to regard your early attendance as an evidence of the promptitude and industry, with which you were anxious to discharge your public duties. It is now in your power, to give me this assurance which I consider *absolutely* necessary to avert the consequences of an opposite conclusion.

That evening there was a conference at the White House, with Forsyth and Silas Wright present as consultants to Van Buren and Jackson. All agreed that Poindexter intended to resort to violence. Meanwhile the conferees decided on this reply:

Washington Jany 6th, 1835.

Sir;

You are quite correct in not permitting yourself to believe that the official act to which you allude, in your letter of yesterday, was designed to arrogate to myself the right of deciding upon the propriety of the Senate's choice of their President pro tempore, or to interfere with the relations in which you or any other member, may stand to that body, and to the country.

Your very proper and explicit disclaimer of all idea of holding me responsible for the commentaries or constructions of the public press has enabled me so far to respect the official relations existing between us, and to which you refer, as to give you this answer.

I am Sir, your humble servt

M. Van Buren.

To the Honble George Poindexter.

Next morning, when Van Buren ascended the Vice President's chair he had a pair of pistols, loaded and cocked, concealed on his person. This was the first time that he had gone armed in his life. Less than four weeks later an incident occurred which convinced Jackson that Poindexter was bent on slaying him as well as Van Buren. While he was descending the east front of the Capitol after attending the funeral services for Representative Warren Ransom Davis, of South Carolina, a house painter named Richard Lawrence fired two pistols point-blank at Jackson. Both flashed in the pan. A local politician charged that the attempted assassination had been instigated by Poindexter. Jackson, in his morbid state of mind and body, believed the falsehood. Poindexter demanded an investigation by the Senate, and was exonerated. Lawrence, unquestionably crazy, was acquitted, and remanded to custody as insane. Poindexter did not carry out his intentions. Van Buren regarded the change in Poindexter's attitude toward him as having been dictated by Henry Clay, who learned of the Mississippian's mad design after the exchange of letters.

In February the Massachusetts Whigs nominated Webster for President. The election of 1836 was twenty-one months off, but the campaign was a month old, as Jackson's own State had nominated Hugh Lawson White, Jackson's successor in the Senate. White was a State-rights Whig. Webster had no strength outside of his own State. The Whigs of other Northern States were planning to make Major General William H. Harrison, the hero of Tippecanoe, their candidate. Harrison was rounding out his life on his farm at North Bend, Ohio, making ends meet with his little salary as clerk of the county court.

When the gavels fell in both houses on March 3, all eyes turned anxiously toward Baltimore, where on May 20, the Democratic-Republicans would hold their national convention. On this third Wednesday in May delegates from every State in the Union excepting Alabama, South Carolina, Illinois, and Tennessee, were in their seats when George Kremer, as temporary chairman, presented a clergyman to offer up prayer. Tennessee was absent because White was her candidate. Alabama had made the cause of White, and that of John Tyler, his running mate, her own. South Carolina, still playing a lone hand, had a candidate for President in Willie P. Mangum, of North Carolina; and supported Tyler for second place. There was more than personal feeling in White's candidacy for President: his supporters were Cotton Whigs, who agreed with their partisans of the North only in believing that Jackson had violated the Constitution. They differed with them on the Bank, the tariff, internal improvements, and State rights. Tennessee disapproved of national conventions, holding that the party in power would dominate their deliberations with "village politicians and placemen."

Although this was the first of the national conventions made up of place holders and others beholden to a Federal administration, it was not as thoroughly drilled as others that followed. When Romulus M. Saunders, of North Carolina, as chairman of the Committee on Rules, offered the undemocratic unit and two-thirds rules, he was outvoted, 231 to 210. The two-thirds rule had been adopted four years before to make Van Buren's nomination for Vice President all the more impressive. On the following day, there was a reconsideration of the vote by which the majority rule had been adopted; and the two-thirds and unit rules were substituted in its stead.

Andrew Stevenson was chosen permanent chairman. On announcing that the next business of the convention was to nominate a candidate for President, he filled the convention with smiles. Van Buren received the unanimous vote of every delegation present, as well as the fifteen votes of absent and unrepresented Tennessee! But one of the fuglemen found a native of Tennessee named Edward Rucker in town; and Rucker was recognized as the "delegation" from Jackson's home State. Rucker was obscure and unknown; but this piece of political magic gave him an unenviable prominence, and enriched the political argot of the day with the verb "to rucker."

The convention balked when the party managers moved the nomination of Senator Johnson of Kentucky. Had the Tennessee delegation—which did not exist save in the fancy of the convention—not been recognized, Johnson would not have been nominated. With the imaginary fifteen votes from Tennessee the total number of accredited delegates was 265; actually there were only 250 delegates present. Under the two-thirds rule, had the fictive fifteen been omitted from the reckoning, it would have taken 167 votes to nominate. The opposition to Johnson mustered 87, three more than the required number to block a nomination. But the fraudulent votes from Jackson's own State saved the day for Johnson, as he received 178 to the 87 cast for William C. Rives of Virginia. The opposition to Johnson was unanimous in the delegations from Maine, New Jersey, Virginia, Georgia, and North Carolina; and ten of the fourteen votes from Massachusetts went to Rives. But all save Virginia agreed to support Johnson. The Virginians adopted a resolution declaring that the Old Dominion had no confidence in either the principles or character of Van Buren's running mate; and chagrined with Van Buren, whom they held responsible for the admission of the non-existent Tennessee delegation, the Virginia delegates also placed on the record that they came to the convention to support principles, not men, and had wandered sufficiently far afield in voting for Van Buren.

On Friday the convention adjourned after an address to the electorate was drafted. No platform was adopted.

Van Buren had remained in Washington during the deliberations of the convention. In his letter of acceptance, Van Buren avoided discussing a single issue. "I am not aware," said he, "that there is any point of interest in the general policy of the Federal Government, in respect to which, my opinions have not been made known by my official acts—my own public avowals, and by the authorized explanations of my friends. If there be any such, however, you may rest assured of my ready disposition to comply, on all suitable occasions, with the wishes of my fellow citizens in this regard."

This letter has been condemned as inane and prolix. It was prolix, but not inane: there were eighteen months of campaign ahead, a hostile Congress, hostile State legislatures, a hostile press, and designing and resourceful enemies. These things he had in mind; and he intended, as the canvass progressed, to discuss new "points of interest" when raised, but only on "suitable occasions": and his foes did not select the occasions. He paid this tribute to Jackson: "I content myself, on this occasion, with saying, that I consider myself the honored instrument, selected by the friends of the present administration, to carry out its principles and policy; and that, as well from inclination as from duty, I shall, if honored with the choice of the American people, endeavor to tread generally in the footsteps of President Jackson —happy, if I shall be able to perfect the work which he has so gloriously begun."

He set the fashion for future nominees by protesting that he had not sought the nomination. He reminded the country of the apprehension entertained by the ruling cliques of the old world that the divine right of kings must give way before the sovereignty of the people. "We hold an immense stake for the weal or woe of mankind, to the importance of which we should not be insensible," he said. "The intense interest manifested abroad in every movement here, that threatens the stability of our system shows the deep conviction which pervades the world that upon its fate depends the cause of Republican Government. The advocates of monarchical systems have not been slow in perceiving danger to such institutions in the permanency of our Constitution, nor backward in seizing upon every passing event by which their predictions of its speedy destruction could be in any degree justified. Thus far, they have been disappointed in their anticipations, and the circumstances by which they were encouraged, however alarming at the time, have in the end only tended to show forth the depth of that devotion to the Union, which is yet, thank God! the master passion of the American bosom."

Every device was employed by the doomed order in its conflict with the inevitable. Less than five years before, a week after the Revolution of July, La Fayette, who had defended his faith in republics with his blood at Brandywine, presented Louis Philippe to the people, with: "We have done a good work. This is what we have been able to make most like a Republic." The monarchists debased this into: "Behold the best of Republics." So widely and zealously was this perversion propagated that it was accepted as truth years later by France's noblest writer. Hugo, too, had fought for freedom. But he missed La Fayette's disclaimer to General Bernard as this passage in his masterpiece indicates: "The 221 made Louis Philippe king, and La Fayette undertook the coronation. He named him *the best of Republics*, and the Town Hall of Paris was substituted for the Cathedral of Rheims." And the bourgeois King's successor, who proclaimed himself Emperor while President of the Republic, was the tool

MARTIN VAN BUREN
From a painting by Inman

used by Europe to attempt the destruction of the Union by setting up the ill-starred Empire to the south of us when secession had become a reality. Van Buren had foreseen it; but in 1835 his adversaries translated his warning into an artful, self-serving appeal to the electors: they had heard the politician so long that they were deaf to the statesman.

The summer boded little good to Van Buren's candidature. The Abolitionists were flooding the Southern mails with incendiary broadsides and pamphlets. It was charged that the intent of these extremists was to incite a servile revolt. Color was lent to the accusation by the unbridled tongue of George Thompson, imported from England by the fanatics, who said that the slaves ought, or at least had the right, to cut the throats of their masters. The South searched the mail bags for the antislavery literature, which was burned publicly, or ceremoniously cast in the water. Slaves suspected of complicity with Abolitionists were summarily hanged. Two gibbets were erected in front of Garrison's home in Boston; and he was manhandled by a mob who were bent on wreaking vengeance on Thompson, who made his escape on a sailing vessel.

A postmaster in Calhoun's State, hoping to enmesh the administration in the fanaticism of the Abolitionists, and thereby hurt Van Buren in the South, placed the question before the Postmaster General. Kendall, who had held this place since May, after it had been shown that the Department under Barry had lost money through jobbery by mail contractors and others, avoided the pitfall by intimating that matter prohibited by State laws should not be transmitted through the mails. While the tumult was at its height Van Buren rested at Saratoga Springs, calm and unruffled, a plenteous supply of wine at his table: for he followed the custom of the day in sending a bottle to the tables of friends and acquaintances.

Toward the end of the summer three campaign biographies of Van Buren were on the presses. Two were the work of friendly hands: one of pamphlet size, by William Emmons; and a more pretentious volume by William M. Holland. The third was by David Crockett, one of the most picturesque and heroic products of the early American frontier, whose crude Falstaffian wit had made him a national figure before he left the Tennessee Legisla-

ture to serve his State in Congress. From a loyal Jacksonite, he
had become a violent partisan of White. A more scurrilous document has not been penned against a candidate for the Presidency.
To quote: "Van Buren is as opposite to General Jackson as dung
is to a diamond. . . . He has no pedigree that I can trace back
farther than his sire. During the war of the revolution, his father
was considered on the *Whig* side, while his uncle, his father's
brother, was a Tory, and it was said, occasionally aided, as a
guide to British scouting parties. I state this fact merely to show
the *breed.* . . . he is what the English call a dandy. When he
enters the senate-chamber in the morning, he struts and swaggers
like a crow in the gutter. He is laced up in corsets, such as women
in town wear, and, if possible, tighter than the best of them. It
would be difficult to say, from his personal appearance, whether
he was man or woman, but for his large *red* [*sic!*] and *gray*
whiskers."

Crockett, in his blind partisanship, believed the worst of the
stories invented when Rufus King was reëlected United States
Senator through the covert influence of Van Buren. After a fair
summary of the extraordinary events leading to the Federal
leader's choice by a Republican Legislature, Crockett wrote:
". . . Mr. King was well known to possess high-toned aristocratic
feelings; and that he would not mix or associate with such men
as Mr. Van Buren and me, who were nothing but the sons of
little, petty, country tavern-keepers, unless it was his intention
to make use of such folks as we were; and for such use he was
willing to *pay;* and, unfortunately, in Mr. Van Buren he found
a person not less willing to *receive* than he was to *pay.*" Van
Buren did not answer this untruthful and unsupported charge.
He did not believe in defensive publications. Then, too, if he had
any thought of replying at the beginning of the spring of 1836,
he had waited too long, as a candidate for office cannot attack a
man whose exit is made glorious by the glamour of heroism.
After the publication of his book, Crockett joined Colonel James
Bowie at the Alamo; and when Santa Anna's vastly superior
numbers took the old Spanish fort, Crockett and five others alone
were living of the little band of defenders. The six prisoners were
taken before the Mexican leader, at whose throat Crockett sprang

with bare hands when the frown of Santa Anna transformed the swords of his soldiers into the knives of butchers.

Following a rest at Saratoga, Van Buren visited Niagara Falls, and while on his way back, a letter from William Schley, of Athens, Georgia, brought forth a fresh disavowal from Van Buren that he entertained "views and opinions that are justly obnoxious to the slaveholding States." He recalled his expressed conviction denying that the Federal Government could interfere, and added: "I should poorly requite the candor with which I have hitherto been treated by the great mass of my fellow-citizens at the South, were I to allow myself to apprehend that those who would otherwise be disposed to give me their confidence could, under such circumstances, suffer me to be prejudiced in their opinion by the unsupported assertions of my enemies, however reckless or vehemently persisted in."

On his return to Washington Van Buren found a vast accumulation of mail. J. M. Van Buren, a cousin, wrote that he had been teaching since he graduated at Union College in June, when "for the special gratification of the Citizens of that Dutch place [Schenectady] I delivered my oration in the Holland, my vernacular language. . . . At Dr. [Eliphalet] Nott's levee he seemed to take uncommon satisfaction in complimenting the Dutch orator. . . ." He had abandoned pedagogy to study at the Theological Seminary at Auburn. He recalled occasions when Van Buren had helped him; and told of having an essay in the July number of the *North American Quarterly*. The subscription, *Yours affectionately*, and the address, *Honored and Respected Friend*, charmed; for there was no mistaking the gratitude and sincerity of the seminarian, who had lost his parents at an early age, and had been brought up by the Hogebooms at Kinderhook. Van Buren had advised him to practice law. "You will excuse me for taking the Ministry instead of Law, my conscience & feelings would not permit me to do otherwise," he explained; and reasoned that since mankind, "generally conceded th[e Minis]try * to be the most honorable calling, it certainly must be so in the sight of God." Van Buren cherished this letter, and at the bottom noted: "Sent him $30."

* Torn.

A letter from Marcy brought him back to his orbit with an inquiry as to what should be said on slavery in his annual message to the New York Legislature. Van Buren's response, although missing, is indicated by Marcy's condemnation of the conduct of the Abolitionists as tending to disturb the harmony of the Union by creating sectional jealousies.

Van Buren also had the papers of Jackson to supervise. The annual message to Congress must also discuss the Abolitionists and the far more pressing question of the nation's claims against France, which had almost led to war in 1834. These claims, arising out of the aggressions on our shipping under the despotic reign of Napoleon, had been a subject of fruitless negotiation for twenty years. European countries had collected similar debts, and Jackson's stern message of the previous year was justified by the advices from Livingston and France's failure to pay the initial instalment of one and one-half millions of francs in accordance with the terms of the treaty signed in the first year of the reign of Louis Philippe. France had agreed to pay twenty-five million francs, a paltry part of what was really due; the United States, in turn, was obligated to settle the claims of French citizens totaling one and one-half million francs. Congress had voted three million dollars, or three-fifths of the sum France owed us, for coastal defense.

We see Van Buren in such lines as these in Jackson's message: ". . . when France was overwhelmed by the military power of united Europe . . . whilst other nations were extorting from her payment of their claims at the point of the bayonet, the United States intermitted their demand for justice, out of respect to the oppressed condition of a gallant people, to whom they felt under obligations for fraternal assistance in their own days of suffering and peril. . . . The conception that it was my intention to menace or insult the Government of France, is as unfounded, as the attempt to extort from the fears of that nation what her sense of justice may deny, would be vain and ridiculous. . . . The people of the United States are justly attached to a pacific system in their intercourse with foreign nations. . . ."

Nowhere was there a withdrawal of a word previously uttered; instead, there was a spirited, yet, inoffensive, defense of what had been said and done. This message was read December 8. On

January 18 Jackson informed Congress that France had demanded that the United States make certain explanations or apologies in writing in terms which she shall dictate, "and which will involve an acknowledgment of her assumed right to interfere in our domestic councils." And, added Jackson, "she will never obtain it."

This second message would have been a preliminary to a formal declaration of war but for the conciliating counsel of Van Buren. Now the President recommended that the importation of French products and the entry of French ships be prohibited until she made "the tardy and imperfect indemnification . . . solemnly agreed upon by the treaty of 1831 . . ." On February 8, when the breach seemed wider than ever, the country learned through another message to Congress that England had offered to mediate. Two weeks later the country was apprised that the friendly offices of our ancient enemy had been successful. Jackson paid high tribute to "the elevated and disinterested part" England had played.

Van Buren's intimates knew that it was his hand which guided the pen of Jackson. Washington Irving, writing to Van Buren on February 1, said: "Much has been calculated on here from your moderation and discretion in this delicate matter, to temper the old General's 'heady valour' into true magnanimity." On February 24 Irving wrote Van Buren: ". . . By heaven you have brought us nobly through this affair and placed the country on a high footing abroad. I have been much pleased with the manner in which all the Messages this year have spoken on this subject. They have corresponded with the tone of some observations which dropped from you in the course of one of our conversations at Washington, and on which I founded hopes of a magnanimous and pacific course of policy. . . . I am inclined to give you great credit for the happy management of this matter, and for the able manner in which the *Collisions* between the two countries have been prevented from *striking fire*. I am happy to find the same opinion is entertained even by those who are usually disposed to gainsay your merits and misrepresent your actions. . . ."

But there was no such happy solution of the problem raised by the Abolitionists. Jackson recommended the enactment of a law to "prohibit, under severe penalties, the circulation in the Southern States, through the mail, of incendiary publications intended to instigate the slaves to insurrection." The opposition still controlled the Senate. A special committee was appointed to consider Jackson's recommendation. Calhoun dominated the deliberations of his associates which submitted a report, as well as a bill, intemperate, unrestrained, and certain to widen the breach between the North and South. It set forth that the States were sovereign and independent communities, and were united by a compact. This, in a word, was nullification. The report assumed that the South was menaced. Typical of the sentiments expressed are the following: ". . . Setting out with the abstract principle that slavery is an evil, the fanatical zealots come at once to the conclusion that it is their duty to abolish it regardless of the disasters which must follow. . . . The inevitable tendency of the means to which the abolitionists have resorted to effect their object must, if persisted in, end in completely alienating the two great sections of the Union. . . ."

The measure accompanying the report went further than Jackson intended. Calhoun demanded that the proposed law, known as the Incendiary Bill, be enacted under pain of secession, not merely of South Carolina, but of the entire South. "If you refuse coöperation with our laws," he said, "and conflict should ensue between your and our law, the Southern States will never yield to the superiority of yours. We have a remedy in our hands, which in such events, we shall not fail to apply. We have high authority for asserting that, in such cases, 'State interposition is the rightful remedy'—a doctrine first announced by Jefferson, adopted by the patriotic and republican State of Kentucky by a solemn resolution in 1798, and finally carried out into successful practice on a recent occasion—ever to be remembered—by the gallant State which I, in part, have the honor to represent." Calhoun was out-Garrisoning Garrison.

Those on the inside knew that the measure had no chance of passage, as at least six Senators from slave-holding States were opposed to the vicious principle of making a censor of every post-office employee in the land. Clay led the opposition; but he was not averse to Calhoun's plot to make it appear that Van Buren alone was responsible for its defeat: this was to be accomplished by throwing the fate of the bill into Van Buren's hands. Calhoun succeeded in effecting a tie vote of eighteen to eighteen to engross the bill: there were twelve absentees. When the vote was taken, Van Buren was out of the chair. Calhoun loudly demanded the presence of the Vice President, calling upon the sergeant-at-arms to produce him. Van Buren was pacing up and down behind the colonnade back of his desk. He let Calhoun enjoy a moment's thought that he had deliberately absented himself, and then took his seat, rising, a moment later, to give the casting vote for the engrossment. Calhoun's plan to inflame the South against Van Buren failed. The measure was defeated later by twenty-five to nineteen, New York's Senators, Wright and Tallmadge, voting with the minority.

Congress adjourned July 4. The disorderly campaign was then approaching its peak. The disorganized Whigs saw no hope save a division in the Electoral College which would throw the election into the House. Van Buren was making the campaign in his own way. Before the adjournment Adams, who had been a member of the House of Representatives since December, 1831, thus appraised, and justly, Van Buren and his principal opponents: "Van Buren's personal character, however, bears a stronger resemblance to that of Mr. Madison than to Jefferson's. These are both remarkable for their extreme caution in avoiding and averting personal collisions. Van Buren, like the Sosie of Molière's Amphitryon, is 'l'ami de tout le monde.' This is perhaps the great secret of his success in public life, and especially against the competitors with whom he is now struggling for the last step on the ladder of his ambition—Henry Clay and John C. Calhoun. They indeed are left upon the field for dead; and men of straw, Hugh L. White, William H. Harrison, and Daniel Webster, are thrust forward in their places. Neither of these has a principle to lean upon. Van Buren's principle is the talisman of democracy, which, so long as this Union lasts, can never fail."

But Van Buren was not "the friend of all the world." Biddle could testify to that. The charter of the Bank expired on March 4; and before its expiration, Van Buren, answering an invitation to be the guest of a partisan gathering in Cincinnati to celebrate "the deliverance of our country from the thralldom of the Bank of the United States," reviewed the various devices to which Biddle's institution resorted to extort a renewal of its charter from Congress, and said: "The people triumphed in that open contest, but before time had been allowed for seasonable celebrations of that triumph—even since your festival has been appointed, and before the day arrived for the expression of your joy—the same power, fighting under the same panoply, but changing altogether its approach, has again entered the field and gained a victory over the popular will . . . But how changed the mode of warfare in this last effort! Instead of commercial distress, public and private embarrassment, and all the concomitants of an uncontrollable panic in the public mind, plenty and even profusion pervaded the city of the Bank, while its noiseless approach to the legislative power was characterized by a dispatch altogether unprecedented in so important a matter in the history of legislation."

These cryptic utterances referred to the granting of a charter to the Bank by the Pennsylvania Legislature, after $400,000 had been mysteriously spent by Biddle's institution: this was unquestionably the price paid to the Pennsylvania lawmakers for extending the life of "the monster." He called the Bank "this aristocratic institution" which "mistook the character of that people whose stubborn necks it proposed to bend to its selfish and sinister designs." He had now reached the fullness of his years; and his belief in the people was no longer disturbed by doubtings.

Before starting for New York he reiterated his views on slavery in replying to six partisans of the town of Jackson, North Carolina, who inquired specifically if he believed Congress had the power to interfere with or abolish slavery in the District of Columbia. Congress at this time was being deluged with petitions from Abolitionists and other anti-slavery groups to prohibit slavery in the national capital. A plain categorical response to this inquiry would have lost him the South, as he would have had to answer: Yes. So he began the reply with repetitions of his avowals on slavery which had endeared him to the South, following them with the expression that "I have not been able to satisfy myself that the grant to Congress, in the Constitution, of the power of 'exclusive legislation in all cases whatsoever' over the Federal District, does not confer on that body the same authority over the subject that would otherwise have been possessed by the States of Maryland

and Virginia; or that Congress might not, in virtue thereof, take such steps upon the subject in this District, as those States might themselves take within their own limits, and consistently with their rights of sovereignty."

As a matter of law there was no doubting the power of Congress to abolish slavery in the district; but as a matter of equity, the national lawmakers should not disturb the existing situation. As Van Buren observed, the cession of the land comprising the seat of government would not have been made by the slave-holding States of Maryland and Virginia had the present agitation been foreseen, except on the express condition that Congress should not exercise this power; "and that with such a condition the cession would, in the then state of public opinion, have been readily accepted." But the rub of the letter lay in this: "I must go into the Presidential Chair the inflexible and uncompromising opponent of any attempt on the part of Congress to abolish slavery in the District of Columbia, against the wishes of the slave-holding States; and also with the determination equally decided, to resist the slightest interference with the subject in the States where it exists." And the high level on which Van Buren sought to keep the campaign was exemplified in the subsequent sentence: "In saying this, I tender neither to them nor to you any pledges, but declare only settled opinions and convictions of duty."

When one of Clay's lieutenants, Sherrod Williams, a Representative from Kentucky, tried to force Van Buren to answer a series of questions before Congress adjourned, he publicly replied he would not reply until after adjournment. Harrison had answered the queries promptly; but Van Buren in declining to do so, said that he would not permit an avowed partisan foe to pick his own time and place to interrogate him; and further, he might, as Vice President, be called upon to vote on some of the matters involved. Williams said these reasons were wholly unsatisfactory. Van Buren curtly responded that Williams must wait. The Kentuckian, openly supporting Harrison, had asked the two chief candidates if they approved of: 1, A distribution of the surplus revenue of the nation among the States according to their population for such uses as they might appoint. 2, A like distribution of the proceeds of the sale of public lands. 3, Federal appropriations to improve navigable streams above ports of entry. 4, Another charter for the Bank if it should become necessary to preserve the revenue and finances of the nation. 5, Expunging records of proceedings of either House of Congress. Harrison had answered the first four in the affirmative, and the fifth in the negative.

Van Buren's answer to the first of these questions, if we had no other record before us, in itself gives the quietus to the oft-repeated line of writers of the period that he was "an echo of Jackson." This related to the proposed distribution of the surplus of $35,000,000 in the national treasury to begin on January 1, 1837. Jackson, who first objected to the measure, signed the bill when it reached him. The financial stringency was being felt everywhere with growing intensity, and the Distribution Act was popular. Van Buren replied that he was opposed to this legislation, insisting that Congress lacked the power to raise money for distribution among the States. "I hope and believe that the public voice will demand that this species of legislation shall terminate with the emergency that produced it." He also disapproved the distribution of the moneys from the sale of public lands to the States, holding that the funds should be applied to the general wants of the Treasury. In this he was one with Jackson. He also opposed, as did Jackson, appropriations for improvements of rivers above ports of entry save for expenditures for lighthouses, buoys, beacons, piers, and the removal of obstructions to navigation. If the people wanted a President who would approve a new charter for the Bank, or any other bank, they must elect some one else, as he was irrevocably opposed to the proposal; he added that it was high time the Federal Government confine itself to the creation of coin and that the States afford it a fair chance for circulation. Answering the last question he said the President would have no voice in expunging proceedings in Congress, but that he believed the adoption of Benton's expunging resolution would be "an act of justice to a faithful and greatly injured public servant, not only constitutional in itself, but imperiously demanded by a proper respect for the well-known will of the people."

The campaign of the opposition was a mild repetition of Jackson's first campaign. Van Buren was "the mistletoe politician, nourished by the sap of the hickory tree." Calhoun stigmatized the followers of Van Buren as "a powerful faction (party it cannot be called) held together by the hopes of public plunder, and marching under the banner whereon is written: 'to the victors belong the spoils.' " The *American,* still edited by Charles King, editorialized on October 28: "Mr. Van Buren . . . consorts most naturally with the degraded and the vile—for among them he is a superior." Six days later: "The good we desire we may not be able to attain: but the evil we dread, the great and menacing evil, the blighting disgrace of placing Martin Van Buren, illiterate, sycophantic, and politically corrupt, at the head of this great republic, and Richard M. Johnson, the husband of a negress and the father of a motley brood, in its second seat of honor; that evil and disgrace, by united exertion, we *can avert* and such a consummation is surely worth some trouble and the sacrifice of personal predilections." This also was fed to its readers: "Gen. Harrison was received with enthusiasm at Columbia, the old military station at the Points of Fork. At night, the citizens procured a tar barrel and several of them proceeded to light it with candles. At the moment of ignition, out popped a snake which had found a residence in the barrel. It was pursued by shouts of 'Van Buren! Van Buren! Here he goes! Put it to him!' amidst an uproar of mirth and applause."

Throughout the closing months of the canvass Van Buren remained in Albany, making occasional visits to lieutenants in other parts of the State who had not found it convenient to call upon him at Saratoga Springs—where he spent most of August— or at his home. Here he received news of his victory, his popular vote being 762,678, to the 735,651 for all his opponents. In the Electoral College the vote was: Van Buren, 170; Harrison, 73; White, 26; Webster, 14; Mangum, 11. Van Buren carried Maine, New Hampshire, Rhode Island, Connecticut, New York, Pennsylvania, Virginia, North Carolina, Alabama, Mississippi, Louisiana, Arkansas, Missouri, Illinois, Michigan; Harrison swept Vermont, New Jersey, Delaware, Maryland, Kentucky, Ohio, Indiana; White polled the votes of Georgia and Tennessee, Webster those of Massachusetts, and Mangum won South Carolina's eleven. Had Van Buren lost his own State, Pennsylvania, or Virginia, the Whigs would have thrown the election into the House, where Harrison would have probably been chosen, as the Whigs and opposing members of the Democratic party—as the party was now generally known—mustered a majority. The Electoral College now consisted of 294 votes, requiring 148 to elect. Virginia, after voting for Van Buren, cast her twenty-three votes for William Smith of Alabama for Vice President. This defection left Johnson with only 147 votes. This threw the contest into the Senate; but here the Van Burenites had a majority, and Johnson was chosen on the first ballot.

Van Buren reached Washington late in November. He spent much time with Jackson; and on learning that John Quincy Adams had reached the capital, immediately paid him a formal visit, which the ex-President returned on December 10. Abraham Van Buren, who had been promoted to a captaincy of dragoons in July, was again aiding his father in the rôle of amanuensis. Yet Van Buren still wrote letters of a personal nature in his own hand; one penned three days before Christmas showed a side known only to his chosen intimates. It also revealed a kindliness of spirit on the part of Marcy on which the record is otherwise silent. This letter, which is addressed to John Van Buren, leaves much to the imagination. It is evident from the letter that a friend of Van Buren, now very old, and too poor to go to Washington to see Van Buren inaugurated, had been inveigled into an absurd election bet by Marcy so that the old man would have the means to gratify his wish. The aged gambler's name is not mentioned by Van Buren, only his initials, V. W.; and we may assume that he was a Van Winkle, a Van Wagenen, or one of the other Van W——'s who were determined to see the first Dutchman inducted into the Presidency. Van Buren wrote: "Gov. M[arcy] suggested to me that our friend V. W. so arranged it with him (by way of a bet) that he was to pay something toward fitting * out Mr. V. W. for Washington to witness the Inauguration, & that he had been requested to suggest to me a contribution, which I cheerfully agreed to make & intimated to him that I would have word with you upon the subject. I have not heard of any thing else & have nothing else in my power. I wish therefore that you would advance him $30 for me to be applied to that object, or if he should when the time comes think the sight not worth the trouble, to any other purpose that suits him better. He is a good natured man . . . but I am sure when he takes into considera-

* Van Buren erroneously wrote *filling*.

tion the time of the year &c he will be inclined to think that he can upon the whole make better use of his money. Advise him frankly what is for his best."

New Year's Day witnessed the distribution to the States of the first instalment of the surplus in the Treasury. This took $9,367,000 from the "pet banks." For a fortnight or so there was no appreciable effect on the strained financial situation of the country, which had been growing more tense since the summer of 1834. Later in the month, after two days' debate, Benton succeeded in having the censure passed upon Jackson three years earlier for removing the Government's funds from the Bank, expunged from the Senate journal.

Van Buren took his leave of the Senate on January 28. King was elected President pro tempore for the remaining five weeks of the term.

When Van Buren began to prepare his message to Congress, the clouds, which were to overshadow his entire administration, began to gather. On Friday, February 10, placards appeared on the dead walls of New York City reading:

BREAD! MEAT! RENT! FUEL!
Their Prices Must Come Down!
The voice of the people shall be heard and will prevail.
The people will meet in the Park, *rain* or *shine,* at
4 o'clock Monday Afternoon,
To enquire into the cause of the present unexampled distress, and to devise a suitable remedy. All friends of humanity, determined to resist monopolists and extortionists, are invited to attend.

Moses Jacques,	Daniel Gorham,
Paulus Hedl,	John Windt,
Daniel A. Robertson,	Alexander Ming, Jr.,
Warden Hayward,	Elijah F. Crane.

New York, February 10th, 1837.

Some of the newspapers carried the same intelligence as paid advertisements. The signers were leaders of the Equal Rights party, composed of radicals who had withdrawn from Tammany two years before as a protest against the control of the organization by Wall Street bankers. Van Buren, who was soon to go further than even the Equal Rights men had planned for themselves, had attempted to compose these differences. But the Equal Rights men, or Loco-focos, as they were derisively called, were determined to clean house in their own way, and nominated a State ticket headed by Isaac L. Smith of Buffalo. Dr. Moses Jacques— he was prominent in the medical profession—was candidate for Lieutenant Governor. It was he who headed the list of signatories for the meeting in the Park. A similar one had been held three weeks earlier in the old Broadway Tabernacle.

At the appointed time the Park was thronged with several thousand men and women. Mayor Lawrence watched the proceedings from the windows of his office. Hundreds in the assemblage came from fuelless and foodless hovels immediately to the north of the City Hall. There were many undernourished boys in the throng. These, or such of them as had homes, lived in the Sixth Ward, the most poverty-stricken section of the city. Present also were many small merchants and professional men who sympathized with the purposes of the meeting. All cheered the attack on the dealers in wheat, who were asking $15 a barrel for flour which a short time before brought $8. "Fellow citizens," said one of the speakers menacingly, "Mr. Hart has fifty-three thousand barrels of flour in his stores. Let us go and offer him $8 a barrel, and if he does not take it—" A friend tapped the speaker on the shoulder, warning him to be careful. "And if he does not take it," he continued, "we shall depart from him in peace."

These last words were uttered in a tone which instantly transformed a small part of the peaceful gathering into a mob, which marched down snow-covered Broadway to Dey street, where it turned west; and in another two or three minutes it was storming the iron doors of the warehouse of Eli Hart. One of the doors was forced, and thirty barrels of flour rolled on the street before Hart returned with a body of policemen. They were instantly charged by the rioters; but by good fortune the police managed to get into the warehouse and drove out the comparatively few who had usurped possession. By this time Mayor Lawrence arrived and addressed the mob.

While he was talking the rest of the hungry or determined ones who had been listening to the speeches in the Park appeared, increasing the number of rioters by many hundreds. They showered the Mayor with snowballs, and as he fled, the handful of policemen were put to rout. Now the mob began its work in earnest: barrels of flour thrown from the upper floors exploded like bombs as they struck the pavement. Six hundred barrels went this way, and more than a thousand bushels of wheat.

Women, covered from head to foot in flour, walked off with their aprons bulging, and the more provident, who brought baskets or boxes, filled these from the street, now knee-deep in flour.

The mob next stormed and took the warehouse of S. H. Herrick & Company, but before they had hurled a hundred barrels of flour to the street, the city's entire police force, with the troops not far behind, drove them off. Many were arrested and sent to prison for long terms, but no attempt was made to apprehend Dr. Jacques or his aides. The convicted men, jobless workers all, save two boys, were fortunate, for they had food and warmth in jail, while many of their fellows, unable to find work, or food, or fuel, died of starvation or were frozen to death. Horace Greeley, who headed the relief committee in the Sixth Ward, was so moved by the scenes of suffering, that he openly embraced the Communistic teachings of Fourier while maintaining his political integrity as a Whig.

The troops stopped the sacking of the flour warehouses, but not the suffering. Van Buren did not relish reading the accounts of starving women risking a shot from a soldier's musket the night of the riot to gather up handfuls of flour from the sidewalks. His inauguration was only a fortnight away. But Jackson was in the seventh heaven. On March 2 the General wrote to Nicholas P. Trist: "On the 4th I hope to be able to go to the Capitol to witness the glorious scene of Mr. Van Buren, once rejected by the Senate, sworn in by Chief Justice Taney, also being rejected by the factious Senate." The next day Captain Abraham Van Buren resigned his commission to accept the post of secretary to the President.

CHAPTER XXXVII

No⊤ since its foundation had Washington known a more pleasant inauguration day than fell on the first Saturday of March, 1837. The sun beamed down with summer splendor. Only the snow on the hills and a nipping breeze remained to remind one that winter had not yet departed. After breakfast Van Buren drove to the White House, which he had insisted must remain the residence of Jackson until he had recovered his health. A little before noon, against the advice of his physician, Jackson took his seat beside Van Buren in the new phaeton, made from wood of the frigate *Constitution*, a present from Tammany to the retiring President. At the crack of the whip the four dappled grays turned out of the grounds and up Pennsylvania avenue, escorted by a small body of cavalry and infantry and a large contingent of civilians. The cheers of twenty thousand greeted their arrival at the Capitol. The crowd parted for them as they made their way up the steps. Reaching the Senate Chamber the procession was formed; and "Van Buren, attended by the ex-President, the Members of the Senate, of the Cabinet, and the diplomatic corps, led the way to the rostrum erected on the ascent to the eastern portico." N. P. Willis described the ensuing scene: ". . . the ex-President and Mr. Van Buren advanced with uncovered heads. A murmur of feeling rose from the moving mass below, and the infirm old man, emerged from a sick chamber, . . . bowed to the people, and still uncovered in the cold air, took his seat . . . Mr. Van Buren then advanced, and with a voice remarkably distinct, and with great dignity, read his address to the people. . . . I stood myself on the outer limit of the crowd, and . . . his words came clearly articulated to my ear."

The address is unmistakably Van Buren; no alien thoughts find lodgment there; but throughout the finishing touches of Butler and of his sons Abraham and John are noticeable. Save for a few sentences, the five thousand words in the document constitute a spirited defense of our experiment in democracy; nay,

400

more, a pæan to the triumph of the test. But this was overlooked
by the Whig journals, which riddled an occasional poorly constructed sentence, notably the observation that he was the first
President born under the Stars and Stripes: "Unlike all who
have preceded me, the revolution that gave us existence as one
people was achieved at the period of my birth; and while I con-
template with grateful remembrance that memorable event, I feel
that I belong to a later age, and that I may not expect my countrymen to weigh my actions with the same kind and impartial
hand." His birth, and not the Revolution, was the memorable
event he had in mind, pedantically observed Charles King in the
American. With Van Buren's capacity for dramatization, what
would he have done, had he but known that, two hundred years before to a day, the first of his ancestors of whom there is record
landed on Manhattan Island, bringing back his bride, the fair
Catelijntje, who hugged their infant child closer as they made
their way to the rude wooden church under the sheltering guns of
the fort?

The whole tenor of the address was to effect an understanding between the North and the South; and so successful was his
effort that Calhoun and his nullificationists acknowledged his
leadership. The conversion of Calhoun was credited to his ambition to succeed Van Buren. Clay, on the Senate floor, recalled that
the South Carolinian had once compared Van Buren to "the most
crafty, most skulking, and the meanest of the quadruped tribe."
Clay testified to his own high appreciation of the personal qualities of Van Buren: "I have always found him . . . civil, courte-
ous, and gentlemanly; and he dispenses . . . a generous and liberal hospitality. An acquaintance with him of more than twenty
years' duration has inspired me with a respect for the man, although I regret to be compelled to say, I detest the magistrate."
The Abolitionists charged that he had sold himself to the South;
yet he thus animadverted to the attacks on them, and to similar
manifestations of mob spirit: "Occasionally, it is true, the ardor
of public sentiment, outrunning the regular progress of the judicial tribunals, or seeking to reach cases not denounced as criminal by the existing law, has displayed itself in a manner
calculated to give pain to the friends of free government, and to
encourage the hopes of those who wish for its overthrow. These

occurrences, however, have been far less frequent in our country than any other of equal population on the globe. . . ."

He noted that the Republic had passed through experiences which the foes of democracy had predicted would mean the wreck of the experiment, especially the extension of its domain, the multiplication of sovereign States, and the increase of population. "Our system was supposed to be adapted to boundaries comparatively narrow. These have been widened beyond conjecture; the members of our confederacy are already doubled; and the numbers of our people are incredibly augmented. . . . Overlooking partial and temporary evils as inseparable from the practical operation of all human institutions, and looking only to the general result, every patriot has reason to be satisfied. . . .

"The last, perhaps the greatest, of the prominent sources of discord and disaster supposed to lurk in our political condition, was the institution of domestic slavery. Our forefathers were deeply impressed with the delicacy of this subject, and they treated it with a forbearance so evidently wise, that, in spite of every sinister foreboding, it never, until the present period, disturbed the tranquillity of our common country. Such a result is sufficient evidence of the justice and patriotism of their course; it is evidence not to be mistaken, that an adherence to it can prevent all embarrassment from this, as well as every other anticipated cause of difficulty or danger . . . the least deviation from this spirit of forbearance is injurious to every interest . . ."

He regarded his election as an indorsement of his opposition to every attempt on the part of Congress to abolish slavery in the District of Columbia against the wishes of the slaveholding States, and gave added assurance that he would veto any such measure if it came before him. Once more he referred to the mob attacks on the Abolitionists; this time as terrifying scenes of local violence. Again he was optimistic of a happy settlement; for "neither masses of the people nor sections of the country have been swerved from their devotion to the bond of union, and the principle it has made sacred. It will ever be thus. Such attempts at dangerous agitation may periodically return . . . That predominating affection for our political system which prevails throughout our territorial limits, that calm and enlightened judgment which ultimately governs our people as one vast body, will always be at hand to resist and control every effort, foreign or domestic, which aims to overthrow our institutions."

Jackson's deep affection for Van Buren was whole-heartedly returned, and his fine tribute to the ailing old man who sat bareheaded, happy in leaving the Presidency, and happier that Van Buren was entering it, was also seized upon by the Whig journals as meet for ridicule. Jackson knew the deep, filial love Van Buren bore him, and we can see his pallid cheeks glow as he hears the sincere voice ring out his praises, which are followed by a prayer that ends with a blessing. "In receiving from the people the sacred trust twice confided to my illustrious predecessor, and which he discharged so faithfully and well," said Van Buren, "I know that I cannot expect to perform the arduous task with equal ability and success. But, united as I have been in his councils, a daily witness of his exclusive and unsurpassed devotion to his country's welfare, agreeing with him in sentiments which his countrymen have warmly supported, and permitted to partake largely of his confidence, I may hope that somewhat of the same cheering approbation will be found to attend upon my path. For him I but express, with my own, the wishes of all—that he may yet long live to enjoy the brilliant evening of his well-spent life; and, for myself, conscious of but one desire, faithfully to serve my country, I throw myself, without fear, on its justice and its kindness. Beyond that I only look to the gracious protection of the Divine Being, whose strengthening support I humbly solicit, and whom I fervently pray to look down upon us all. May it be among the dispensations of His providence to bless our beloved country with honors and with length of days; may her ways be ways of pleasantness, and all her paths be peace."

When Van Buren finished his address, Taney, Chief Justice of the United States Supreme Court, whom the Senate had rejected as Attorney General, administered the oath of office to the eighth President of the United States. Jackson's happiness was now complete. The scene restored his health, and in the evening he attended the inaugural ball at Carusi's.

What Van Buren's emotions were as he returned that evening to the house which had been his home during the past four years we can only fancy. Thirteen years earlier he had made his début as a Warwick of democracy, a circumstance due, in no small measure, to the advice given him by Burr a decade earlier as they rode from Schenectady to Albany. Burr was now at rest in the family plot at Princeton. He had died penniless the preceding September, the object of charity of a woman who had known him in his days of prosperity. Others, who had had great expectations of Van Buren, had also set forth on their last adventure. He could not avoid thinking of her who had never doubted his greatness as he saw their four children gathered round him; all save the youngest had voted for him: Smith Thompson had lacked two months of his majority when the balloting was on.

Before the summer was out Van Buren started to finish what Jackson had commenced: the divorce of the bank and state. This was to be accomplished through the establishment of a depository for the nation's funds, the Sub-Treasury, the great achievement of his administration. The power that had been Biddle's was not destroyed: it had merely been transferred to the host of state banks in which the government had placed its money. These "pet" banks had labored for Van Buren's election; their opposition would have spelled his defeat. To oppose this vast aggregate of wealth, with the tremendous influence that went with it, took courage.

Jackson had advantages in his fight on the Bank on which his successor could not count: the glamour of glory won on the battlefield; a prosperous people who had long venerated him; and powerful allies in the very institutions Van Buren would have for foes.

Jackson had sufficiently regained his health to start for the Hermitage three days after the inauguration. Van Buren accompanied him to the station of the new railroad, where the Orestes and Pylades of American politics took an affectionate leave of each other. Van Buren was deaf to Jackson's plea that he did not want a doctor to travel with him; but Van Buren was President, and the Surgeon-General of the United States Army was under his orders; so the old hero smilingly accepted the medical officer as a traveling companion on his way home.

At the outset of his administration Van Buren learned that he need expect not even the suggestion of a fair deal from the opposition press. His very utterances were distorted. His most implacable foe among the Washington correspondents was

Matthew L. Davis, the literary executor of Burr, then working on the latter's life and letters. That we may not have an unjust measure of Davis, who signed his articles in the *Morning Courier* and *New York Enquirer* "The Spy in Washington," this story should be retold: He was showing a friend hundreds of love letters to Burr, some signed by women of wealth and position. When Davis's companion observed that these billets-doux could enrich a blackmailer, Davis cast them into the open fire. Yet in describing Van Buren's reception to the diplomatic corps, Davis wrote that the President was flurried, ill at ease, and blunderingly addressed them as the Democratic corps. In commenting on the President's address in the same issue of March 10, the journal, addressing the Chief Magistrate as "Mr. Matty Van Buren," said: "As for the Presidency's being 'the highest of all marks of the country's confidence' we are compelled to say that the fact of your election utterly overturns that idea."

Van Buren made only one appointment in the Cabinet, naming Joel R. Poinsett, an uncompromising Union man from South Carolina, Secretary of War to succeed Lewis Cass, whom Jackson named Minister to France. John Forsyth, of Georgia, was Secretary of State; Levi Woodbury, of New Hampshire, Secretary of the Treasury; Mahlon Dickerson, of New Jersey, Secretary of the Navy; Amos Kendall, of Kentucky, Postmaster General; and his old law student and partner, Benjamin F. Butler, was prevailed upon to continue as Attorney General. Although the Cabinet, with the exception noted, was named by Jackson, it was largely of Van Buren's selection; and all were friends of long standing save Kendall. As Cabinets go, it was far above the average in ability and capacity.

But no group of men, however able, could check the financial panic which distressed the nation shortly after the adjournment of Congress. It has been the fashion to attribute the upheaval to Jackson's fight on the Bank. His specie circular of July 11, 1836, is regarded by those who hold this view as an immediate cause of the crash. These were minor factors. The panic had its genesis in the opening of the Erie Canal in 1825. This started the country on a career of canal and road building, followed by the construction of railroads and steamboat lines. These improvements led to the settlement of new villages and towns. All this called for the extension of credits. Until the speculator entered the field, the expansion had no effect on the resources of the country's financial institutions. The speculator projected improvements which included villages, towns, and even cities, for which there were neither settlers nor demand. The unprecedented prosperity attracted European capital, and conservative business men were ensnared by the mania for speculation, which reached its peak in 1835. The sales of public lands afford us the best indicia of the extremes into which the unwary had plunged. In 1834 the sales of public lands amounted to $4,500,000; in the ensuing two years $39,500,000—mostly paper signed by favorites of the banks—was invested in these unproductive lands. To check this evil the Treasury Department ordered that payments for public lands be in specie. An exception was made of bona fide settlers, who were granted an additional six months' grace. As the nation sold its land for $1.25 an acre, the actual tiller of the soil was not hard pressed, as he owned little, and had little to find. The speculating frenzy extended into every realm of trade and commerce, the total loans and discounts of all the banks being increased from $354,000,000 in 1834 to $457,000,000 in 1836.

Two weeks after the adjournment of Congress Hone noted: "The prospects in Wall street are getting worse and worse. . . . The accounts from England are very alarming; the panic prevails there as bad as here." On March 28 the New York merchants, seeing ruin staring at them, drafted a letter appealing to Biddle to save them. They might as well have asked the mill wheel to stem the stream which turned it. Within the next ten days ninety-eight New York business houses went bankrupt, and thereafter the failures were so numerous that count was lost of them. Land at Broadway and 100th street, which had sold seven months before for $480 a lot, now changed hands for $50. This was symptomatic of what was happening in other commercial and industrial communities.

At the end of April the New York merchants met in Masonic Hall and appointed a committee to urge Van Buren to repeal the specie circular and call an extra session of Congress. This had been Biddle's advice. Hone thus appraised the situation: "No man can calculate to escape ruin but he who owes no money. Happy is he who has a little, and is free from debt."

While the committee was vainly importuning Van Buren one of the New York banks failed. The next evening, May 9, all the New York banks agreed to suspend payment in specie. The paper they offered in lieu of gold and silver had greatly depreciated. "Where will it all end?" asked Hone, who answered: "In ruin, revolution, perhaps civil war."

A packet brought intelligence that fears were entertained for the stability of the Bank of England. Hone, who regarded Jackson and Van Buren as the cause of the distress, ironically observed: "Markets continue extravagantly high; meat of all kinds and poultry are dear as ever. The farmers (or rather the market speculators) tell us this is owing to the scarcity of corn; but the shad, the cheapness of which in ordinary seasons makes them, as long as they last, a great resource for the poor, are not being bought under seventy-five cents and a dollar. Is this owing to the scarcity of corn, or are the fish afraid to come into our waters lest they be caught in the vortex of Wall street?"

The suspension of the New York banks led to bank suspensions throughout the country. Many shared Hone's alarm of revolution or civil rage. The suffering among the laborers and mechanics in the cities now extended to the ranks of clerks, professional men, and merchants. The only classes which did not feel the pinch of want, or the absence of customary luxuries, were the very rich and the farmers: the panic did not affect the fecundity of the soil, the fertility of the hens, or the productivity of the cattle.

The effrontery of Biddle, whom Van Buren regarded as a contributory cause of the panic, was shown by his visit to the White House. Van Buren received him and talked about everything save banking and commercial distress. Biddle published a card informing the public of Van Buren's silence "upon the great and interesting topics of the day." This was followed by an editorial by Bennett in his *New York Herald* reading: "The first symptoms of the mania which has produced the present revolution, developed themselves in the Spring of 1829, when Mr. Van Buren, a common country lawyer, who began life by trundling cabbages to market in Kinderhook, perfumed with Cologne water, and his yellow whiskers arranged *à la Paris,* presented the famous Safety Fund scheme of banking in Albany. . . . Martin

Van Buren and his atrocious associates form one of the original causes of the terrible moral, political, and commercial desolation which spreads over the country. . . . Nicholas Biddle . . . is such an aristocrat as you will find in heaven—Martin Van Buren such a democrat as you will discover coiled up in any burning corner in the other place— . . ." A blackmailing snob makes a contemptible foe.

On May 15, less than six weeks after Van Buren had declined to call an extra session, the demand became so general that he issued a proclamation convening Congress on the first Monday in September. This gave him three and a half months in which to formulate a remedy, or at least a palliative, for the crisis. Two days later, Abbott Lawrence, head of the largest cotton and woolen commission houses in the country, told a mass meeting of fellow Bostonians that no other people were so abused, cheated, plundered, and trampled upon by their rulers as Americans. He advanced sinister counsel: no overt act should be committed by the people until the laws of self-preservation compelled a forcible resistance; "but the time might come when the crew must seize the ship." In New York, where the Whigs had been triumphant in the April charter elections, Van Buren's refusal to repeal the specie circular was described as "a more high handed measure of tyranny than that which cost Charles the First his crown and his head—more illegal and unconstitutional than the act of the British ministry which caused the patriots of the Revolution to destroy the tea in the harbor of Boston—one which calls more loudly for resistance than any act of Great Britain which led to the Declaration of Independence."

The friends of the administration countered with meetings equally large and fiery. Thousands of Philadelphians commended Van Buren's course, and adopted resolutions wherein occurred: "We hereby pledge our lives, if necessary, for the support of the same." A Baltimore gathering denounced the demand for the repeal of the specie circular as "the senseless clamors of the British party." Down with paper currency! and Give us hard money; were the passwords of the Van Burenites. The Whigs responded by printing debased paper currency and coining tokens in tin, lead, brass, and iron adorned with caricatures of Van Buren and Jackson. Many establishments in all parts of the country issued tokens with real value. Scrip, too, was printed by business houses of all sorts.

Webster and other Whig leaders thundered at Van Buren from the hustings. But Van Buren was as silent under these attacks as he was to the strictures of their journalistic supporters. He intended to meet the crisis in his own way and at a time and place of his own selection. With his son Abraham he took daily rides over the roads he and Jackson had traveled. On May 23, in a letter to Jackson, he said: "I have sent by the same vessel that conveys to you the *Constitutional Carriage* a quarter cask of old & excellent gold sherry, which has been ordered for me by our friend Capt Nicholson. I find it to be of superior quality, & beg you to accept of it, & shall feel most highly honored to be occasionally remembered by yourself and friends in the use of it." Van Buren himself drank Madeira, or the rarer product of the hills between Caserta and Naples, the exquisite Monte Pulciano.

Under orders from Van Buren, the Secretary of the Treasury on June 23 instructed all subordinates to discontinue depositing the government's moneys in banks that had refused to pay in specie. This was the first indication of what Van Buren's recommendations to the special session would be. On Tuesday, September 5, the second day of the sitting, his son Abraham delivered his message to Congress. Rare courage and statesmanship were blended in this historic document. It was more than a message to Congress; it was an appeal to the people to sustain him in his revolutionary design. The bills carrying out his proposal for a Sub-Treasury, or Independent Treasury—as it was first known —and suggestions for immediate relief, were in the hands of Silas Wright. The message not only considered the immediate causes of the financial and commercial crisis, but answered those who looked to the government for material relief by thus reminding them of the designs of the Republic:

It was not intended to confer special favors on individuals, or on any classes of them; to create systems of agriculture, manufactures, or trade; or to engage in them, either separately or in connection with individual citizens or organized associations. . . . If its operations were to be directed for the benefit of any one class, equivalent favors, must in justice, be extended to the rest; and the attempt to bestow favors with an equal hand, or even to select those who most deserve them, would never be successful. All communities are apt to look to Government for far too much. Even in our own country, where its powers and duties are so strictly limited, we are prone to do so, especially at periods of sudden embarrassments and distress. But this ought not to be. The framers of our excellent constitution, and the people who approved it with calm and sagacious deliberation, acted at the time on a sounder principle. They wisely judged that the less Government interferes with private pursuits, the better for general prosperity. It is not its legitimate object to make men rich, or to repair, by direct grants of money or legislation in favor of particular pursuits, losses not incurred in the public service. This would be substantially to use the property of some for the benefit of others. But its real duty—that duty the performance of which makes a good Government the most precious of human blessings—is to enact and enforce a system of general laws commensurate with, but not exceeding, the objects of its establishment, and to leave every citizen and every interest to reap, under its benign protection, the rewards of virtue, industry, and prudence.

Equally sound was his lacerating arraignment of the paper-bottomed financial system of the time. To understand his fear of financial institutions as a menace to the integrity of the Republic, we must go beyond his message. In his *Inquiry into the Origin of Political Parties* Van Buren wrote: "Such aggregations of wealth and influence, connected as they usually are with social distinctions, naturally come to be regarded as the fountains of patronage by those who are in search of it. The press, men of letters, artists, and professional men of every denomination, and those engaged in subordinate pursuits who live upon the luxurious indulgences of the rich, are all brought within the scope of their influence." He apprehended that "these aggregations of wealth and influence," unless checked, would lead to the formation of a party "constructed principally of a network of special interests." There is a hint of this in his message. In recounting to Congress his objections to the reëstablishment of a national bank, he said that it "would impair the rightful supremacy of the popular will; injure the character and diminish the influence of our political system; and bring once more into existence a concentrated money power, hostile to the spirit, and threatening the permanency, of our republican institutions."

He justly attributed the immediate cause of the panic to

"over-action in all departments of business; an over-action deriving, perhaps, its first impulses from antecedent causes, but
stimulated to its destructive consequences by excessive issues of
bank paper and other facilities, for the acquisition and enlarge-
ment of credit." In addition to the domestic inflation and "the
spirit of reckless speculation engendered by it, were a foreign
debt, estimated in March last at thirty million dollars; . . . the
diversion of much of the labor [to needless improvements projected by speculators] that should have been applied to agriculture, thereby contributing to the expenditure of large sums in
the importation of grain from Europe—an expenditure which,
amounting in 1834 to two hundred and fifty thousand dollars,
was, in the first two quarters of the present year, increased to
more than two millions of dollars; and finally, without enumer-
ating other injurious results, the rapid growth, among all classes,
and especially in our great commercial towns, of luxurious habits,
founded too often on merely fancied wealth . . ."

Then he surveyed the panic as it affected other countries:
"It has appeared that evils, similar to those suffered by ourselves,
have been experienced in Great Britain, on the continent, and indeed, throughout the commercial world. . . . Two nations
[Great Britain and the United States], . . . but recently enjoying the highest degree of prosperity, and maintaining with each
other the closest relations, are suddenly, in a time of profound
peace, and without any national disaster, arrested in their career,
and plunged into a state of embarrassment and distress. . . .
The history of these causes and effects in Great Britain and the
United States, is substantially the history of the revulsion in all
other commercial countries."

Speaking of the failure of the banks to honor the government drafts in gold, as required by law, he said: "A system which
can, in a time of profound peace, when there is a large revenue laid
by, thus suddenly prevent the application and the use of the
money of the people, in the manner and for the objects they have
directed, cannot be wise; but who can think, without painful
reflection, that, under it, the same unforeseen events might have
befallen us in the midst of a war . . . To such embarrassments
and to such dangers will this Government be always exposed,
whilst it takes the moneys raised for, and necessary to, the public

service, out of the hands of its own officers, and converts them into a mere right of action against corporations entrusted with them. . . . The money received from the people, instead of being kept till it is needed for their use, is . . . a fund, on which discounts are made for the profit of those who happen to be owners of stock in the banks selected as depositories. . . ."

Van Buren thus voiced his faith in the class from which he sprang, the tillers of the soil: "The proceeds of our great staples will soon furnish the means of liquidating debts at home and abroad, and contribute equally to the revival of commercial activity, and the restoration of commercial credit." He closed his message with a regret that he had to dwell on anything but the history of the country's unalloyed prosperity. "Since it is otherwise, we can only feel more deeply the responsibility of the respective trusts that have been confided to us, and under the pressure of difficulties, unite in invoking the guidance and aid of the Supreme Ruler of nations, and in laboring with zealous resolution to overcome the difficulties by which we are environed."

The opposition met this sound analysis with the balderdash of the hustings. Clay said the panic was due to the fight against the Bank. He attacked hard money with: "It was paper money that carried us through the Revolution, established our liberties, and made us a free and independent people." He characterized Van Buren's proposals as "a cold and heartless insensibility to a bleeding people." After noting the Whig victories in the spring and summer elections he truthfully observed that instead of a majority of Democrats in the Senate, "there would be thirty-two or thirty-four Whigs to eighteen or twenty friends of the administration." This was followed by: "We are told that it is necessary to divorce the Government from the banks. Let us not be deluded by sounds. Senators might as well talk of separating the Government from the States, or from the people, or from the country. We are all—people—States—Union—banks, bound up and interwoven together, united in fortune and destiny, and all entitled to the protecting care of a parental government. . . . A hard money Government and a paper money people! A Government, an official corps—the servants of the people—glittering in gold, and the people themselves, their masters, buried in ruin and surrounded with rags." He twitted Calhoun on what he had said about the official corps when he was fighting Van Buren—"one hundred thousand office holders and their dependents, directed by the will of a single man."

Wright and Benton reiterated all Van Buren's arguments in defense of the Sub-Treasury measure, but witnessed a defection of many Democrats in the House and the Senate. These styled themselves Conservative Democrats. The bill passed in the Senate 26 to 20. One who voted against the bill was taking his first step out of the party. This was Tallmadge of New York, whose speech reads as if it were written by a committee from the "pet" banks. He uttered one grain of truth worth recording here: "The tendency of this scheme [the Sub-Treasury] is to bring this country, virtually, to an exclusive metallic currency."

The Sub-Treasury bill was lost in the House on October 16 by a vote of 120 to 106. Four days earlier Webster and three other Senators presented petitions against the annexation of Texas. Many of these protests contained several thousand names each. Most of the signers were from the Northern and Eastern States. Jackson, just before leaving office, had acknowledged the independence of Texas. The slave-holding states were clamoring for her admission, as it would add to their representation in Congress. Jackson covertly and shamelessly aided the insurrection against Mexican dominion; but Van Buren was against annexation, and had so informed Memucan Hunt, envoy and minister extraordinary of the Republic of Texas, when he presented his country's plea for admission to the Union.

The Panic Session, as the first sitting of the Twenty-fifth Congress became known, adjourned *sine die* October 16 after six weeks of talk. It accomplished nothing of moment beyond the enactment of two of Van Buren's recommendations: empowering the Treasury Department to issue $10,000,000 in interest-bearing notes for the Government's current obligations—a singular situation for a country that had wiped out its national debt; permitting importers to pay custom dues in paper.

The coalition of the Conservative Democrats and the Whigs in the lower house of Congress anticipated the sentiment of the people in the November elections. The Whigs carried the legislatures of most of the Northern and Eastern States. In New York there had never been such a rout of any party since the early days of the nation. Of the one hundred and twenty-eight candidates for the Assembly, the Whigs elected one hundred and one; six of the eight Senators chosen were of the same faith. Throughout most of November the Whigs celebrated: news of the results from some distant community being a sufficient excuse for more torchlight processions.

One of these celebrations was out of the ordinary, and bore the earmarks of careful planning. Some three hundred Whigs roused Washington from its sleep on the night of Tuesday, November 22. About midnight the celebrants, mildly described by Adams as riotous, staged mock demonstrations before the homes of the members of the Cabinet. They were equipped with a heavy ·brass cannon. They first visited the White House and awakened its occupants with jeering huzzas and the rumble of the gun carriage. What Van Buren and other inmates of the Presidential mansion thought when the cannoneers discharged the piece of artillery, has not been recorded. The merry mob then made the rounds of the houses of the heads of Departments, cheering and firing a salute of mockery before each.

Van Buren continued on his plotted course. When Congress reassembled in December it heard the President's analysis of the elections. In again recommending the enactment of the Sub-Treasury bill he made light of the Whig victories by saying that "questions of far deeper and more immediate local interest than the fiscal plan of the National Treasury were involved in those elections. Above all, we cannot overlook the striking fact, that there were at the time in those States more than one hundred and sixty millions of bank capital, of which large portions were subject to actual—and most of it, if not all, to a greater or less extent, dependent for a continuance of its corporate existence upon the will of the State legislatures to be then chosen." He assailed all financial institutions with: "Indeed, I am more than ever convinced of the dangers to which the free and unbiased exercise of political opinion—the only sure foundation and safeguard of republican Government—would be exposed by any further increase of the already overgrown influences of corporate authorities." In the State elections not only the State banks, but the influences of insurance companies, mercantile houses, and other "large aggregations of wealth" were "spread through all the ramifications of society." All the forces of entrenched wealth were at war with him because of his advocacy of the Sub-Treasury. He was asking no quarter. He called attention to the nation's balance of more than $34,000,000, of which only a little more than $1,000,000 was immediately available: most of the rest was in banks which had suspended specie payments.

The Senate was still with Van Buren; but the House was again controlled by the continued coalition of Whigs and Conservative Democrats. Until there was a change in the political complexion of the House he could not hope to enact the Sub-Treasury bill. The November results had not shattered his faith in the people. They had erred; but he was relying on their inherent righteousness; and consoled himself by calling to mind his favorite phrase, which Matthew Henry, the English divine, had coined in 1710: "the sober second thought of the people." He knew that the return of the mass mind to sane thinking could be hastened by the propagation of easily assimilable truths.

In his message he blazed away at Biddle and the Bank for reissuing some ten million dollars in notes under the charter which had expired on March 4, 1836. It was improper, he told Congress; but the Government was powerless, as this dishonesty had not been anticipated by the lawmakers. He spoke regretfully of the non-realization of his expectations for a settlement of the country's claims against Mexico which Jackson had pressed; there was his familiar conciliatory note in his references to the dispute over the Northeastern Boundary, which remained in the unsettled state the signers of the Treaty of Peace had left it in, in 1783; and he discussed minor topics of domestic concern.

Washington society was disappointed. It had expected frequent and colorful receptions at the White House in keeping with the reputation Van Buren had earned during his long residence in the national capital. But not until New Year's Day were the doors thrown open. In this he had no choice: it was traditional to keep the President's house open from eleven in the morning until eight in the evening. The day was like a bit of June. An endless stream passed in and out of the house. In the afternoon Henry Clay called. He sardonically observed to Van Buren that he must feel happy in being surrounded by so many friends. Van

Buren looked out on the sun-kissed lawn as he parried the thrust with: "The weather is very fine."

Dolly Madison also kept open house this day. She had returned to Washington in October after an absence of twenty years. Age had been kind to her; and suffering had not robbed her eyes of their girlish winsomeness, nor her face of its beauty. She was queenly as ever. When Clay entered the room, she "rose at his approach, extended her hand, and gave him one of those smiles which no doubt helped to make the dominant party adhesive, in the days of her [husband's] presidency."

The fashionables among these New Year's callers discussed "the shabby court of Martin the First": they had dubbed Jackson King Andrew. He was patronizing letters: first it was Washington Irving; now he had named George Bancroft Collector of the Port of Boston; and Bancroft appointed a young author named Nathaniel Hawthorne to a subordinate place. But they preferred Lucullus to Mæcenas. And all hoped that his son Abraham would marry a daughter of The Patroon, as gossip had it. That would make the court of Martin the First endurable, and the White House the heart of the city's social life, as it should be. We can see Dolly Madison nodding acquiescently to these idle chatterers, and smiling to herself. She could have told them that the daughter of The Patroon would not be the lady of the White House; for she herself, within a month after her return to Washington, had presented her cousin, Angelica Singleton, at the White House. This charming daughter of a South Carolina planter, with her corkscrew curls, fresh from Madame Grelaud's seminary at Philadelphia, had won the affection of Van Buren and the love of his son. But Dolly Madison said nothing of this: she was a perfect matchmaker.

Another morsel of gossip concerned the insurrection of Upper Canada. Rensselaer Van Rensselaer, a son of Solomon, had been made Commander-in-chief of the revolting Canadians, and as a consequence, many Americans were joining the Patriot Army, as the insurrectionists styled themselves. This revolt was giving Van Buren concern. There was much sympathy with the followers of William Lyon Mackenzie, Toronto's first Mayor, who had been routed by royal troops early in the month of December.

This was the second insurrection within a month. The first

SMITH THOMPSON VAN BUREN
From a tintype owned by Ellen Van Buren Pell

was led by Louis Joseph Papineau, Speaker of the Legislative Assembly of Lower Canada, and Thomas Storrow Brown; but the military quelled it after three weeks.

Both had their origin in the same causes: corruption and misrule. Reform was impossible while the upper house of each parliament, appointed by the Governor General, who owed his office to London, could negative all acts of the lower house, whose representatives were chosen by the people. Mackenzie, a journalist, had been elected five successive times to the Provincial Parliament, and as often expelled, for having published the truth about the venal ruling clique. Five years before the revolt Mackenzie went to London and induced the Whig ministry to dismiss the Solicitor General and the Attorney General of Upper Canada, and to veto a vicious bank act. On his return conditions grew more intolerable, and the despotic acts of Sir Francis Bond Head, the Lieutenant Governor, culminating in interference in elections, led to the establishment of a provisional republic.

Before the actual outbreak of hostilities, Rensselaer Van Rensselaer, who had been secretary to William H. Harrison when he was Minister to Colombia, had left Albany "for the purpose of picking up news and new subscribers for the *Albany Daily Advertiser*." When Van Rensselaer reached Buffalo, his name and his training at West Point induced Mackenzie and two of his aides, Dr. John Rolph, and M. S. Bidwell, Speaker of the Legislative Assembly of Upper Canada, to offer him the commission of Commander of the Patriot Army. Van Rensselaer assumed command on December 14, and shortly thereafter seized Navy Island, in the Niagara River, and within speaking distance of the Canadian shore. When Van Rensselaer took the island he had twenty-eight men, and two six-pounders; but within a few days his force was augmented to nearly eight hundred. Mackenzie and other leaders of the uprising were in various parts of the United States enlisting fresh recruits.

On December 27 the royal forces began to shell Navy Island. News traveled slowly then, and the gossips at Washington on New Year's Day knew nothing of this, nor of the indefensible atrocity committed at the American village of Schlosser, opposite the island, at midnight on the 29th. January 1 fell on a Monday. On the following Saturday Van Buren received a letter from H.

W. Rogers, District Attorney for Erie County, dated Buffalo, December 30, reading: "Our whole frontier is in commotion, and I fear it will be difficult to restrain our citizens from revenging, by a resort to arms, this flagrant invasion of our territory. Every thing that can be done will be by the public authorities to prevent so injudicious a movement. The respective sheriffs of Erie and Niagara have taken the responsibility of calling out the militia, to guard the frontier, and prevent any further depredations."

An affidavit, sworn to by Gilman Appleby, captain of the steamboat *Caroline*, and supported by nine other Americans, recited that the boat had made three trips between Schlosser and Navy Island during the day, landing men and freight (recruits and ammunition for Van Rensselaer), and had tied up to the dock at Schlosser for the night. ". . . the crew and officers of the *Caroline* numbered ten; . . . in the course of the evening, twenty-three . . . citizens of the United States, came on board . . . and requested to remain . . . during the night, as they were unable to get lodgings at the tavern nearby; these requests were acceded to, and the persons thus coming on board retired to rest, as did also all of the crew and officers of the *Caroline*, except such as were stationed to watch . . . about midnight, this deponent was informed by one of the watch that several boats filled with men were making toward the *Caroline* . . . this deponent immediately gave the alarm and before he was able to reach the deck the *Caroline* was boarded by seventy or eighty men . . . they immediately commenced a warfare with muskets, swords, and cutlasses upon the defenseless crew and passengers of the *Caroline*, under the fierce cry of 'G—d damn them, give them no quarter; kill every man; fire; fire!' . . . the *Caroline* was abandoned without resistance, and the only effort made by either crew or passengers seemed to be to escape slaughter. . . ."

Only twenty-one of the passengers and crew escaped. The boat was set adrift in the river and fired by the invaders, who then returned to the Canadian side, where their return was received with loud cheers. The following morning the charred fragments of the slaughtered were seen swirling in the eddies below the Falls.

On January 8 Van Buren transmitted to Congress the documents quoted with a message which made no attempt to palliate the "extraordinary outrage," yet couched in language to obviate hostile discussion. A demand for redress would be made, and while he did not doubt that the Government of Upper Canada would "do its duty in punishing the aggressors and preventing future outrage, the President notwithstanding, had deemed it necessary to order a sufficient force on the frontier to repel any attempt of a like character, and to make it known to you that if it should occur, he cannot be answerable for the effects of the indignation of the neighboring people of the United States." The restrained tone of the message was dictated by Van Buren's dominating idea since he had been Secretary of State, to "lay a lasting foundation for perpetual peace & harmony between the two countries." The phrase is from a letter marked "Private & confidential," written by Jackson to Van Buren on December 17, 1831.

Actual hostilities ended on January 14, when Van Rensselaer and his troops evacuated Navy Island after parleys with General Winfield Scott and Governor Marcy. Van Rensselaer was arrested on a charge of accepting a commission from a foreign government and released on bail; but subsequently imprisoned. A Canadian who boasted that he was in command of the force which slaughtered the crew and passengers of the *Caroline* was arrested in New York, tried, and acquitted. Mackenzie was taken in Rochester, where he was publishing a newspaper, and imprisoned. Mackenzie, described by Van Rensselaer—after they had quarreled—as "a meddling little body but fully devoted to the cause of freedom," had a long memory and an effective pen. We shall meet him eight years hence, a member of the *Tribune* staff, and a successful pamphleteer. While Mackenzie remained a citizen of the United States, the reforms for which the Canadian liberals had fought were largely realized. An act of amnesty was passed; Mackenzie returned to Toronto; served in Parliament; and published a weekly, *Mackenzie's Message*.

It was not until March that the White House drawing room was opened. Van Buren, fond as he was of society, had little heart for it while the financial crisis, and the suffering it entailed, was at its height. But relief was in sight: England was relieving the stringency by shipping gold here, and most of the banks would resume the payment of gold and silver in a month or two at the most. In April Van Buren gave another reception at the White House. These were his contributions to the social side of Washington for the season. He entertained members of Congress at the traditional Saturday night dinners. At one of these a servant whispered: "The house is on fire." Excusing himself, Van Buren went to the kitchen: a few pailfuls of water quenched the blaze. On returning to the table he explained the reason for his absence. Clay, his hand on his heart, protested loudly: "Mr. President, I am doing all I can to get you out of this house; but believe me, I do not want to burn you out."

On April 11, Butler, who had consented to remain with his old preceptor and law partner for a year, resigned as Attorney General. Senator Felix Grundy, of Tennessee, was appointed his successor. Once, when Van Buren inquired what Hugh Lawson White was doing in his retirement, Grundy gave this picture of a defeated aspirant for Presidential honors: "I will tell you: he sits all day long in the chimney corner, spitting tobacco juice by the gallon, cursing everything and everybody, except his Creator, but thinking devilishly hard of him."

Dickerson was anxious to retire from the Navy Department. Van Buren offered the post to Irving. When the author declined, Van Buren tendered the post to another man of letters in his cabinet, James K. Paulding, satirist, humorist, poet, and novelist, related by marriage to Irving, with whom he collaborated on the first numbers of *Salmagundi*. Paulding accepted.

Congress sat until July 9, and one of its last acts was to pass one of Van Buren's recommendations: making the reissuance of old notes of the Bank of the United States a crime. About three weeks before adjournment, Senator William C. Preston, of South Carolina, who did not share Calhoun's support of the administration, withdrew his resolution for the annexation of Texas. The Washington house of the Prestons was also the home of their charming kinswoman, Angelica Singleton, since the preceding fall. And after the adjournment of Congress she returned with them to South Carolina, where, in her father's house, in the month of November, she was married to Captain Abraham Van Buren; and shortly after started north with him to be the mistress of the White House.

Van Buren also left Washington after the adjournment of

Congress. It was his first vacation in two years. From early in July until late in September he rested at White Sulphur Springs. We have this glimpse of him on the way down, sent by the correspondent of the *Richmond Enquirer* on his arrival at Louisa Court-house: "About one o'clock he arrived, travelling in the plainest manner, with two of his sons, drawn by four horses; his servant riding the horse presented to him by the late John Randolph, of Roanoke." His two sons were Abraham and Martin.

On his return to Washington, Van Buren appraised the surveys of the Democratic canvassers in States which went Whig in the preceding fall. The reports showed that the panic was little more than a painful memory; the banks that had survived were paying in specie, and credit was gradually being restored. News came from London of the regal time Van Buren's son John was having in the British capital. John had left for England in the late spring. At the state dinner given by Queen Victoria on July 25 the Queen received him with marked consideration. The *Courier*, the British court journal, on July 26, published the list of guests in this wise: "Prince Nicholas Esterhazy; Prince Windisch Gratz; John Van Buren, son of the President of the United States; the Lord Chancellor and Lady Cottenham; . . ." Then followed dukes and duchesses; marquises and marchionesses; earls; counts, viscounts, lords, baronets, and commoners of distinction.

The Whig journals seized upon this list as a choice morsel. Who were the princes at Queen Victoria's state dinner? Prince Nicholas Esterhazy; Prince Windisch Gratz; Prince John Van Buren. And then they told, with much fanciful elaboration, how Prince John danced with Queen Victoria; and how Prince John was given precedence over the Hero of Waterloo and other lesser and greater dukes. And they dwelt on the dinner given a few days later by the Lord Mayor and Corporation of London to illustrious foreigners, where Prince John was placed on the right hand of the Lord Mayor with the Prince de Nemours, son of Louis Philippe. Now the Whig press talked of Prince de Nemours and Prince John van Buren; for to heighten the effect, some printed the surname with a small *v*. Mockingly they called him "our Prince John."

Prince John—the name thereafter clung to him—returned in time to take active part in the November elections. The slavery question was playing a large part. This was due to the autocratic attitude of the slaveholders in Congress; they forced upon the lower house a rule prohibiting debate on petitions relating to slavery, or even their reference to a committee. This was the undemocratic "gag rule" which Adams mocked daily in the House by presenting petitions from Abolitionists, whose course he disapproved, but whose right of free speech he defended. The Abolitionists asked candidates if they were for or against the gag rule. In New York, Marcy, candidate for reëlection, when asked: "Do you believe in the right of Abolitionists to petition Congress?" replied: "No." Seward, who again opposed him, answered: "Yes." Seward was elected Governor by 10,000 majority. But it was not a complete rout of the Regency: they reduced the Whig majority in the Assembly to 79, and maintained their ascendancy in the upper house.

Van Buren found consolation in the country-wide returns. The Whigs carried only four States besides New York: Rhode Island, Indiana, Kentucky, and North Carolina. The loss of Ohio, Harrison's home State, offset the loss of New York to the Democrats. The Whigs made slight gains in Illinois and Missouri. But for the Canadian insurrections the Democratic gains in New York and elsewhere in the North would have been more pronounced; for Van Buren's laudable neutrality earned for him and his administration the unwarranted charge that they were "the tools of Victoria." Solomon Southwick, now a bitter foe of Van Buren, told Mackenzie during the canvass that Washington was "a sink of iniquity, corruption, and British influence." The Whig vote, generally, was a conservative poll. Outside of the South, the Democratic ranks were augmented by the addition of most of the liberal element. The Equal Rights, or Loco-focos, had returned to the party because of Van Buren's demand for a Sub-Treasury and his radical pronouncements in advocating it. His insistence upon the divorcement of bank and state signally embraced the twin objectives of the Loco-focos: no special privileges, and no class legislation.

On the second day of its sitting Van Buren communicated his annual message to Congress. He spoke cheerfully of the state of the country: the harvest had been abundant; industry was prospering; plague had not visited us; peace reigned among us.

"These blessings, which evince the care and beneficence of Providence, call for our devout and fervent gratitude." He noted that "the present year closes the first half century of our Federal institutions; and our system—differing from all others in the acknowledged, practical, and unlimited operation which it has for so long a period given to the sovereignty of the people—has now been fully tested by experience. . . . It was reserved for the American Union to test the advantage of a Government entirely dependent on the continual exercise of the popular will; and our experience has shown that it is as beneficent in practice as it is in theory."

The major part of his report was a reiteration of his sound economic theories in advocating the Sub-Treasury. He regarded the rapid recovery of the nation without the aid of the Bank (which had done what it could to prevent the State banks from resuming specie payments) as refutation of the arguments of the opposition. "The scenes through which we have passed conclusively prove how little our commerce, agriculture, manufactures, or finances, require such an institution, and what dangers are attendant on its power—a power, I trust, never to be conferred by the American people upon their Government, and still less upon individuals not responsible to it for its unavoidable abuses."

He told of the progress made by the administration, of the settled policy of the nation, dating back to Monroe, to move the Indians "to a country west of the Mississippi, much more extensive, and better adapted to their condition, than that on which they then resided; the guarantee to them, by the United States, of their exclusive possession of that country forever, exempt from all intrusions by white men . . ." He noted a regrettable exception: 2,000 Seminoles in Florida under Osceola were unwilling to leave their old hunting grounds. "The continued treacherous conduct of these people; the savage and unprovoked murders they have lately committed, butchering whole families of the settlers of the Territory, without distinction of age or sex, and making their way into the very center and heart of the country, so that no part of it is free from their ravages; their frequent attacks on the lighthouses along that dangerous coast; and the barbarity with which they have murdered the passengers and crews of such vessels as have been wrecked upon the reefs and keys which border the Gulf, leave the Government no alternative but to continue the military operations against them until they are totally expelled from Florida." The Florida War was an inheritance from the Jackson administration, and it was to outlast Van Buren's by a year.

Van Buren, although expressing a hope that Congress would pass his Sub-Treasury bill at this session, knew that the House was still controlled by a coalition of Conservative Democrats and Whigs.

England's provocative colonial policy was threatening Van Buren's hope of an enduring peace between the two countries. Adams thus described the English colonial attitude: "The policy of the British government has been to maintain and excite divisions of interest among the colonies themselves, as well as to nourish and stimulate their animosities against the neighboring States [of the United States]. . . . There are very perceptible mutual rivalries and jealousies between the provinces, and a great indifference in both the Canadas. They levy an impost duty of five per cent upon all imported goods from one to the other, and it is very apparently part of the political system at home to keep them as much as possible alienated from each other, that all may be perfectly dependent upon the common parent. Another precaution at home is a rigorous prohibition to recruit any of the regiments in the provinces. . . . The men are enlisted for life, and as they are all taken from the paupers of the three kingdoms, and are fed, clothed, and lodged at the King's expense, and trained exclusively to the performance of military service, they are nested in a condition of existence from which they have little temptation to depart, especially at the risk of capture and severe imprisonment. . . ."

A series of high-handed acts of aggression by the Canadian authorities, having their origin in the disputed Northeastern Boundary, culminated this winter in the seizure of an agent of the State of Maine who had been sent to investigate reports that bands of trespassers from Canada were cutting timber in the Aroostook region. This agent was taken to Fredericton, the capital of New Brunswick, where he was held by Sir John Harvey, Lieutenant Governor of the province. Sir John then dispatched more of his lawless lot to the timber lands within Maine's boundary; but they were driven back into Canada by the State militia.

As soon as credible information of the border trouble reached Washington, Van Buren—after negotiations between the Secretary of State and the British Minister had failed—transmitted the correspondence to Congress with a message sustaining the action of Maine. He hoped that mutual exercise of jurisdiction over the disputed territory by the authorities of Maine and New Brunswick would be continued pending arbitration, which had been agreed upon by the two nations years back. But "if the authorities of New Brunswick should attempt to enforce the claim of exclusive jurisdiction set up by them, by means of a military occupation of the disputed territory, I shall feel myself bound to consider the contingency provided by the Constitution as having occurred on the happening of which a State has the right to call for the aid of the Federal government to repel invasion. . . . As, however, the session of Congress is about to terminate, and the agency of the Executive may become necessary during the recess, it is important that the attention of the Legislature should be drawn to the consideration of such measures as may be calculated to obviate the call for an extra session. . . ."

Congress unanimously empowered the President to call out fifty thousand volunteers to aid Maine if he deemed it necessary. On the day the measure reached the Senate, March 2, it was immediately acted upon and unanimously passed.

No necessity arose for a military demonstration, as a memorandum was signed binding Maine and the Province of New Brunswick to release all prisoners, and to act "in concert, jointly or separately, according to agreements between the Governments of Maine and New Brunswick" to disperse intruders or trespassers in the disputed territory.

Before this amicable solution had been reached, the border States were in a ferment. In New York when it seemed as if the militia of the several States would be ordered to Maine, Solomon Van Rensselaer, now approaching his sixty-eighth year, called on Governor Seward. And lest his gold-headed cane be mistaken as an old man's support, he carried it under his arm when he asked for command of the State troops in the event of war. Seward humored the old veteran, who then called on Judge John Sanders and asked him to be one of his aides. The local newspapers, under such heads as "Fire of the Old Flint" published: "We learn from the highest authority that Maj. Gen. Solomon Van Rensselaer, who was distinguished in the Indian War of the last century, and who led the American troops at the Battle of Queenstown, has promptly tendered his services as the senior major general of New York State infantry to the commander-in-chief in the event of war between England and America. This hero of two wars . . ." A few weeks later, in the same paper, the *Albany Evening Journal*, under date of March 18, there appeared a story which began: "General Solomon Van Rensselaer, our excellent and respected Post Master, has received a letter from Amos Kendall announcing that he has been instructed by the President of the United States to say that in his judgment the public interests will be promoted by a change of Post Master at Albany, and that such change will be made at the close of the present quarter." But the old man, pretending not to mind, raised his head higher, and continued with his preparations for the war with his old enemy. He thought the foe would be England: but it was his still older foe, the fear of want.

Van Rensselaer was the first of the victims to fall in Van Buren's campaign to capture the next Congress as a preliminary to his campaign for reëlection in 1840. Some six months before the blow fell, the old veteran, in writing to Vice President Johnson to thank him for being reappointed, said that many in Albany were seeking his place. Had he written in like strain to Van Buren —but he was a Dutchman, too, and could not—he would have been permitted to end his years overseeing the mails at the ancient seat of the Manor of the Van Rensselaers. We have evidence tending to support this belief in Van Buren's refusal, shortly after his inauguration, to permit the removal of the old soldier on fictive charges of shortage in his accounts. The Regency persisted in its demand for his place; and Van Buren could not continue deaf to it. It was an important office, as the spoilsmen saw it, and one of the faithful must fill it. Yet within a month after the proscription of the most picturesque of the Van Rensselaers, Van Buren showed his other side. William Leggett, a brilliant journalist, whose caustic pen had often made Van Buren wince, was dying of tuberculosis at his home in New Rochelle. Since the *Plaindealer* had failed in 1836, Leggett had been too weak to work. Doctors advised a trip to a warmer climate; but Leggett was penniless and in debt. Van Buren solved the problem by appointing him diplomatic agent to Guatemala. With a lighter heart than he had known in many months, Leggett made ready; but on May 29, a few days before his ship was to sail, he died.

CHAPTER XXXVIII

In the last week of June Van Buren left for New York. His progress was deliberately slow. In several places in Pennsylvania he addressed partisans. Gradually it dawned upon the nation that Van Buren was campaigning for a Democratic Congress, and for his own reëlection, although it would be a year or so before he would be renominated. The stage was carefully set for his return. He arrived in Newark "in the railroad cars at half past 9 a.m." The *New Era*, which alone of New York journals assigned a reporter to meet him, then continued: "At a quarter before 11 o'clock, the President and a procession of vehicles and equestrians which extended apparently more than a mile in length, departed for Jersey City amidst cheers . . . At the several villages of Bergen County on his way, Mr. Van Buren was honored with repeated salutes of cannon procured for the occasion. . . ."

From Jersey City Van Buren saw New York for the first time since November, 1836. The whole Upper Bay and the mouth of the Hudson were dotted with gayly decorated craft when he stepped aboard the *Utica*. Midway between the New Jersey and New York shores the frigate *North Carolina* lay at anchor. Instead of heading straight for the opposite shore, the *Utica* plied her way "gracefully for some time among the vessels that thronged the bay." As she approached the frigate, whose yards were covered "by rows of sailors in white uniforms," the forty-four pound guns fired a double-broadside salute. This was returned by the forts on Bedloe's Island, Staten Island, and Governor's Island; and the several companies of artillery on the Battery thundered a welcome home; and for more than half an hour "the whole atmosphere was filled with the smoke and rent by the thunder of the continued discharge of cannon."

Not since the visit of La Fayette had New York seen such a spectacle. At least one hundred thousand men and women, in gaudy summer raiment, cheered Van Buren as he stepped ashore at the Battery. He was escorted into Castle Garden, where a citizens' committee, headed by John W. Edmonds, a former State Senator, received him. In his greeting, Edmonds repeatedly referred to the Democratic party of the State. The *Evening Post* —William Cullen Bryant was his most loyal and steadfast editorial supporter in his fight for a Sub-Treasury and other reforms—thus quotes Van Buren's response: "Gentlemen: I am deeply and gratefully affected by this cordial reception on the part of my Democratic fellow citizens of the City and County of New York. . . . Your observations upon an . . . independent treasury show a very mature and just consideration of the subject in all its bearings; tested by the principle which has been opposed to it—that of giving a temporary use of the public money, and a consequent control over it, to private corporations irresponsible to the people—it may well be regarded as a question of involving the nature, and to some extent the existence of republican institutions, as well as a consideration of the main purposes for which our government was established; whether for the safety of the many or the aggrandizement of the few, whether or not to secure the greatest good to the greatest number, in our view, the only legitimate object of the government among men. . . ."

In his reference to the Canadian insurrectionists, he answered his critics who accused him of being a foe to the spread of republican principles: ". . . we may, I am sure, count, with confidence upon a vigilant support, by our citizens, of those great principles of international justice, the maintenance of which is alike indispensable to the preservation of social order and the peace of the world. In doing so it does not follow that we are either to surrender the right of opinion, to suppress a solicitude for the spread of free government, or, to withhold our best wishes for the success of all who are in good faith laboring for their establishment."

"At the conclusion of the ceremonies in the garden," the *Evening Post* chronicled, "the President, mounted on a very graceful and spirited black horse, reviewed the six thousand troops gathered at the battery, when they were formed into ranks and the procession began slowly to move up Broadway, surrounded on all sides by multitudes of persons of both sexes and of all ages. The line of march was from Broadway up Chatham street [now Park Row] and the Bowery, through Broome street into Broadway again from whence it returned to the park. . . ." Here he dismounted and was escorted into the City Hall, where Isaac L. Varian presented him to the members of the Common Council. Both the Council and the Mayor were of his own political faith, the Democrats having regained control of the city in the April election.

Van Buren's ill-chosen phrase in his opening sentence—"my Democratic fellow citizens"—was included by the Whig press in its array of exhibits assembled to support the charge that Van Buren was violating the unwritten law forbidding a President to canvass for office.

The following day Van Buren received local political leaders and a large number of citizens in his suite at the Washington Hotel. The third day of his stay he journeyed to Staten Island in Captain Cornelius Vanderbilt's boat to attend the Fourth of July celebration of the Sunday schools of the metropolitan district. On Friday nine thousand people called to shake his hand. Commenting on this demonstration, the *New Era* said: "And this is the man that the Whigs, a year ago, asserted did not dare to come to our city for fear of assassination." Not even a member of the local police force was detailed to guard him.

From Hone's diary we learn that toward the end of the week he attended a performance at the Bowery Theater, where *The Lion King, or The Bandit's Doom* was showing nightly, followed by some other popular melodrama, such as *Nick of the Woods, or The Jibbenainosay*. It had not become the fashion for newspapers to assign reporters to record the movements of a President. Van Buren went to the playhouse with several Loco-focos, including Alexander Ming. This was the same Ming who had signed the call for the meeting in the Park in February, 1837, when he and other speakers incited their hungry listeners to storm and sack the flour warehouses. Ming was still shouting "Down with monopolists and extortionists!" It distressed Hone to see Van Buren associating with such radicals. On Monday morning Hone paid his respects to the President. Later in the day Van Buren visited the Navy Yard in Brooklyn, whose citizens turned out to honor him.

The next morning he left the city to visit friends in Westchester County. He was accompanied through the sylvan roads of upper Manhattan by Mayor Varian and several Councilmen in barouches. Mounted members of the Young Men's Democratic Club escorted them to the village of Harlem. Farmers, on horseback and in wagons, joined the procession along the route, now massed with skyscraping apartment houses. An *Evening Post* reporter noted: ". . . before reaching Harlem the train extended for more than a mile."

After spending a night with Colonel Hunter on his island estate in the East River, he shared the hospitality of Irving at his home at Sunnyside. Then he journeyed to Sing Sing, where several villages united in an official welcome. Three old farmers were so overjoyed to see one of their own blood elevated to the Presidency, that they kissed his hand. It was a fair stretch from the scene of the ceremonies to the boat landing. Van Buren walked the distance, the center of a cheering crowd that moved with him. From the windows women waved handkerchiefs. Hat in hand, he bowed right and left in acknowledgment. A venerable graybeard decided he must protect the President from the scorching sun, and persisted in keeping an umbrella over his head until the landing was reached. These spontaneous attentions were distorted by the local Whig weekly, the *Hudson River Chronicle*, in this wise: "We are not disposed to withhold from Mr. Van Buren any of the glory he received at Sing Sing, and therefore, though we confess it a disgrace to our place, we state the fact, that three of his faithful followers kissed his hand, with which he seemed greatly gratified. . . . On the way to the boat, a person was appointed to hold over his head an umbrella, after the fashion set by slaves of the Chinese emperor."

At Peekskill some little schoolboys, who had learned their pieces by heart, bade him welcome. This surprise moved Van Buren; for the children mentioned Kinderhook. And as he shook hands with each, he doubled the tiny fist over a five-dollar gold piece. The small boys now knew why he was called the Little Magician.

Van Buren was making his way by easy stages, the guest of the local authorities of every village and town on the east bank of the Hudson, until he reached the city of Hudson. It was here, as we remember, that he first practiced law on a large scale; here his first child was born. Here, at the seat of Columbia County, he had sat as Surrogate; and it was while a resident of Hudson that he was elected to the State Senate. He arrived in Hudson Friday, July 19, ten days after he left New York. He had been prepared for the rebuff, as he had received several days before a copy of the churlish resolutions the Whig Common Council of "the city of his adoption" had adopted the preceding Saturday. These resolves read in part:

It is therefore plain—beyond the power of argument to make it plainer, that Mr. Van Buren's tour is one of a political and partizan character.—Therefore be it

Resolved, by the Mayor and Common Council of the city of Hudson, in Common Council assembled, that we do not feel bound by any consideration of *justice, prudence,* or *hospitality,* to expend the people's money, or descend from the dignity of our official stations, for the purpose of aiding political partizans in their endeavors to carry out their favorite schemes.

These exalted ones had taken their cue from the Jovian Seward, who in declining to attend the celebration in New York City, wrote: "I have regarded his policies and his measures as injurious to the country. . . . It would be an extraordinary demonstration of respect on the part of the Chief Magistrate of this State towards any public functionary, were he to leave his duties at the capital to receive such functionary in your city."

The "discourtesy and illiberality"—as the Albany *Argus* characterized it—of the common Council, reacted to Van Buren's advantage; for many thousands journeyed from Ulster, Albany, and Rensselaer counties to make certain that he was not greeted by a handful. Several detachments of militia, including a company of artillery, participated in the celebration. Impartial witnesses of the reception to Van Buren who had been present at La Fayette's visit to Hudson a decade and a half earlier compared the two favorably. After the cannon had roared a Presidential salute, and the citizens' committee had formally welcomed him back to the "city of his adoption" and the county of his birth, Van Buren spoke. There was no suggestion of politics in his utterances, so the Democratic papers of New York City did not republish the report in the *Argus*. "Let me add," said Van Buren midway in his short response, "that to me it is a source of pleasure to meet so many of the associates of my youth, and of

my maturer years." As we read we hear him speak, not in his usual
rapid delivery, but slowly, in the manner of one who has been un-
expectedly called upon to speak and searches his heart for something to say.

That night he slept in Hudson. In the morning, at nine
o'clock, accompanied by his youngest son and sixteen friends,
most of them blood relatives, he set out for Kinderhook. They
rode in four barouches and two one-horse wagons. There were
no outriders. A mile outside his native village the six vehicles
halted as they came within earshot of a group of horsemen. They
were the reception committee of Kinderhook. At their head was
Mordecai Myers, President of the village. His aides were officers
in the militia and veterans of the War of 1812 who had not grown
too rotund for their faded uniforms. The mounted men flanked
themselves on either side of the Presidential party, and presently
the little procession moved forward at a brisk trot. It lacked a
few minutes of noon, the hour fixed for Van Buren's arrival at
Stranahan's Hotel, which was set in the heart of Kinderhook, three
miles north. They could barely make it in the time remaining.

A four-page draft, in Van Buren's hand, of the speech he
was to make that day, is in the archives of Congress. The only
printed record is found under "Kinderhook Correspondence" in
the *Argus* of the following Tuesday. The unknown chronicler has
placed Van Buren on the balcony of the squat, two-story village
hotel. From his vantage Van Buren glimpses the weather-beaten
pile of shingles and clapboards—now untenanted—the tavern
where he was born. In front of the doorway has been raised a
flagpole from whose top the Stars and Stripes floats in the noon-
day sun. Through the trees to the northwest, a few rods away,
bits of marble gleam against the restful green of the grass. He
cannot avoid seeing these, and recalling, as he does, the sentiment
he uttered the day before at Hudson: "I am happy in finding
myself once more in the midst of those with whom my career in
life commenced, and among whom I hope to be permitted to close
it." The Parian shafts marking the resting places of his wife and
parents grow indistinct as the closely packed mass in the square
below cheers again. The chairman has finished speaking: it is now
his turn.

After Van Buren formally acknowledged the welcome, he

began to talk of his toil-filled childhood; of scenes that had changed or were now no more; of his father and mother, and others whose voices had long been silent, from whom he had learned his first concepts of truth and honor. He was back home among them all. None of them had died; for their spirits lived. And when he laid down the cares of the Presidency he would come back again, this time to stay as long as the hills of Kinderhook endured. The surging mass in the village square became still; eyes moistened, and many sobbed softly. Tears coursed down Van Buren's cheeks, and he had to struggle with his emotions to keep his voice. There is mute supporting evidence of this scene, which local tradition has hallowed, but could not embroider. We find in the *Argus* of July 23: ". . . His reply was one of the most effective and beautiful addresses I have ever heard . . . the feeling allusions to the scenes he had passed through from the time he was a youth to the present, was such that all hearts were melted; and he himself was almost overcome by the bare repetition of them. . . ."

The soul-baring speech is over, and there is "another outburst of feeling in the repeated cheers." And we will let the unknown correspondent of the *Argus* continue: "He now took all by the hand that approached him, and exchanged congratulations with old neighbors and friends. When dinner was announced he sat down with them at the public table [in Stranahan's Hotel]. It was, however, understood beforehand that there were to be no set speeches nor toasts. . . ."

We have not used Van Buren's draft of the speech he intended to deliver on this day; for the things he said from the balcony of the inn are not put down on paper in advance.

Four days he remained in Kinderhook. He lived at the old Van Ness home, to which he had recently acquired title. Part of his stay was spent in devising improvements. But—these were his imperative instructions—under no circumstances was the half-door with its brass knocker to be altered in any manner. He wanted them to remain as souvenirs of that day, thirty-five years ago, when he hurried to the house in answer to the call for help from Billy Van Ness, a fugitive after the Burr-Hamilton duel, and found Billy's father seated under the brass knocker, oblivious to his presence and to his repeated rapping. A sad smile played around Van Buren's mouth as he recalled the scene which ended when Billy came down the long hall and whispered to his father, who never forgave Van Buren for supporting Morgan Lewis against Burr for Governor in the April election of 1804.

Van Buren's youngest son remained a day at Kinderhook, and then went on to Albany, where the father followed him. Here, the Whig municipal authorities followed the example set by their partisans in Hudson, and declined to welcome the President. But the citizens of the State Capital organized a celebration, which ended with speeches on the steps of the City Hall. In his reply to ex-Governor Marcy's address of welcome, Van Buren uttered a thought worth recording: "Deception and delusion may, for a time, depress the worthy and elevate the undeserving, but the final judgment of this people as to the tendency of public measures and the motives of public men, is alike unerring and inflexible."

Van Buren and his son stopped at Congress Hall while in the capital. The Whig authorities of two other cities on his way to Saratoga—Schenectady and Troy—also snubbed him. Said the Trojans: "Resolved, That the occasion of the President's visit calls for no public action on the part of the city authorities." Before leaving Albany Van Buren wrote to Jackson recounting the splendid receptions he had, and voiced the conviction that the State was redeemed politically. The next day his son wrote to his brother Martin in Washington:

My dear Mat,

The old man has just gone to Schenectady—and intends to bring up at the United States Hotel, Saratoga, tomorrow. I shall follow on this afternoon with the luggage. We have had a very pleasant time since I last wrote you. At Kinderhook we spent a day & dined at the Van Ness Place—Kleirood no more! We had a capital dinner of Fricasse [*sic!*] and ham, washed down with champaigne [*sic!*] We tried hard to get up a good name; but it is very tough work. The present favorite is "The Locusts" of which there are a great number about. The only objection is that the same name is used by Cooper in the "Spy" for one of his places. . . .

Believe me
Yrs ever affectionately
S. T. Van Buren
Albany July 31st 1839

Mat's younger brother should have added his brother's title to his name; for he was Acting Secretary to the President of the United States. Abraham and his bride were enjoying a brief holiday in Europe. No American couple received such attentions. He was the Secretary and son of the President, and she the niece of Andrew Stevenson, Minister to Great Britain. They were accorded regal honors. After dinner at St. Cloud, Louis Philippe conducted them through the palace; and all doors opened to them save the entrance to the sleeping apartment of the Comte de Paris, the grandson of the Citizen King. When Mrs. Van Buren told the Queen of their failure to obtain admittance, she explained laughingly: "Ah! that is all the King knows about it! After his mother left with the Duc d'Orléans for Algiers, I caused the child to be removed to a room nearer my own." Victoria was equally gracious in her informal reception of America's first lady of the land and her amiable husband.

While Van Buren was at Saratoga he wrote to Abraham to be home for the opening of Congress; for he depended on his daily reports for his news of the two houses. We have glimpses of Van Buren at Saratoga. Hone and Mrs. Hone are there, and Van Buren sends his bottle of wine to their table. Morgan Lewis, still active despite his eighty-three years, at whose home Van Buren has often been a guest, is seen walking with him. Henry Clay is expected, and the Democratic papers copy this thrust at him in the *Cincinnati Advertiser and Journal:* "The vindictive demagogue may meet the Little Magician there who may conjure him into a nonentity." Secretary Forsyth arrives with "others of the faithful," notes Hone. Another member of the Cabinet, Poinsett, follows. Van Buren "is conducting himself with his usual politeness and making the best of everything, as he is wont to do. . . . I have studied to treat him with all the respect due to his high station and the regard I have for an old friend, and I acknowledge the kindness with which my advances have been received." And all have forgotten old hatreds. But there has been "one exception, on the part of a lady, which, in my judgment, was equally at variance with good taste and proper feeling." This reference was the public snub administered to Van Buren by the widow of De Witt Clinton. Members of the gentle sex do not forgive a wrong done to the man they love.

There are two common tables in the dining room. "The President takes the head of one of the tables," writes Hone, "and the *modest* Mr. Bennett of the *Herald*, the other. The President cannot help this, to be sure, and the juxtaposition is somewhat awkward. Bennett will make a great thing of this with those who are not aware that any person may take this seat who has impudence enough . . ."

Clay arrived on Friday, August 9. Van Buren had been escorted to the hotel by a motley horde. The local Whigs had been divided over the nature of the reception to their leader, a minority protesting against an elaborate welcome because of the presence of Van Buren. Their problem was solved by Van Buren himself, who told them that he would leave before Clay arrived, and would return on Monday. He went to Troy where the citizens made amends for the inhospitality of the Whig municipal governing body. Clay was led to the hotel at the head of a formal procession which moved to the martial music of a brass band. As he was entering the hotel, he was detained on the porch long enough to enable a chaplet of roses and hyacinths to be lowered from the window of Mrs. Clinton's room. Clay suspected nothing until the garland touched his brow, when he pushed it to one side.

Clay had been looking forward to a visit to the battlefield of Saratoga. Van Buren anticipated this, and arranged that Morgan Lewis be his guide. This thoughtfulness, and the honor involved, delighted Clay. And Lewis enjoyed it just as much. There was the spot where his regiment first came in contact with Burgoyne's troops; and there the British broke; and . . . Clay warmed the spry old hero's heart by observing that a colonel of a fighting unit should not have been saddled with the duties of Quartermaster General of the entire Northern Army. And he talked of other battles Lewis fought in the fight for freedom. Clay had been well primed.

General Winfield Scott, another aspirant for the Whig nomination for President, arrived during Van Buren's absence. The three met in the drawing room on Van Buren's return. Clay was unable to get close enough to shake Van Buren's hand because of a group of ladies in the promenade, so he called out to him. Van Buren smiled as he saw Clay's predicament, and returning his greeting, exclaimed: "I hope I don't obstruct your progress."

"Not at all," came the quick response: "I have found the utmost facility in my progress since I entered your dominions." Scott, from a distance spied the meeting, and joined them, and "for an hour the three luminaries continued their promenade."

Van Buren threw no obstacles in Clay's path while he was in his "dominions." When the Kentuckian arrived in New York City, nine days later, Van Buren saw to it that the Loco-foco municipality placed the Governor's Room in the City Hall at Clay's disposal. Here the hosts of Whigs thronged to do Clay homage. This unusual mark of respect accentuated the lack of sportsmanship—to use a most charitable expression—of Van Buren's political adversaries.

The Whig papers afforded Van Buren and his friends a hearty laugh, somewhat at his expense. Black Bess, the horse he had ridden in the New York parade, had been loaned by Thomas S. Hamblin, the Shakespearian actor, and a Whig. The *New York Express* said that had it the power it would confer the privilege of suffrage on Black Bess that she might always vote the Whig ticket. The *Era* retorted: "A horse vote for the Whig ticket! What does that show?" "Shows that he is not a jackass," riposted the *Louisville Courier*.

Van Buren took his leave of the Springs on August 20; and on the following day was the center of a celebration in the village of Whitehall. Other large villages and cities were thereafter visited, including Buffalo ar 1 Auburn; and in the third week of September, the political tour ended, he enjoyed a fortnight's rest in Kinderhook. This was followed by a brief stay in New York on his return to Washington.

The November elections justified his expectations, the Democrats electing a bare majority in the House, thus giving him control of both branches for the first time since he began his fight for a Sub-Treasury. Congress convened on December 2. The House of Representatives was thrown into a turmoil by ten rival claimants for five of New Jersey's six seats. Governor William Pennington, a Whig, had given commissions to five of his partisans who had lost to their Democratic opponents on the face of the official returns. The Whigs charged that returns in the contested districts had been falsified. Excluding these seats, the Democrats had 119, and the opposition 118. At noon, the Clerk of the House, Hugh A. Garland, of Virginia, began calling the roll. When he reached New Jersey, he called the name of Joseph F. Randolph, and "then said that there were five other seats from the State of New Jersey which were contested; and not feeling himself authorized to decide the question between the contending parties, he would, if it were the pleasure of the House, pass over the names of those members and proceed with the call till a House shall be formed, who will then decide the question." Adams, who has left us the most replete account of the two weeks' tumult which this announcement started, continued: "This gave rise to a debate, which continued until past four o'clock, when a motion was made to adjourn. The Clerk said he could put no question, not even for adjournment, until the House itself should be formed. . . . There was a general call to adjourn; and, although one voice cried 'No!' and others called out to adjourn to eleven o'clock, the Clerk declared the House adjourned to twelve o'clock. This movement has been evidently prepared to exclude the five members from New Jersey from voting for Speaker; and the Clerk has had his lesson prepared for him. . . . His two decisions form together an insurmountable objection to the transaction of any business and an impossibility of organizing the House."

For three days the House of Representatives was made a mock parliament by the Clerk. The fiery Henry A. Wise, of Virginia, in leaving the chamber on the second evening, observed to those near him: "We are a mob." Not until the evening of the third day did the Clerk condescend to put a question, and then only on a motion to adjourn. On the fourth day, Adams addressed his associates, summed up their predicament, and said: "If we cannot organize in any other way,—if this Clerk will not consent to our discharging the trusts confided to us by our constituents, —then let us imitate the example of the Virginia House of Burgesses when the colonial governor [Dinwiddie] ordered it to disperse, and like men—"

Adams never finished the sentence, although his corrected speech has rounded it out. The House broke into cheers; the galleries, forgetting that visitors must remain silent, joined in the boisterous demonstration to the "old man eloquent." He offered a resolution directing the Clerk to call the names of the five Whigs from New Jersey who had credentials, explaining that any member might offer an amendment to his resolve, and thus bring the question to an immediate issue. To the more exasperated this seemed ineffectual, and they shouted from all parts of the House: "Who will put the question?" and "How shall the question be put?" Adams, still holding the floor, astonished all with his answer, which rang out clear like the peal of cathedral chimes above the roar of an angry mob on the square below: "I intend to put the question myself." This was usurpation; but it was also a solution. Now the Clerk tried to define his position. But his words were drowned in the uproarious shouts of "Organize without him!" Robert Barnwell Rhett, of South Carolina, mounted a desk and moved that Lewis Williams, of North Carolina, dean of the House, take the chair. Williams objected: his choice was Adams. "Adams! Adams!" chorused the House. Rhett, who named Williams solely because he was older than any other man in the House, instantly substituted the name of the ex-President, who was chosen by a thunderous volley of ayes.

A ten-day struggle to elect a Speaker began, the House having decided to suspend the inquiry into the New Jersey elections until a presiding officer was chosen. On the 16th Robert M. T. Hunter, of Virginia, was chosen. It took another week to organize the House, and then the President's annual message was read. The five Democrats from New Jersey were thereafter seated. They had as much color to their claims as their Whig opponents; both sides had been guilty of frauds in the election.

During the first week of the sitting the Whigs met at Harrisburg and again nominated General Harrison for President. John Tyler, of Virginia, a Democrat, and a Strict Constructionist, was named for Vice President. Clay, who never doubted that he would be the choice of the convention, "was sitting in a room at Brown's Hotel, anxiously waiting to hear of his nomination." Wise, who called on him, relates that Clay "made most singular exhibitions of himself in that moment of ardent expectancy. He was open and exceedingly profane in his denunciation of the intriguers against his nomination. We had taken two Whig friends of our district to see him; and after they had sat some time listening to him, in utter surprise at his remarks, full of the most impudent, coarse crimination of others, in words befitting only a bar-room in vulgar broil, of a sudden he stopped, and turning to the two gentlemen, who were dressed in black and both strangers to him, he said, 'But, gentlemen, for aught I know, from your cloth you may be parsons, and shocked at my words. Let us take a glass of wine.' And, rising from his seat, he walked to a well-loaded sideboard, at which, evidently, he had been imbibing deeply before we entered."

When word was brought that Clay had been defeated, Wise noted: "Such an exhibition we never witnessed before, and pray never again to witness such an ebullition of passion, such a storm of desperation and curses. He rose from his chair, and, walking backwards and forwards rapidly, lifting his feet like a horse string-halted in both legs, stamped his steps upon the floor, exclaiming, 'My friends are not worth the powder and shot it would take to kill them!' He mentioned the names of several, invoking upon them the most horrid imprecations. . . . 'It is a diabolical intrigue, I now know, which has betrayed me. I am the most unfortunate man in the history of parties: always run by my friends when sure to be defeated, and now betrayed for a nomination when I, or any one, would be sure of an election.' "

Clay had not overstated the nature of the intrigue. The younger Joseph Gales had told Adams "that the nomination of Harrison at Harrisburg was the triumph of Anti-Masonry and was entirely the work of W. H. Seward, the present Governor of New York." Seward effected Clay's defeat through a most ingenious invention. This was the famed Triangular Correspondence. Seward, knowing that New York would control the nomination, induced his aides, pretended friends of Clay, residing in Rochester, Utica, and New York City, to write each other to this effect: "Do all you can for Mr. Clay in your district, for I am sorry to say that he has no strength in this." These letters were then shown to Whig leaders in the three great sections of the State. In this manner Clay's strength was destroyed before the New York delegation went to Harrisburg, and the delegates were committed by Seward to support Scott, the stalking horse for Harrison.

On Christmas Eve Congress heard Van Buren's annual message. He again assailed the paper banking system in his fourth plea for the Sub-Treasury. The collapse of Biddle's Bank of the United States in the second week of October, with the consequent suspension of banks in the West and South, he adverted to in the course of a plea for regulation of the banks. The several State governments, he said, ought to limit the activities of banks to banking, and "take from them . . . the unjust character of monopolies; to check . . . by prudent legislation, those temptations of interest, and those opportunities for their dangerous indulgence which beset them on every side . . ." After dwelling on the immense power of the banks over politics and trade, and the wholesome effect the Sub-Treasury and other imperative reforms would have on them and on the nation, he observed that in most other countries the ends aimed at could be achieved only "through that series of revolutionary movements, which are too often found necessary to effect any great and radical reform; but it is the crowning merit of our institutions that they create and nourish in the vast majority of our people, a disposition and a power peacefully to remedy abuses which have elsewhere caused the effusion of rivers of blood, and the sacrifice of thousands of the human race."

When the message was read, in the Senate, William Allen, of Ohio, moved that it be printed. Allen, ever coining phrases—it was he who invented five years later, during the Oregon boundary dispute, "Fifty-four forty, or fight!"—was at his happiest on this occasion. He was brief, and did not construct a bewildering labyrinth of rhetorical expressions. Thus he summed the evils of paper money and Van Buren's struggle:

> To guarantee forever the rights, the happiness of individual man —to protect the feeble against the rapacity of the strong—the whole against the combinations of the parts, by an equal distribution of burdens and of blessings among all—was the cardinal object of our civil institutions. But, notwithstanding this, these rights have been violated —this happiness perilled—this rapacity allowed—these combinations formed—and this equality destroyed. These things have been done, and that, too, under the authority of law. Corporations innumerable freckle the face of the land. Corporations which, not content with absolute power over the currency—over the property—over the labor of the entire people, now seek to render themselves immortal, and their dominion complete, by political associations. . . .

When, in 1837, after the universal crash of the banking system, the President recommended its severance from the Government, and the Government's restoration to its ancient policy, the people, unprepared alike for the ruin around them, or the remedy proposed, remained for a moment, equally confounded by both. State after State reeled from its perpendicular and slid from its support; politician after politician fled for safety or for succor to the arms of his foes; yet he, almost alone, amidst the general consternation, amidst the desertions of the venal and the shrieks of the timid, stood unappalled —confiding, as he ever has, does, and ever will, in that "sober second thought" of his countrymen which is "never wrong, and always efficient."

The opposition realized that Van Buren's stand on the Sub-Treasury would not lend itself to a popular form of attack. But they were not in a dilemma because of this, as Van Buren's supporters had forged the very steel they sought. When Harrison was nominated, the *Baltimore Republican* sneered at his poverty with: "Give him a barrel of hard cider, and settle a pension of two thousand a year on him, and my word for it he will sit the remainder of his days in his log cabin . . ." The Washington correspondent of the *Evening Post* defiled the columns of Van Buren's metropolitan organ with this: "General Harrison's poverty has awakened the sympathy of the ladies of this District, and they are now at work getting up a subscription to supply the 'war-worn hero' with a suit of clothes. If you have any old shoes, old boots, old hats, or old stockings, send them on, and they will be forwarded to the Hero of North Bend."

Shortly after the Senate confirmed a new Cabinet officer. The election of Grundy in November to succeed Senator Ephraim H. Foster had created the vacancy. Van Buren at first invited Buchanan to be Attorney General. When he declined, he named another Pennsylvanian, Henry D. Gilpin, author of several legal tomes, patron of the arts, and philanthropist. Until he joined Van Buren's official family, Gilpin had been Solicitor General of the Treasury. Grundy, an old friend of Calhoun, had been laboring for some months to effect a personal reconciliation between the Great Nullifier and the President. He was aided by Francis W. Pickens, a Representative from South Carolina.

The day following Christmas, Calhoun was a guest at the White House. No one was astonished, as the South Carolinian had been a zealous supporter of Van Buren's policies for some time. Had Grundy alone attended this little dinner, and participated in reuniting the two, the Whig press would have been furnished with fresh ammunition for the impending campaign. Pickens had been one of the most caustic critics of the Van Buren administration. No one had played more on Marcy's "to the victor belong the spoils."

The bellwether of the opposition journals, the *American,* in satirizing the reconciliation, recalled the speech Pickens made at the opening of the regular session of Congress in 1837, when he said: "The rooks, together with the obscene birds, have perched themselves in the high places of the land, and we sit here beneath, surrounded by their filth and corruption."

On January 27 the *American* said that the enactment of the Sub-Treasury bill would reduce "the wages of free labor in the United States to the lowest standards of overtaxed and overpopulated Europe." This, of course, Rufus King's son, and those who reëchoed his editorialisms, knew to be untrue. But canards of this type were leaving their impress on the masses in the cities, who were again beginning to feel the pinch of poverty, as they had felt it in 1837.

Through Hone we have a glimpse of Van Buren on the last day of the month, at one of his Saturday night dinners. "The party consisted of about five and twenty gentlemen; a splendid affair . . . The President does the honours with dignity and graciousness. There is no fuss in the business, and every guest has his full share of the attentions of his host. I thought myself particularly favoured, and so I presume others did. The President sat on one side of the table, with Mr. Southard on his right, and Mr. Sturgeon, the new senator from Pennsylvania, on his left. Immediately opposite to him was Mr. Forsyth, Secretary of State, with General Scott on his right and me on his left,—an arrangement which the Secretary informed me before the dinner was made by the President's order. The President's first glass of wine was drunk with General Scott, and the second with me." This was typical of Van Buren: distinguished Whigs who visited Washington were invited to these Cabinet dinners and shown marked attention at his table.

The Whig campaign was actively under way in the month of February. The slurs on Harrison's poverty were the materials out of which the opposition beclouded issues and fashioned the most dramatic appeal ever submitted to the American electorate. The log-cabin home of the Whig nominee symbolized not only the struggles of the frontiersman, but the simple ways of the majority; and to their prejudices the Whig journals made daily appeals. In the month of March, during the height of the New York charter elections, the log cabin was first used as the Whig emblem, and hard cider was distributed free and freely at Whig rallies. On Friday, April 10, four days before election, Hone noted: "Immense meetings take place every night at the general and ward places of rendezvous. Processions parade the streets at night with music, torches, and banners; the prevailing device for the latter is the *log-cabin;* and we had hard cider, which has become the fountain of Whig inspiration. . . . on all their banners and transparencies the temple of Liberty is transformed into a hovel of unhewn logs; the military garb of the general, into the frock and shirt-sleeves of a laboring man. The American eagle has taken his flight, which is supplied by a hard cider barrel, and the long established emblem of the ship has given way to the plough." Biddle and his host of paper bankers had become more democratic than the most radical of the Loco-focos. The Whigs lost the city; but the Democratic majority was greatly lessened.

The following day Van Buren was the victim of a most virulent attack in the House of Representatives by Charles Ogle, of Pennsylvania. This speech is an unexcelled example of partisanship run riot. For almost the entire day the Whigs sat enthralled as their spokesman wove a record with warp of fact and woof of fancy. Ogle fabricated a figure so like Van Buren as to deceive the unknowing. More than twenty years before this speech was made, William Lee, American Consul at Bordeaux, purchased for the Presidential mansion many exquisite pieces of French cabinetry, and other furnishings, including a service of gold spoons. Monroe, the second Adams, and Jackson had used these things. Ogle said that Van Buren had bought these luxuries: and plated spoons and divers other articles of base metal, became, in the orator's crucible, expensive examples of the goldsmith's art. This, and similar ridicule, was heaped on Van Buren:

And now, sir, having seen that this democratic President's house is furnished in a style of magnificence and regal splendor that might well satisfy a monarch, let us examine the manners, habits, conduct, and political principles of the person who dwells in it, and see if they correspond to the grandeur of the mansion. I do this to show the People some facts, from which they may judge whether this is that plain, simple, humble, hard-handed democrat whom they have been taught to believe is at the head of the democratic party. . . . He may call himself a democrat—such, no doubt, he professes to be—but then there is a great difference between names and things. You have heard the story of the farmer's son, who said to his father, "Father, if I should call that calf's tail a leg, how many legs would the calf have?" "Why, five to be sure," said his father. "Why, no it wouldn't," says the boy, "because my calling it a leg wouldn't make it so."

So, in this case, I strongly suspect that, when we look a little closely, we shall find that the democratic leg is nothing but a tail, after all.

Ogle next transformed the White House into a palace, and Van Buren into His Majesty. Even the President's churchgoing came in for Ogle's gibes, who contrasted Henry Clay walking from his lodgings to St. John's Church, with Van Buren riding the short three hundred yards between the White House and the Episcopal church "in His Democratic Majesty's British State-coach." It should be noted that Van Buren had not embraced Episcopalianism: he was but following the example of the Patroon and other New York Dutchmen in worshiping at the historic edifice on La Fayette Square, there being no Dutch Reformed Church in Washington.

Ogle assailed Van Buren through Prince John, who "had been honored with wine-sipping with 'the pretty little Queen,' and 'the Queen was highly delighted' with 'our Prince!'" Here Ogle exclaimed: "Our Prince! mind you. We must get familiar with these things, for we must come to them. We have a President who was so great a favorite with the English nobility that when his son goes there they rank him above their titled noblemen." Ogle was certain that Jackson or Harrison or any other heroes of the War of 1812 would not have received any honors from British hands. "What has John Van Buren done for his country to distinguish him? Nothing. . . . But our Prince, I am informed, is a very clever gentleman, and by the way, possesses a great deal of drollery. I am told that one day he went into the palace, and seeing his father rather melancholy at the prospect of Old Tippecanoe coming in, he patted him on the back, and said: 'Pa, you need not despair, because, if you are beat, I will take you in to practice law with me.' " He told how the Secretary to the President was honored by British royalty. "Is not this all enough to sicken an old-fashioned democrat? And this is Van Buren democracy! This is bringing up the sons of a democratic President in fine style!"

Many wild tales were told of Prince John, most of them sheer inventions. His mad pranks suggested many of them. A few months before Ogle's speech, with other members of New York State's Board of Law Examiners, he was a guest of the budding Solons. John Bigelow, who had just passed the examinations, was one of the youthful hosts. He recounts that immediately after all had risen and drunk solemnly to the toast, "To George Washington, the Father of his country!"—many impromptu toasts had been drunk earlier in the evening—Prince John rose and proposed: "To the health of Martha Washington, the Mother of Her Country!" A few had difficulty swallowing their wine because of the merriment that convulsed them.

Van Buren—we have Ogle's partisan speech for it—never mingled with the people on the street: he always rode in his "gilded coach." "He was out, to be sure, at the ball at Carusi's on the 22d of February. He appeared about 9 o'clock . . . the bank struck up 'Hail to the Chief.' What a glorious chief to be sure! I wonder where he fought his battles." And where was Van Buren in the War of 1812? Opposed to Madison and the war along with the Federalists and the Peace party who supported De Witt Clinton for President. Ogle appealed to the prejudices of the South by recalling that one of the reasons advanced by Clinton's friend for their opposition to Madison in 1812 was that Madison "is devoted to the Southern policy." Continued Ogle: "Was it a crime then to be 'devoted to Southern policy'? And is it a virtue now to be 'a Northern man with Southern principles'? . . ."

Ogle played with the phrase "a Northern man with Southern principles." What would the Southerners think of a Southern man with Northern principles?

After reading "the base assaults on General Harrison's poverty" in the New York *Evening Post*, Ogle said: "I can inform this insolent Loco-foco that General Harrison, though not rich, has always had money sufficient to pay for hemming his own dish rags and grinding his own knives, and that he would scorn to charge the people of the United States with foreign cut wine coolers, liquor stands, and golden chains to hang golden labels around the necks of barrel-shape flute decanters with cone stoppers. And I can further inform this Loco-foco calumniator that the hands of the 'Hero of North Bend' have become so hard by the use of the flail and the plough tail, that a cordial grasp of his dexter would cause the big tears to flow from the eyes of the taper, lily fingered aristocrat who made the people pay for his Fanny Kemble green finger-cups, larding needles, and certain other articles which dare not be named to ears polite."

We had forgotten to mention that the Countess of Westmorland stayed at Saratoga when Van Buren was there. She was beautiful, and all who made her acquaintance paid her homage. But Ogle, to perfect his fictive figure of the aristocratic Van Buren, imaged Saratoga as a lonely trysting place where Van Buren spent all his time "in gallanting the Countess of Westmorland."

Ogle had sneers for "the cabbage garden at Kinderhook," and Van Buren's fondness for society. He was not an ordinary aristocrat, but a leader of cotillions in the gay salons of the opulent, a fop who used pomatum on his hair, powder on face, and perfume—the most expensive French *Triple Distillée Savon Daveline Mons Sens*—on his whiskers and lily-fingered hands.

Ogle had made a campaign text book—typical of these quadrennial imprints—for the Whig spouters.

A fortnight later Congress was deserted by Whig and Democratic leaders. All were headed for Baltimore, where the Democrats were holding their National Convention, and the Whigs had staged a rival gathering to divert attention from the proceedings of the Democrats. From all parts of the country the Whigs came to the number of thirty thousand. They had a procession with floats, including log cabins on wheels and barrels of hard cider. The Baltimore *Patriot* tells us that "a thousand banners, burnished by the sun, floating in the breeze, ten thousand handkerchiefs waved by the fair daughters of the city, gave seeming life and motion to the very air."

Hoodlums attacked the procession. Stones and brickbats

ANGELINA SINGLETON VAN BUREN
After an engraving by J. C. Buttre

injured several; and a local carpenter who was marching in the parade was slain. Webster and his fellows from Massachusetts raised more than $1,000 for the dead Whig's family. Other delegates contributed more than $6,000. No one was permitted to contribute more than a dollar.

The next day, Tuesday, May 5, the convention renominated Van Buren. The presiding officer was William Carroll, sometime Governor of Tennessee, whose duel with Jesse Benton in 1813 led to the street brawl in which dirks, sword canes and pistols were used, Jackson receiving an ugly pistol wound. On motion of Buchanan there was no ballot for President, there being no opposition to Van Buren. There were many objections to renaming Johnson for second place; several States, in local convention by legislative caucuses, had nominated favorite sons for Vice President. In the resolution placing Van Buren before the people, it was also resolved, "That the convention deem it expedient at the present time not to choose between the individuals in nomination, but to leave the decision to their Republican [*sic!*] fellow-citizens in the several states, trusting that before the election shall take place, their opinions shall become so concentrated as to secure the choice of a vice president by the electoral college." In an appeal to the people the Convention denounced the Abolitionists, and accused the Whigs of enlisting them in support of Harrison. The hard cider and log cabin processions were properly described as costly and stately pageants addressed merely to the senses, which would be met with the truth and reason of democracy. The document unjustly reflected on Harrison's military achievements; and with a like disregard of truth, wrote him down a Federalist.

Letters which passed between Van Buren and Jackson indicate that the failure to name a Vice President was an expedient devised by Van Buren. On April 3 Jackson wrote to Van Buren that a Vice President ought to be named: he was against the renomination of Johnson and favored James Knox Polk, long a member of Congress from Tennessee, several times Speaker of the House. Forsyth, supported by his fellow Georgians and friends in other States, was an open aspirant for the place. Tazewell, of Virginia, was a candidate. Van Buren remained loyal to Johnson, holding that the personal habits of a man, provided they did not interfere with his labors as a public servant, were not a bar to office. But he did not dare assert himself openly.

Unlike the Whigs, the Democrats adopted a platform epitomizing the cardinal principles of Van Buren's political faith. He was for a strict construction of the Constitution, and a Sub-Treasury, and economy in government; he was against government aid to private enterprise or internal improvements; he denied that Congress had the power to interfere with slavery in the States, or to create a national bank; he denounced Abolitionists as enemies of the Union, and the few who sought to abridge the privilege of citizenship as kin to the advocates of the Alien and Sedition Laws of the first Adams.

On the day he was renominated Van Buren received a letter that effaced politics and Washington from his mind, and conjured up a picture of his childhood, of Kinderhook blanketed in snow, when young and old sang: *"Sint Nikolaas goed heilig man!"* And what was it they asked Santa Claus to bring from Muscat? Ah, yes, it ran: *"Noten van Muskaat."* Never till now had he thought of anything save nuts coming from Muscat. This was the letter:

To His Excellency Martin Van Buren, President of the United States of North America, Washington:

Sir: Hope the Almighty God will protect you, and keep you in good health. From this part of the world, having no news to communicate them to your Excellency; and, whenever opportunity offers for this place, we shall feel happy to hear from your Excellency. With any thing that we can do for you, little or plenty, shall feel happy.

Written by the order of His Highness,

Seyd Seyd Bin Sultan Bin Ahmed,

Imaum of Muscat.

Seyd Bin, Calfaun.

Dated Muscat, 25th December, 1839.

He could not help noting that the quaint letter was dated Christmas Day—the day associated with the song. And then there was a second note from the merchant house of Barclay and Livingston advising him that on His Highness's ship, *Sultanee,* there arrived in the Metropolis on May 2, these gifts from the Imaum of Muscat: two Arabian horses, one case of attar of roses, five demijohns of rose water, one package of Cashmere shawls, one bale of Persian rugs, one box of pearls, a box containing a sword. The Constitution prohibited the acceptance of presents "from any King, Prince, or Foreign State" without the consent of Congress, which had never yet granted this permission. Van Buren intended to shatter this tradition, as he had so many others. The third day following the receipt of the Imaum's letter, Van Buren, with the aid of an Oriental epistolarian, penned this answer:

To His Highness Seyd Seyd Bin Sultan Bin Ahmed, Imaum of Muscat, from Martin Van Buren, President of the United States of America—Greeting:

Great and Good Friend: By the hands of Ahmed Ben Haman, commanding your Highness's ship Sultanee, I had the satisfaction of receiving your Highness's letter of the 19th of the Moon of Shawal, the 1,255 of the Hegira. It has been a source of lively satisfaction to me, in my desire that frequent and beneficial intercourse should be established between our respective countries, to behold a vessel bearing your Highness's flag enter a port of the United States, to testify, I hope, that such relations will be reciprocal and lasting.

I am informed that Ahmed Ben Haman had it in charge from your Highness to offer for my acceptance, in your name, a munificent present. I look upon this friendly proceeding on your part as a new proof of your Highness's desire to cultivate with us amicable relations; but a fundamental law of the Republic which forbids its servants from accepting presents from foreign States or Princes, precludes me from receiving those your Highness intended for me. I beg your Highness to be assured that, in thus declining your valuable gift, I do but perform a paramount duty to my country, and that my sense of the kindness which prompted the offer is not thereby in any degree abated.

Wishing health and prosperity to your Highness, power and stability to your Government, and to your people tranquillity and happiness, I pray that God may have you, great and good friend, in his holy keeping.

                                        M. Van Buren

By the President:
    John Forsyth,
        Secretary of State.
Washington, May 8, 1840.

The Emperor of Morocco, not to be outdone, sent a lion and a lioness to Van Buren, who induced the Senate to permit him to accept the gifts and sell them and place the proceeds in the Treasury, and the House ratified. A number of Whigs, persuaded by Adams to respect the ancient tradition, voted in the negative.

Kendall tendered his resignation as Postmaster General on May 16. He was not too robust and wanted to conserve his energies to spit Van Buren's enemies on his pen. Kendall privately recommended that John Milton Niles, Senator from Connecticut, be named in his stead. Van Buren doubted that Niles would accept: he was a philanthropist, a distinguished writer, and founder of the Hartford *Times*. He wrote Niles immediately, marking the communication "Strictly confidential," so that his declination could not be capitalized by the opposition. Niles, to Van Buren's delight, accepted.

It was a long session, after the manner of sittings in Presidential years. The Whigs assailed Van Buren for the expensive campaign against the Seminoles, and for using bloodhounds to track the Indians through the swamps of Florida; he was accused of trying to emulate Napoleon, Cromwell, and Cæsar, because Poinsett recommended a Federal organization of the militia— this was "Van Buren's standing army of 250,000"; he was not a Democrat, but a Kinderhook man, and his followers were the men of Kinderhook, although occasionally they were referred to as the Kinderhook Democrats. The Bank men were making their last stand against the Sub-Treasury. As had been the case since he first recommended the measure, the real battle was in the House: the Senate, following its practice, passed the bill shortly after Congress was convened. On the last day of June the House sent the bill to the President. A few Whigs, realizing that this was the most forward-looking measure that had been submitted to any Congress, voted for it. On July 4 Van Buren signed the Sub-Treasury Act, thus striking the golden chains of the banks from the hands of government.

When Congress adjourned on July 21, the campaign was rapidly approaching the high note of its hilarious crescendo. Adams was far from sanguine of Whig success in June. At this time Van Buren wrote Jackson that the prospects of reëlection were favorable. Adams and others of conservative leanings did not approve the mob appeals of the Whigs, who were erecting log cabins in every important community in the country where barrels of hard cider were the principal furnishings, and where all comers might drink themselves into a drunken stupor. Banners adorned these free saloons depicting Harrison in the buckskins of a frontiersman trapping the Red Fox of Kinderhook, or bearing some kindred device. Raccoon skins adorned the walls, and quite frequently live raccoons ran around the cabins within the orbits of their chains. In commemoration of Harrison's farewell to his soldiers, when he invited them to call at their pleasure, assuring them that his door would be never shut, or the string of the latch pulled in; the doors of these log cabins had conspicuous latchstrings, always out.

The largest of these log cabins was erected a few streets north of New York's City Hall, on Broadway, at the corner of Prince street, and covered a plot of ground fifty by one hundred feet. It was formally dedicated on the night of June 16 with speeches by Whigs from Kentucky, Indiana, and Ohio. One of the local attractions was Joseph Hoxie, a wealthy importer of textiles, a dabbler in politics, and with no pretensions to oratory. He sang. Before the summer was well under way he had organized a glee club and toured the country. Whig glee clubs sprang up everywhere, in imitation of Hoxie's. To the air of "Little Pig's Tail" they sang—and the audiences sang it with them:

> What has caused this great commotion, motion,
>   Our country through?
>   It is the ball a-rolling on,
> For Tippecanoe and Tyler too, Tippecanoe and Tyler too.
> And with them we'll beat little Van, Van, Van;
>   Van is a used-up man.

The ball referred to was taken from Benton's speech on the night the expunging resolution was adopted by the Senate, when he boasted that "solitary and alone" he had "put the ball in motion." Another of the many uses of this figure ran:

> As rolls the ball,
> Van's reign doth fall,
> And he may look
> To Kinderhook.

There was more of it, and soon the Whigs everywhere were singing it, for the melody was popular. They mocked Van Buren's ruffled shirt and golden plate in sounding the praises of Harrison's simple garb:

> Ole Tip he wears a homespun suit,
> He has no ruffled shirt—wirt—wirt;
> But Mat he has the golden plate,
> And he's a little squirt—wirt—wirt.

When this was sung in the taprooms by those who chewed tobacco, the *wirt—wirt* was simulated by ejecting tobacco juice through the clenched teeth. A parody on "John Anderson, My Jo, John!" found favor in the drawing rooms as well as on the hustings and in the taverns. The first three verses ran:

> O Matty Van, my jo, Mat,
>   I wonder what you mean
> By such a naughty act as that
>   Which lately has been seen.
> What want you with an army, Mat?
>   Ah, why do you do so?
> 'Twill march you back to Kinderhook,
>   O Matty Van, my jo.
>
> O Van Buren, my jo, Van,
>   You've clomb the hill o' State,
> And monie a cunnin' trick, mon,
>   Was fathered in your pate;
> But now you're tottering down, Van;
>   How rapidly you go!
> You'll soon be sprawling at the fit,
>   O Matty Van, my jo.
>
> O Matty Van, my jo, Mat,
>   When we were first acquaint,
> 'Tis true you were not slow, Mat,
>   With sinner or with saint;
> But now you have grown ould, Mat,
>   You never seem to know
> How fast you're goin' "bock agen,"
>   O Matty Van, my jo.

Nor did the Whig versifiers forget those who preferred recitations. The most noted of these pieces told of Tippecanoe coming out of the West, where his fame was best; "for, save his log cabin, he station had none." Of course he boldly entered the President's hall; and Van Buren, overwhelmed by Harrison's goodly form and honest face, surrendered the White House to him. And then:

> One touch to Blair's hand and one word in his ear,
> As Van reached the door, and his carriage was near:
> "We are gone, we are gone, by hook or by crook,
> I must wend my way back to my own Kinderhook;
> My light English coach, though often it flew,
> Couldn't match the hard gray of old Tippecanoe."
>
> There was mounting and tramping of Cabinet clan,
> And the Kitchen concern, some rode and some ran;
> There was racing and chasing o'er Capitol lea,
> But the little Magician no more could they see!
> So dauntless in war, to his country so true,
> Who could clear the Kitchen but Tippecanoe?

Picturesque as were the meetings, they were outdone by the parades. As the campaign progressed, women and children were infected by the enthusiasm; they rode in wagons from which they chorused partisan ditties to the accompaniment of brass bands or fife and drum corps. The fusion of the Conservative Democrats with the Whigs was epitomized in the couplet emblazoned on nearly every third banner:

> National Republicans in Tippecanoe,
> And Democratic Republicans in Tyler too.

Lurid daubs of paint on transparencies depicted Harrison on a charger bidding farewell to his soldiers; a log cabin with the legend, "The latchstring will be always out"; Harrison attired as a hunter standing beside a trapped fox with the face of Van Buren; Harrison building a rude stockade; Harrison leading a charge; Harrison guiding a plow; Harrison fighting Indians; Van Buren riding in a gilded coach—a British state-coach—driven by a redcoat; and plain white banners on which the cabalistic K.K.K.K.K. was inscribed in black. There was not a child in the land who did not know that this stood for Kinderhook

Kandidate Kant Kome it Kwite. No parade was complete without this rude couplet borne aloft:

> With Tip and Tyler
> We'll burst Van's biler.

These artificially stimulated demonstrations of popular protest against Van Buren were, in themselves, insufficient to move the mass behind Harrison. No one expected that the thinking element of the electorate would be swayed by theatrical claptrap. Webster and others who knew better, using the hustings and the press as their vehicles, sought to drive fear into homes not moved by the costly street pageants or swigs of hard cider. Day after day the prostitute press sang the praises of paper banknotes, denounced gold and silver, and cried the need of another national bank to save the nation from financial ruin. The Sub-Treasury was pictured as a menace to our institutions.

Van Buren, citing the record, said that the Bank had been originally devised by friends of privileged orders.

Webster, in one of his most dramatic outbursts, recalling that the first Bank of the United States had been chartered when Washington was President, and the second Biddle institution created under Madison, argued that this statement of Van Buren's was a direct accusation of corruption against Madison and Washington. Still essaying the rôle of a debased demagogue on the hustings, Webster added: "I may forgive this; but I shall not forget it." Biddle could not say that this laborer was not worthy of his hire.

It is an old device of politicians to accuse their opponents of traducing the venerated dead. Old Federalists were reminded that Washington had been their leader. Democrats had Van Buren held up to them as the quondam campaign manager of Rufus King, "Federalist, Missouri restrictionist, and advocate of negro suffrage." And most monstrous crime of all, Van Buren had supported Clinton and opposed Madison and the war. There was no reference to his advocacy and aid of the war after the people had spoken at the polls, nor of his intense democracy in his maturer years.

The officers of the suspended banks, still hoping to see the day return when the Sub-Treasury Act would be repealed, and the vast revenues of the government once more placed in their hands —without interest—were still powers in their respective communities. These civic and social leaders had no difficulty in persuading commission merchants and other middlemen to advertise in this manner: "The subscriber will pay five dollars a hundred for pork if Harrison is elected, and two and a half if Van Buren is." and "The subscriber will pay six dollars a barrel for flour if Harrison is elected, and three dollars if Van Buren is." Employers appealed to Democratic workmen to abandon Van Buren, saying if Harrison were not the next President their wages, then at a low ebb, would be still further reduced—provided any work was to be had. Similar appeals were made editorially, of which this from the *Morning Courier and New York Enquirer*, of October 2, is typical:

"To the Laboring Classes and Workingmen in the City and State of New York—If you wish to be poor and trodden down, and to see your wife starving and your children in ignorance, vote for Martin Van Buren."

The Whig spouters repeated the fiction of the gold spoons and falsely charged Van Buren with extravagance in the administration of government. They truthfully said the payments from the Treasury during his term had exceeded $130,000,000: they neglected to say that $14,000,000 had been spent in removing the Indians west of the Mississippi; that the pension roll had been increased to more than $10,000,000; $3,000,000 for public buildings, and nearly $7,000,000 which had been received from foreign governments for indemnities had been transferred through the Treasury to citizens.

Throughout the campaign Van Buren remained in Washington, answering letters of Whigs and his own partisans, confining his replies to the issues of the campaign. He knew that if the election was to be decided on the issues, he would receive a larger Electoral vote than any President save Washington and Madison. He knew also that if the canvass was to turn solely on the relative values of himself and Harrison, "Old Tippecanoe" would not receive a single vote.

Harrison, following the precedent established by Van Buren, campaigned for the office. In a speech at Dayton he asked himself if he was in favor of paper money, and answered: "I am." He branded the charge that he was an Abolitionist as a slander. He made an appeal to the South by declaring that the Constitution did not sanction the discussion of slavery in slave states by citizens of free states. He dodged the question of what should be done with petitions to Congress to abolish slavery with the announcement that he stood for the right of petition. The "gag rule," while prohibiting the discussion, or even the reference to a committee, of Abolitionist petitions, conceded the right to petition. No one denied this right.

Van Buren dramatized Harrison's evasion when he was interrogated concerning the "gag rule." He replied that as President he had no concern with the "gag rule." He could have stopped here; but he added that Congress was justified in its treatment of the memorials from Garrison and his followers. Not an inquiry addressed to him remained unanswered by Van Buren.

Jackson was restless. His health prevented a country-wide tour, but he canvassed western Tennessee where the Whigs were making heavy inroads. Historians have doubted that in a tavern on this tour Jackson said: "The Whigs sent Daniel Webster over to England to negotiate for a great Bank of America; the dukes, lords, and ladies over there are to be the stockholders, and the Whigs' campaign expenses are being defrayed by British gold sent here for that very purpose." Had they access to Jackson's private correspondence with Van Buren they would not have questioned that the Old Hero believed that "the combined money power of England, and the Federalists"—the phrase is Jackson's—was being used to bribe the electorate. Without Van Buren at his side, the victor of New Orleans was feeding on his old hate. In a public letter Jackson charged the opposition with resorting to "falsehood and slander of the basest kind"; but he was confident that the "virtue of the people" would triumph over the "money power." He pitilessly compared the two candidates. Harrison had only military achievements of small merit to commend him: Van Buren by his firmness and ability had earned a rank not inferior to Jefferson or Madison.

As the election drew near Van Buren's friends centered their efforts on New York, knowing that if he did not hold the State, he would not only lose the election, but suffer a severe blow to his prestige. Here the Whigs were repeating Marcy's "To the victor belong the spoils," and warning the people against corruption at the polls in the Metropolis. Two years earlier the Whigs had outdone the city Democrats in the use of repeaters, and in making false returns. There had been current for many months rumors that in 1838 Whig ballot box stuffers had been paid with money furnished by five distinguished citizens, including Moses H. Grinnell, one of our merchant princes, as friendly journals alluded to him.

A fortnight before election James B. Glentworth, an appointee of Governor Seward, was imprisoned on sworn charges that at the instance of Grinnell—then a member of Congress—and others he had imported repeaters from Philadelphia. Letters of the accused were impounded and made public. One referred to the repeaters as pipe-layers for the Croton Aqueduct. Grinnell and his associates were in a tight box. Their guilt was beyond question. They could not deny that they had supplied money which went to the repeaters; so they posed as philanthropists, and said that they had drawn upon their private funds, not to corrupt the electorate, but to prevent illegal voting. A friendly grand jury returned their reputations restored.

Nine days after the balloting in New York Jackson wrote Van Buren:

Hermitage
Nov^{br}. 12th 1840

My dear Sir,
Your letter of the 1st instant * has been rec^{d}. its contents duly noted, and which will be passed in review by me in a letter to you soon—Corruption, bribery & fraud has been extended over the whole Union—still, altho our friends here are all gloom, and the Federal Whigg [*sic!*] pipe layers are rejoicing, and saying they have carried Pennsylvania and will have New York, I do not believe one word of it, nor will I believe that you are not elected untill [*sic!*] I see *all* the official returns—I trust in a kind providence that he has not so early doomed us to fall by bribery, & corruption. Corruption, bribery & fraud has been resorted to over the whole Union—Tennessee & Ohio has fell victims to it—I am sure good old Pennsylvania will prove proof against the mass of corruption, & bribery that has been lavished upon her,—if New York proves democratic your election is safe—I

* Van Buren's letter to Jackson is not extant.

cannot believe otherwise—My Household join me in kind regards & success to you—

Yr friend

Andrew Jackson

M. van Buren
    President, U. S.

Not only had Van Buren lost his own State, but he carried only three States in the South: Alabama, Virginia and South Carolina: Calhoun had been faithful. He lost the entire East save New Hampshire; and carried only three western States: Illinois, Missouri, Arkansas. These seven gave him only sixty votes in the Electoral College to the two hundred and thirty-four in the twenty States that went for Harrison and Tyler. One of the Virginia electors voted for Polk for Vice President; and South Carolina's eleven votes were cast for Tazewell. The popular vote was far from being four to one against him; it stood: Harrison, 1,275,017; Van Buren, 1,128,702. James G. Birney, candidate of the Abolitionists, polled 7,059 votes. New York's count for the two major candidates was: Harrison, 225,812; Van Buren, 212,519.

Before the complete returns from the entire State were tabulated, Rufus King's son Charles printed in his *American:* "The Empire State casts out her recreant son; and by a voice of 10,000 at least condemns his measure, and supplants his power." He let no opportunity pass to void his venom on Van Buren. Six days after the election he printed a half-column of doggerel slurring the President. The first verse ran:

> Who killed small Matty?
> We, says Tippecanoe,
> I and Tyler too:
> We killed small Matty.

This attack was not sheer wantonness. King was only one of many. The Whig press, or more precisely, the journals under control of the paper-money bankers were beginning a new campaign of scurrility and vilification against Van Buren. He must be destroyed politically to serve as a warning. He had dealt them a wound which they thought the next administration would heal.

They expected to recover; but all they could hope for was a respite: Van Buren's blow was mortal. Van Buren had asked no quarter, and the banks were giving none. The leading New York morning opposition daily, the *Courier and Enquirer*, commenting on his defeat, said:

In 1836, the State of New York, anxious to do honor to one of her citizens, gave Martin Van Buren her electoral vote by a majority of twenty-eight thousand, two hundred and seventy-two! After a period of four years, during which he has been at the head of the nation, the people of his native state have again been called upon to give him their confidence and support, and the result is that he has been declared unworthy of his station, and an enemy to the welfare of the Republic by a majority of more than ten thousand of the very people who only four years since, gave him a majority of 28,272! Let the advocates of corrupt and unprincipled politicians and demagogues who dare to trample upon the rights of the people, bear in mind this rebuke of a profligate and unscrupulous public functionary. The history of the United States can furnish no such instance of an unworthy public servant being thus severely rebuked by his fellow citizens. . . .

Van Buren ignored these attacks. Nor did he bear any ill-will toward his journalistic libelers, save King: they had to live. Years later, when King was President of Columbia College, he conversed familiarly with Van Buren at the opening of a new club house. Van Buren mistook him for his brother James, and made him feel perfectly at home. Suddenly he discovered his error: His whole attitude changed. King, sensing the situation, withdrew as gracefully as the circumstances permitted. As King walked away, Van Buren's eldest son joined him and smiling said: "I saw that you did not at first recognize your old friend Charles." This restored Van Buren to his amiable self. Years had elapsed since King had assailed him: he had made an overture for peace: Van Buren immediately sought him out and resumed the conversation.

Three days after the *Courier and Enquirer* attack, Van Buren wrote to Jackson. We get a suggestion of the tenor of his missing letter of November 1 in the opening sentence: "The apprehensions expressed in my last have been fully realized." He then continued:

"The experience in N York had the effect of assisting, at that place, in Philadelphia & the neighbouring Counties, the frauds of the opposition, but it came too late for general effect. We carried all the counties with only one exception on both sides of the River to Albany, and a majority of 5000 to the margin of the last District in the State composed of but six Counties, and have these overthrown by a majority of three or four thousand. So complete was our success in the old parts of the State that I can go from the City to my Home 150 miles without touching a Whig County. You will recollect the caution expressed in my last about Penn. not to trust to the results in the City and County until we heard whether the business of pipe laying had been extensively carried on in the interior. The result you have seen. . . . Time will unravel the means by which these results have been produced, & the people will then do justice to all. Having pursued a course in which my confidence was daily increased and which has left me nothing to regret, it is, I hope, unnecessary to say to you, you know me well, that the result causes me no personal regrets. Of this my enemies shall have abundant evidence. . . ."

After reading Van Buren's letter Jackson was more convinced that the election had been bought by English and Federalist gold. There is a touch of unconscious humor in Jackson's explanation of the reverse in Tennessee. The Old Hero began by noting Van Buren's mistake in writing October in dating his last. Jackson then continued:

The democracy of the United States have been shamefully beaten, *but I trust not conquered.* I still hope there is sufficient virtue in the unbought people of this Union, to stay the perjury, bribery, fraud, and imposition upon the people by the vilest system of slander, that ever before has existed, even in the most corrupt days of Ancient Rome, who will unight [*sic!*], and by their moral force check this hydra of corruption in its bud, or our republican system is gone, and the Federalists doctrine will be verifyed [*sic!*], "that the people are incapable of self government," and that they must be governed by corruption and fraud. I do not yet despair of the Republick, altho the scenes of corruption at our late elections, are now so probable, and so general, that unless soon met by the indignant powers of the virtuous portion of the whole community, and all those who have been engaged in these monstrous scenes of fraud perjury & imposition upon the unsuspecting portion of the people, hurled from their confidence, we will [be] ruled by the combined money power of England and the Federalists of this Union. But I trust, still, in the virtue of the great working class, that they will rally & check at once this combined corrupt coalition & on their native dunghills set them down.

I would be thankful to be informed of the componant [*sic!*] parts of the next Congress that is to say the congress of 1841—will Harrison have a majority in both Houses.

The census law—I mean the foolish questions of how much soop [*sic!*] how many chickens, geese, &c. &c. &c. lost us the State of Tennessee—the Whiggs [*sic!*] used it with great dexterity—they had their whoppers in [*sic!*], in every precinct in the State & alarmed all the old ladies with the idea that all soop [*sic!*] &c &c &c were to be taken to support your standing army of 200,000 men—& I have no doubt now but that scamp Goodlow of Louisiana, had the amendment proposed by him introduced for this purpose. But the scene is now for the present, closed, and it must be the duty *now* of all the democratic papers, to hold forth in flowing [*sic!*] colors before the people these base slanders and frauds, and the people must & will reflect on the baseness of these demagogues who originated & circulated them throughout our whole country—this is the only way by which the people can be brought to know the great injustice done you, and the democracy of the country.

For yourself you have nothing to regret, altho your Secretary of War may—you have done your duty well and I trust the people will do you justice yet, by hailing you with the approbation of "well done [thou] good & faithfull [*sic!*] servant.["]

My whole Household with Major A. J. Donelson joins me in kind regards & best wishes for your future prosperity, fame & happiness and believe me Sincerely your friend,

Andrew Jackson

Martin Van Buren
P. U. States

P. S. Some of our Republican friends—Genl Armstrong & Marshall &c was determined to resign—I have said to them no—this would be playing into the hands of the Harrisonites—Let him remove them—*Tip* has said in his speeches, that he would turn out no man for his political opinion. let us therefore test it.

Van Buren's answer to this letter is also lost. Replying to Jackson's query on party divisions in the Congress which would go into office with Harrison, he would have said that the Whigs would

control the Senate by seven, and would have a comfortable working majority of nearly fifty in the House. One of the Democratic
seats would be held by his son John. He had expectations that
there would be a second family of which it could be said that the
father and son had filled the highest office in the land.

CHAPTER XXXIX

VISITORS to the White House found Van Buren as amiable and cheerful as if he had been given another four years' lease on the President's mansion. On the opening day of Congress, he was in his office engaged in lively conversation with a dozen or more members of both houses. A few had supported Harrison. All had been received with the same cordiality. While the friends were chatting pleasantly, Senator Preston entered. Van Buren received him with marked respect, and invited him to a chair. Preston noticed that the greeting had not been as cordial as usual. When Preston had settled himself in his seat, Van Buren remarked on the unusual severity of the weather. Talking about the weather . . . and in that frigid tone. But Preston understood. He immediately rose, bowed, and withdrew. Senator William H. Roane, of Virginia, on finding Preston gone, exclaimed: "What has become of Preston—what made him leave so soon?" All knew the intimate relations that existed between the Van Burens and the Prestons since Abraham began paying court to his future wife under the roof of the Prestons. No one had noticed anything singular in Van Buren's attitude toward Preston; and he diverted the discussion to other channels. But all Washington was talking of it within a few days as Preston made no secret of his sudden departure. Meeting a common friend almost immediately after leaving the White House, he volunteered:

"Well, I have been to pay my respects to the President. He received me with all the respect that was due to a Senator of the United States. Spoke of the coldness of the weather, and treated me and received me in a way that was a damned deal colder than the weather. But that was not the worst of it; he was perfectly right, and treated me no worse than I had deserved. . . . I was goose enough during the recent canvass to make myself a party in one of my Virginia speeches to the absurd gold spoon story. . . . I was heartily ashamed the moment I had done it, and have been so ever since."

Van Buren would readily forgive and forget unfairness in the heat of a canvass from an ordinary political foe, but not where his adversaries, as in the cases of Preston and Charles King, had risen from his table to malign him. No one had campaigned more zealously against him than Clay; but the Kentuckian had fought fair; and when he called two days after the rebuke to Preston, Van Buren received him privately, and for an hour they were closeted together. They had one thing in common: their dislike of Webster, which with Clay was gradually assuming the dimensions of aˉ hatred. The sagacious and wily New Englander—to borrow one of Van Buren's milder descriptions of Webster— had already succeeded in convincing Harrison that Clay must have no voice in the incoming Administration. Clay was not discreet in his speech when Webster was involved. He loathed venality; Webster was not avaricious, but he had expensive habits: money trickled through his fingers. Back in the session of 1825, when Buchanan was about beginning his career, Clay, in discussing the payment of the Spanish claims then pending in the House, told Buchanan that Webster had a financial interest in the legislation. "That ——— yellow rascal is to have $70,000 of the money," said Clay.

On the day of Clay's visit to Van Buren, the President's fourth and last annual message was read in Congress. He had been working on it for weeks. As in his other public documents, there is a polish of which he was incapable; but the sentiments are his. "Fellow Citizens of the Senate and House of Representatives" was the greeting, followed by: "Our devout gratitude is due to the Supreme Being for having graciously continued to our beloved country, through the vicissitudes of another year, the invaluable blessings of health, plenty and peace. . . . With all the powers of the world our relations are those of honorable peace. . . . If clouds have lowered above the other hemisphere, they have not cast their portentous shadows upon our happy shores. Bound by no entangling alliances, yet linked by a common nature and interest with the other nations of mankind, our aspirations are for the preservation of peace, in whose solid and civilizing triumphs all may participate with a generous emulation. Yet it behooves us to be prepared for any event, and to be always ready to maintain those just and enlightened principles of national intercourse, for which this Government has ever contended. In the shock of contending empires, it is only by assuming a resolute bearing, and clothing themselves with defensive armor, that neutral nations can maintain their independent rights. . . ."

After a review of the suspension of specie payments at the outset of his term, "and the excesses in banking and commerce out of which it arose," and the consequent losses to the government, he said:

Among the reflections arising from the contemplation of these circumstances, one, not the least gratifying, is the consciousness that the Government had the resolution and ability to adhere, in every emergency, to the sacred obligations of law; to execute all its contracts according to the requirements of the constitution, and thus to present, when most needed, a rallying point by which the business of the whole country might be brought back to a safe and unvarying standard—a result vitally important as well to the interests as to the morals of the people. . . .

The policy of the Federal Government in extinguishing, as rapidly as possible the national debt, and consequently, in resisting every temptation to create a new one, deserves to be regarded in the same favorable light. Among the many objections to a national debt, the certain tendency of public securities to concentrate ultimately in the coffers of foreign stockholders, is one which is every day gathering strength. Already have the resources of many of the States, and the future industry of their citizens, been indefinitely mortgaged to the subjects of European Governments, to the amount of twelve millions annually, to pay the constantly accruing interest on borrowed money —a sum exceeding half the ordinary revenues of the whole United States. The pretext which this relation affords to foreigners to scrutinize the management of our domestic affairs, if not actually to intermeddle with them, presents a subject for earnest attention, not to say, of serious alarm. Fortunately, the Federal Government, with the exception of an obligation entered into on behalf of the District of Columbia, which must soon be discharged, is wholly exempt from any such embarrassment. It is also, as is believed, the only Government which, having fully and faithfully paid all its creditors, has also relieved itself entirely from debt. . . . Never should a free people, if it be possible to avoid it, expose themselves to the necessity of having to treat of the peace, the honor, or the safety of the Republic, with the Governments of foreign creditors, who, however well disposed they may be to cultivate with us in general friendly relations, are nevertheless, by the law of their own condition, made hostile to the success and permanency of institutions like ours.

This last note we find dominating the mental processes of Van Buren in all his later years. No man, since Jefferson, had a more profound knowledge of foreign affairs, or a deeper understanding of the varied and subtle influences set in motion by the ruling classes of the Old World to destroy our experiment in democracy. After sounding this warning, he continued:

Another objection, scarcely less formidable, to the commencement of a new debt, is its inevitable tendency to increase in magnitude, and to foster national extravagance. He has been an unprofitable observer of events, who needs at this day to be admonished of the difficulties a Government, habitually dependent on loans to sustain its ordinary expenditures, has to encounter in resisting the influences constantly exerted in favor of additional loans; by capitalists, who enrich themselves by Government securities for amounts much exceeding the money they actually advance—a prolific source of individual aggrandizement in all borrowing countries; by stockholders, who seek their gains in the rise and fall of public stocks, and by the selfish importunities of applicants for appropriations for works avowedly for the accommodation of the public, but the real objects of which are, too frequently, the advancement of private interests.

He answered the false charges of extravagance his foes had made during the canvass with a presentation of the state of the Government's finances. He observed that in the few months the Sub-Treasury had functioned nothing had occurred "in the practical operation of the system to weaken in the slightest degree . . . the confident anticipation of its friends." He assailed the Whig proposal for a new Bank because "it had been so clearly demonstrated that a concentrated money power, wielding so vast a capital, and combining such incalculable means of influence, may, in those peculiar conjunctures to which this Government is unavoidably exposed, prove an overmatch for the political power of the people themselves; when the true capacity of its character to regulate, according to its will and its interests, and the interests of its favorites, the value and production of the labor and property of every man in this extended country, had been so full and fearfully developed . . ."

To avoid a national debt, he advised economy; in lieu of a Bank, he urged the continuance of the Sub-Treasury. And thus he summed up his stand against subsidizing private enterprise: ". . . Not deeming it within the constitutional powers of the General Government to repair private losses sustained by reverses in business having no connection with the public service, either by direct appropriations from the Treasury, or by special legislation designed to secure exclusive privileges and immunities to individuals or classes in preference to, and at the expense of, the great majority necessarily debarred from any participation in them, no attempt to do so has been either made, recommended, or encouraged, by the present Executive."

He had nailed his colors to the mast.

Six days after the message had been read, Clay introduced a resolution to repeal the Sub-Treasury Act. He knew that the repealer had no chance in this Congress; but it was a dutiful gesture, as he explained. Calhoun rebuked him for assuming that the people had decided against the Sub-Treasury in the late election, and reminded the Whigs that at their national convention they had "solemnly resolved that they would make no declaration of their opinions." On motion of William Allen of Ohio, Clay's resolution was amended by striking out all its language after the word, resolved, and inserting an indorsement of the Sub-Treasury. It was a temporary triumph for the people.

New Year was ushered in by a blinding storm of snow, hail, and sleet, which did not abate until nightfall. At the White House Van Buren's daughter-in-law stood in the receiving line with the members of his Cabinet and their wives. Clay was there. Other members of Congress, with their wives and daughters, had braved the weather to pay their respects. Most of the callers were Whigs. Democrats who knew him only politically remained beside their own hearths. They could not get anything more from him; he had nothing more to give. Van Buren had a keen appreciation of dramatic contrasts. As he greeted Clay, he could not but recall his first New Year's Day in the White House; the endless stream of visitors; Clay sardonically complimenting him on being surrounded by so many friends; and his own cynical retort: "The weather is very fine." He had anticipated the loss of his fair-weather friends.

caMan

On Tuesday, February 9, Harrison arrived in Washington, and he called the following day at the White House. For half an hour they chatted pleasantly.

On Thursday Van Buren shattered another tradition, when, accompanied by his entire Cabinet, he returned the visit by calling on Harrison at his lodgings in Gadsby's Hotel. The strict etiquette of official Washington is that the President shall not return visits. He next played host to Harrison. The President-elect was the only Whig at this White House dinner. The Democratic leaders of Congress, and the heads of departments, assisted in entertaining Harrison, whose heart was warmed by these unexpected attentions. Turning to Van Buren's spokesman in the upper house, he exclaimed: "Benton, I beg you not to be harpooning me in the Senate; if you dislike anything in my administration, put it into Clay or Webster, but don't harpoon me."

Hone reached the city on the Thursday following the dinner to Harrison. The next morning he called at the White House. Van Buren escorted him into his study. Van Buren was "fat and jolly," and "a stranger would be greatly at a loss to discover anything to indicate that he was a defeated candidate for the high office he is about to vacate." Van Buren assured Hone that his opposition during the campaign had not diminished his friendship for him, and expressed his gratification because Hone had not indulged in personalities. The few Whigs who had not maligned him had earned his gratitude. To be grateful because one is not basely slandered: this is the pathos we would expect to find in a Greek tragedy. Yet Sumner, in his life of Jackson, said: "He [Van Buren] was thick-skinned, elastic, and tough." Yale's professor of political and social sciences had found a well drilled by the hirelings of the corrupt financial system Van Buren destroyed.

The last day of February fell on Sunday. While driving to St. John's, Van Buren saw Hone walking churchward. As Hone ascended the steps he was greeted by Van Buren's son Smith, who extended his father's invitation to share his pew. Hone had "to stand some shots from the Whigs who have not the taste to understand how a man may continue on good terms with a gentleman whose election he has worked hard to defeat." Hone naïvely added: "I . . . did not find my devotions interfered with, nor my political principles contaminated, by the company I had the honor to be placed in."

Van Buren vacated the White House the day before the inauguration, and took his lodgings with his Attorney General. He had offered to break up his household on February 20 so Harrison might have a needed rest: this was impossible at any of the overcrowded hotels. At Gadsby's, where Harrison lodged, the dining room had been converted into a dormitory. A rude shed, seating four hundred, hastily erected in the court, housed the hungry diners. Harrison would not permit Van Buren to make this sacrifice. Harrison's enfeebled frame and sixty-eight years had badly weathered the buffetings of the campaign.

The visiting Whigs made the inauguration the climax of the Presidential campaign. In the taprooms of hotels and taverns they celebrated. Joseph Hoxie was welcomed by every drinking group; and the *Evening Post* correspondent wrote that "he has already made a deep impression on the *profanum vulgus* by his splendid execution of some choice Tippecanoe songs, although hardly in the city forty-eight hours." The small boys, who always run with the herd, paraded Pennsylvania Avenue, singing:

> Couldn't come it over Tip,
> Couldn't come it nohow,
> Couldn't come it over Tip,
> Because they didn't know how.

The custom of a retiring President participating in the inauguration of his successor had not been established. Van Buren remained in Gilpin's home. Van Buren had work to do. The Legislature of Missouri had nominated him for President four years hence, and had also honored him by naming a new county after his native village. In his reply, addressed to Governor Thomas Reynolds, he avoided saying that he would run again. "I did not on that occasion [when first nominated], nor do I now, profess to be indifferent to a station to which every citizen of the United States may aspire. . . . No one can expect, or should desire, to be always in office under a government and institutions like ours; and I have enjoyed that privilege long enough to satisfy my utmost ambitions. . . . The circumstances under which the Democracy of my native county, of my native State, and of the sister

States, have raised me from the first to the last step of advancement, the opportunities they have afforded me to exemplify to the world the principles by which I have been governed, and the indomitable spirit with which they have sustained me in the late struggle to baffle the exertions and appliances of selfish and political interests combined against me, and against the measures which I have uniformly advocated, and in part succeeded in establishing, have imposed upon me an obligation lasting as life, and leaving on my heart a debt of gratitude I can never discharge."

This letter was dispatched on March 6. Two days later he wrote to the Tammany leaders planning a welcome home that he would be in the Metropolis on the 23rd. He informed the committee: "I come to you now with a political ambition more than satisfied by the many and distinguished honors which have been conferred upon me, and with no higher aspirations, if there be higher, than to occupy the station, enjoy the privileges, and discharge the duties of an American citizen."

He returned home by easy stages. He was entertained at Baltimore and Philadelphia. On March 17 he reached the Quaker City, accompanied by Silas Wright, and in the evening visited the Democratic Reading Room at 8th and Chestnut streets. New York impatiently awaited the day of his arrival, and when it came, wished that any other day in the year had been chosen. A gusty wind from the ocean swept sheets of rain through the city streets. At three o'clock Van Buren and Wright arrived in Jersey City. It was still pouring. Half an hour later he landed at Castle Garden, and the waiting thousands at the Battery were wet to the skin.

He laughed at the suggestion that he ride in a closed barouche. There was "a corps of lancers . . . beautifully dressed and equipped" and "a numerous body of armed firemen" to escort him to Tammany Hall. He insisted that he and Wright sit in the barouche with its top down. Several times the parade was halted in its course up Broadway by mobs massed around the ex-President's carriage. Women waved handkerchiefs from windows draped with dripping flags. At Bleecker street the cortège turned east, and thence south on the Bowery to Chatham street [renamed Park Row] to Tammany Hall, where Robert H. Morris formally welcomed Van Buren back to his native State. The response was very short. He expressed the hope "that Providence may enable me to demean myself worthily toward the great cause to which I have been long and devotedly attached, and toward the virtuous and devoted yeomanry by whom I have been intrepidly sustained in the hour of difficulty."

After dinner Van Buren went to the Bowery Theater where he saw the "immense Attraction—Dramatic and Equestrian— . . . The Greek Warrior's Return . . . followed by varied and beautiful selections of Arena Entertainment by the whole Equestrian Company . . . concluded with the Equestrian Drama in 3 acts, of El Hyder, or, Love and Glory." He visited the menagerie of wild animals. We also learn from the advertisement for the evening's bill that there was no advance in prices, which remained: "boxes 50c, pit 25c, gallery 12½c." All evening long the audience took turns in applauding the performers and huzzaing for Van Buren.

That night he slept at the house of his law partner. Butler had a home on Waverly place and Greene street. On the morrow he rested. Thursday found him in the City Hall where he received eight thousand admirers. Friday evening he attended the Park Theater where Mrs. Sutton played the leading part in "The Ladder of Love," followed by "the grand opera of Norma," Mrs. Sutton singing the title rôle; and as soon as the curtain had been rung down on Bellini's work, Mrs. Sutton sang "a grand *scena* from Otello" and "Woodman, Spare That Tree!" The evening was rounded out as it began—with a farce, "Shocking Events," in which the versatile and tireless Mrs. Sutton appeared as the leading lady.

When Van Buren had been in New York a week, Webster visited the city. Webster not only had succeeded in making Clay an unwelcome visitor at the White House, but had so played upon Harrison that the Kentuckian was constrained to write the President:

. . . I was mortified by the suggestion you made to me on Saturday, that I had been represented as dictating to you, or to the new Administration—mortified, because it is unfounded in fact, and because there is danger of the fears, that I intimated to you at Frankfort, of my enemies poisoning your mind toward me.

In what, in truth, can they allege a dictation, or even interference, on my part? In the formation of your Cabinet? You can contradict them. In the administration of the public patronage? The whole Cabinet as well as yourself can say that I have recommended nobody for any office. I have sought none for myself, or my friends. I desire none. A thousand times have my feelings been wounded, by communicating to those who have applied to me, that I am obliged to abstain inflexibly from all interference in official appointments. . . .

If to express freely my opinion, as a citizen and as a Senator, in regard to public matters, be dictation, then I have dictated, and not otherwise. There is but one alternative which I could embrace, to prevent the exercise of this common right of freedom of opinion, and that is retirement to private life. That I am most desirous of, and if I do not promptly indulge the feeling, it is because I entertain the hope—perhaps vain hope—that by remaining a little longer in the Senate, I may possibly render some service to a country to whose interests my life has been dedicated. . . .

The new Administration was heading into a storm. Webster and Clay were each ambitious to succeed Harrison; his age precluded any thought of a renomination. Toward the end of March New York heard that Harrison was gravely ill; and on April 4, "thirty minutes before one in the morning" as the official announcement had it, he died. Van Buren was the principal mourner at the obsequies held in the Metropolis.

Saturday morning, May 8, Van Buren boarded the *Albany* at the foot of Barclay street. He was at last going home. "Early in the afternoon, a numerous and respectable portion of the citizens of Kinderhook, Stuyvesant and the adjoining towns assembled on the steam-boat wharf, to await the arrival of the Ex-President. When the . . . boat . . . came in sight, she was saluted by a heavy piece of artillery which continued firing until the boat reached the wharf. Several popular airs were also played by the Spencertown Brass Band the members of which, without distinction of party, volunteered for the occasion." Butler was with him, and together they entered Van Buren's private carriage and led a procession "composed of a long line of citizens in carriages and on horseback." Their approach to the village "was announced by the firing of cannon and ringing of bells. . . . The procession having arrived in front of Stranahan's hotel, Mr. Van Buren was conducted . . . to the piazza of the spacious building, which was already graced by a goodly company of ladies. . . ." Again, as two summers ago, Mordecai Myers spoke the welcome.

The outside world learned of Van Buren's return from the *Albany Argus* of three days later, which published a paragraph beginning: "We understand that Mr. Van Buren came up the river on Saturday last, on the steam-boat. . . ." A full week later, the *Argus* reprinted the account of the reception from the *Kinderhook Sentinel.* Van Buren had not given up hopes of again presiding over the destinies of the nation as this excerpt from Myers's speech indicates: "Here, surrounded by friends and connections, may you, under the protection of Divine Providence, pass many and happy years under the shade of your own vine and fig tree, unless again called by the voice of the people into public life, a mandate which you ever have and doubtless ever will obey."

All else in the "thrice welcome home" was devoid of politics. Van Buren ended his response with: ". . . I come to take up my final residence with you, not, I assure you, in the character of a repining, but in that of a satisfied and contented man. Of this even my opponents, if they are not already, will soon, I trust, be entirely satisfied." He emphasized that he had no regrets, defended the financial system he had given to the country, and added: ". . . all I desire is, that my future political standing with the people of the United States shall be graduated by the opinion which they may ultimately form of the soundness of the principles and measures referred to." There was to be no compromise with the social and economic forces which defeated him.

Van Buren evidently sent a clipping from the *Sentinel* to Jackson in the first known letter that he wrote after his return, from which we quote: "You will see by the enclosed that I have at last got home. My health has never been better, nor my spirits either. I found the improvements I had directed on my place in great forwardness, & hope to get into it by the 1st of June. How greatly would its value be encreased [*sic!*] if I could promise myself to see you at it. To come as near that as is practicable, I have our friend Col. Earle's likeness of you (which is the best he took) well framed, & mean to surrender to it, and to an excellent likeness of Mr. Jefferson which I have had the good fortune to procure, in my dining room."

Extensive alterations were made on the old red brick pile, built by Billy Van Ness's father in 1797. The plain brick mantels in the fireplaces on the first floor gave way to chaste marble, worked in Ionic design. Two additional kitchens were built at the rear of the house: there would be large gatherings at Lindenwald. An observation tower, from which the Hudson could be seen, was raised four stories above the old gables. A new pump was installed outside the original kitchen door, and the well in the cellar—still used in old country houses in the north when the pump freezes—cleaned out. The spacious hall was papered with a colorful hunting scene designed by an Alsatian craftsman toward the end of the eighteenth century. A lodge at either end of the arched driveway lent a manorial tone to the place. New chicken houses, a stable, and a cattle shed had been built in the rear of the house.

For two months Van Buren lived alone. Every morning, before breakfast, he would mount the gift of John Randolph of Roanoke and ride to the village, exchanging salutations with neighbors, and pleased when greeted in Dutch. He would have liked to have one of his children with him; but Prince John was in Washington, serving his first term as a member of Congress in the special session convoked by President Tyler on May 31; and he was marrying sometime in June. His bride was Elizabeth Vanderpoel, a native of Kinderhook. It would be a long session; he would like to be near John; but all accounts concerning him were highly flattering. As July was ending, Abraham came to Lindenwald, bringing his wife and their infant son. Van Buren was a grandfather. The old house was now worth living in. He turned to politics with added zest. He kept up a voluminous correspondence with lieutenants throughout the country, and directed the contest to reclaim New York from the Whig control.

The Whigs in Congress were in a sorry state. In his inaugural message Tyler voiced disapproval of a new Bank of the United States and of Van Buren's Sub-Treasury. He signed a bill repealing the act creating the crowning achievement of Van Buren's administration; and on August 16, vetoed a bill creating another Bank. The Whigs regarded Tyler as a traitor to the banks who had lavished their money to elect him and Harrison. Had he forgotten what had happened to Van Buren? A second bank bill

—the word bank was omitted, and corporation used throughout the measure, in the hope that Tyler would accept this puerile substitution—was rushed through both houses. On September 9 Tyler vetoed it. Within forty-eight hours, the entire Cabinet, save Webster, resigned. Mighty was the power of the men who could bribe legislatures to yield them bank charters, and with this grant in their vaults—and little else beside—turn out paper money as fast as the presses could print it.

The November elections justified Van Buren's expectations. In New York the Democrats captured some sixty Whig seats in the Assembly: it would take another year to win the Senate, where only a third of the membership was chosen annually; and all indications pointed to the election of a Democratic Governor twelve months hence. Democratic gains in other States showed the trend of the next Presidential election.

Congratulations poured in on Kinderhook. Letters from Judge John Law, of Indiana, and John Hastings, one of Ohio's Representatives in Congress, especially pleased him: both described the elections as the return of "the sober second thought of the people." Not since Jefferson had any President out of office wielded such influence with the masses. Lindenwald was becoming another Monticello.

His old enemies talked of Calhoun for President in 1844 with Silas Wright for Vice President. They uncooped a canard that Van Buren declared he would not run again. In denying this he volunteered that he would take no step toward being the party's choice for President.

Shortly after the election John A. Dix visited Kinderhook. Dix, who was distinguished as an educator and a lawyer, had been elected to the Assembly from an Albany district: service in humble places was not then regarded as bemeaning. When he returned to his home, he wrote an editorial for the *Argus*. It appeared December 1 under the heading: "Mr. Van Buren in Retirement." It was a tactless production, and in sum, said that Van Buren must be nominated by the next Democratic National Convention, whether he wished it or not. Bryant, ever loyal to Van Buren, apologized in his *Evening Post* for the dictatorial tone of the editorial. Thurlow Weed, the bellwether of the Whig journalists, disposed of it in his *Albany Journal* with: "Written by

Dix, revised by Butler, approved by Van Buren." To which the *Argus* rejoined that neither Van Buren nor Butler had any hand in preparing it.

On December 14 a grand jury in Philadelphia indicted Biddle and several directors of the defunct Bank of the United States for looting the institution. Biddle was specifically charged with having conspired to rob the stockholders of $400,000. He succeeded in escaping jail on a technicality. This did not destroy his unholy sway over the politics of the land.

In the second week of February Van Buren began a tour of the South. The announced reason was a visit to the Hermitage, but its immediate purpose was to circumvent the moves Calhoun and his friends were making to destroy Van Buren's strength in the South. He was accompanied by his former Navy head, James K. Paulding, who acted as secretary. When Clay learned that Van Buren had started, he invited him to be his guest. Clay's invitation overtook Van Buren at the High Hills of Santee, South Carolina, on March 26, five days before Clay delivered his valedictory to the Senate. His retirement emphasized the Whig party's repudiation of Tyler, who now occupied the unique position of a President without a party. Van Buren replied that, plans permitting, he would be in Kentucky early in May. He was declining numerous invitations from Southern communities anxious to do him honor. Nashville and Jackson greeted him affectionately.

Early in May Van Buren bade farewell to the most devoted friend he ever had. On arriving in Lexington, he and Paulding were met by Clay and invited to his home. The next morning Van Buren and Paulding went to Ashland where they remained two days. No one enjoying Jackson's friendship, save Van Buren, could have gone from the Hermitage to Ashland without forfeiting the Old Hero's esteem; for Jackson cherished the delusion that Clay had corruptly robbed him of the Presidency in 1828. There was drama in this meeting—and mystery. No one knows what passed between these potential rivals for the Presidency in another two years. The general surmise was that they agreed to keep the question of the annexation of Texas out of the campaign. Both saw eye to eye on this problem which the servilocracy hoped to make the issue in 1844. Annexation would stop the reconquest of Texas by Mexico. The slave-owners were ready to plunge the nation into war if necessary to add Texas to the Union, and thus increase their strength in Congress. Jackson, whose encounters with Spaniards made him detest the whole race, sympathized with the Texans; but since Van Buren had taken a position against admitting Texas without Mexico's consent, he had maintained silence.

Van Buren's reception in Lexington so delighted him that he made special mention of it in a letter to Jackson telling of his visit to Clay, and his departure for Frankfort. At St. Louis he was regally received. This was repeated at Cincinnati, Columbus, Indianapolis, and elsewhere on the route. On his return to Kinderhook Van Buren went over his broad acres—there were more than a hundred cleared and nearly as many in timber—and was satisfied with the husbandry. On July 30 he wrote to Jackson: ". . . I find my farm in excellent condition, crops good and promising & hope to sell *enough of it to pay the workmen in the garden, & on the farm* which is my ultimatum. . . ." He marketed his large potato crop in New York.

The New York Whigs made Van Buren an issue in the fall campaign and met defeat. William C. Bouck was elected Governor. Seward, sensing the shift, had declined to run again. The Democratic gains throughout the Union were acclaimed by Van Buren's friends as evidence of his return to popular esteem. He had now several rivals for the nomination; the most formidable, next to Calhoun, were Buchanan and Cass.

Tyler was feeling the long arm of the Bank through its controlled press. These were almost wholly Whig. Van Buren organs in quoting from their rivals invariably distinguished them in this wise: "We copy the following from the Boston *Courier*, a Whig paper independent of Bank influence." Whig journals not of the type of the Joseph Tinker Buckingham paper had maintained a vituperative campaign against Tyler since he vetoed the two measures designed to incorporate another Bank of the United States. When a mild form of influenza was epidemic, the Bank papers called it the "Tyler grippe." He was branded as a tyrant and a traitor, and all to one end: to prepare the people for his impeachment. Their intentions were known when Congress convened, and on January 10 the impeachment resolution was presented to the House. Tyler's spokesman in the House and biographer, the fiery Wise, does not name the author of the resolution, merely indicating him as "the coarse creature" and "the ogre of Whig politics." Nor would Wise name the State which sent him to Congress. The mover of the resolution was John Minor Botts, of Virginia. Appended to the resolution calling for a committee to institute the impeachment proceedings were the charges on which the Bank men sought to remove from office the President of the United States. Wise fairly disposes of the accusations as "foul, false, pointless, and offensive to every sense of good morals and good taste." This first attempt to indict a President has one count which betrayed the motive of Botts:

I charge him with the high crime and misdemeanor of withholding his assent to laws indispensable to the just operations of government, which involved no constitutional difficulty on his part; of depriving the Government of all legal sources of revenue; and of assuming to himself the whole power of taxation, and of collecting duties of the people without the authority or sanction of law.

This was the rub of it: Tyler had vetoed the Bank's bills. The resolution was defeated 127 to 83. All save ten who voted for impeachment had voted for the Bank bills which Tyler disapproved. Only six New York representatives voted for the proposal, Prince John and twenty-one other Democrats from New York voting no. Millard Fillmore, who was to reach the Presidency after the manner of Tyler, was one of the New York Whigs to support the Botts resolution.

Had Botts the evidence of the secret negotiations then being carried on between agents of Tyler and Texas, he would have had ample reason for moving an impeachment. This intrigue to annex Texas was conducted without even the actual knowledge of Tyler's Secretary of State. Only the arch-leaders of the servilocracy knew, although Joshua R. Giddings, of Ohio, and other Congressmen suspected that they were under way as early as the second week in February. There was no secret, however, of the intentions of the South. Wise in a speech on the floor of the House thus voiced them: "True, if Iowa be added on the one side, Florida will be added on the other. But there the equation must stop. Let one more northern state be admitted, and the equilibrium is gone—

MARTIN VAN BUREN
After an engraving by H. B. Hall, Jr.

gone for ever. The balance of interests is gone—the safeguard
of American property—of the American constitution—of the
American union, vanished into thin air. This must be the inevitable
result, unless, by a treaty with Mexico, the south can add more
weight to her end of the lever! Let the south stop at the Sabine
[the eastern boundary of Texas], while the north may spread
unchecked beyond the Rocky Mountains, and the southern scale
must kick the beam."

There was little likelihood that the plot could be consum-
mated in Tyler's term: it was essential, therefore, that his
successor be favorable to the scheme. Accordingly a second conspiracy was contrived against Van Buren because he opposed annexation. This design began with the publication of a letter signed
by Thomas W. Gilmer, a member of the House, and former Governor of Virginia, urging that Texas be annexed "soon, or not
at all" to prevent Great Britain from imposing a military and
political control over Texas. The *quid pro quo* was to be a loan
and the guarantee of the independence of Texas. The political
control would lead to the abolition of slavery. Many believed all
the representations in the Gilmer letter, whose authorship has
been traced to Duff Green, the steadfast ally of Calhoun. In the
month of February, Aaron Vail Brown, a member from Tennessee, and an avowed friend of Van Buren, was induced by Representative George W. Hopkins, of Virginia, to mail a copy of the
Gilmer letter to Jackson with a request for his opinion.

It did not require much to rouse Jackson's suspicions of
Great Britain. Moreover, he favored annexation from the beginning, and in 1829 directed Van Buren, then Secretary of State,
to instruct Poinsett to negotiate the purchase of Texas from
Mexico. In 1835 the offer was renewed and, again, Mexico declined to sell, although this time the offer was increased. The sentiment for annexation in the North was universal, provided it
could be accomplished honorably and did not increase the power
of the servilocracy. On March 12, three days before Jackson celebrated his seventy-sixth birthday, he wrote to Brown that he
favored immediate annexation. Gilmer obtained possession of the
letter, and exhibiting it in confidence to a friend of Benton,
boasted it would destroy Van Buren. He explained he would have
Van Buren and Calhoun interrogated on immediate annexation

just before the convention; after Van Buren had declared against it, it was planned to read Jackson's letter to the delegates: this would drive Van Buren's Southern delegates to Calhoun.

About this time it became desirable that the Secretary of State be made a party to the secret negotiations carried on with Texas. Webster was inflexibly opposed to annexation as proposed: he must be supplanted. A few months back he had successfully completed the most important foreign undertaking Van Buren had left unfinished—the settlement of the Northeastern Boundary question. On May 8 he resigned. Neither he nor Tyler gave any reason. Wise, with delightful naïveté, recites that Webster "magnanimously retired to make way for a Southern statesman, when the time came to take up the next most important matter of foreign relations,—Texas." The "Southern Statesman" was Abel Parker Upshur, of Virginia. Webster left office undoubtedly ignorant of the moves that had been already made in that direction; but he could not have been unaware of the rumors which reached Adams and other New Englanders. Six weeks after his resignation he accompanied Tyler to the dedication of the Bunker Hill monument on the anniversary of the battle it commemorated. On this particular June 17 Adams entered in his diary: ". . . Daniel Webster is a heartless traitor to the cause of human freedom; John Tyler is a slave-monger. What have they to do with the Quincy granite pile on the brow of Bunker's Hill? What have these to do with a dinner in Faneuil Hall, but to swill like swine, and grunt about the rights of man? . . ." These sentiments are explained by an entry made nine days earlier: "Webster has undertaken to dragoon the Whigs of this State [Massachusetts] from their allegiance to Henry Clay, whom he proposes to supplant as a supplementary candidate for the Presidency by a double coalition with John Tyler and John C. Calhoun. . . . This is but a step to that flagitious coalition which is to prostrate the freedom of this Union to its slavery." Webster's silence made many suspect him of a secret bargain with the servilocracy; but he was not found wanting when the hour arrived.

While the plot against him was in being, Van Buren continued to answer interrogatories on political subjects. In proclaiming himself a low-tariff advocate, he said that the chief sufferers from a high protective tariff were the mechanics and laborers. All aspirants for the nomination were asked if they would abide the result of the convention. Calhoun in his reply volunteered that he was not a candidate.

Bancroft and other friends advised Van Buren during the summer not to write letters, or at least confine himself to short responses to interrogatories. They did not want him to jeopardize his strength before the convention. But Van Buren, intent as he was on getting the nomination, was not ready to purchase it with silence or evasions. He continued to answer frankly all inquiries. No one disputed his leadership, openly, at least. The Whig journals rounded on the Democrats in the fall campaign as the Van Buren party. The people, surfeited with Whigs and paper money bankers, elected a Democratic Congress. The Whigs had fewer than half as many members in the House as the Democrats, who elected John W. Jones, of Virginia, Speaker, by a vote of 128 to 59.

The national conventions were to have been held in December, but were postponed to May. The Whigs, whose nomination of Clay was a foregone conclusion, agreed to postponement at the suggestion of Democratic leaders. Van Buren's friends, scenting no intrigue in the proposal, joined in the request. This delay was to the success of the plot of the Texas annexationists. Van Buren, unsuspecting, on January 13, wrote Jackson that he expected a harmonious outcome at the convention.

Toward the end of the month the intrigue against Van Buren began to appear in the open. Advices from Indiana and Illinois revealed his enemies at work among the delegates. In the latter State the feeling over annexation was bitter; here a mob, in the first months of Van Buren's administration, had shot to death Elijah P. Lovejoy, a Presbyterian minister, publisher of an Abolitionist newspaper. The pro-slavery men had thrice before destroyed Lovejoy's printing presses. Wright wrote Van Buren on March 1 that Washington teemed with rumors that he intended to withdraw as a candidate. A copy of the *Evening Post* reached him about the same time with comment on Biddle's death. Bryant wrote that Biddle died "at his country seat, where he passed the last of his days in elegant retirement, which, if justice had taken place, would have been spent in the penitentiary."

The next day New York was shocked by news which arrived

by express from Washington. The preceding afternoon a new gun, called the "Peacemaker," exploded on the steam-frigate *Princeton*, killing several officials, including two of Tyler's Cabinet, Upshur and Gilmer. The latter had resigned from Congress only ten days before to become Secretary of the Navy. Wives, sisters and daughters of the distinguished guests had prevailed on the President to remain below decks while the big gun was being fired. Tyler escaped death through the timidity of the women.

A week later Calhoun was named Secretary of State to complete the secret negotiations with Texas. Within two weeks of his taking office, the conspirators passed the word that a treaty of annexation had been signed and would soon be submitted to the Senate. Stocks and bonds tumbled, as a war would hurt commerce. But a bloody conflict was nothing if it prevented the southern scale from kicking the beam—to borrow Wise's image. It was not, however, until April 12, that the treaty was signed by Calhoun. Some speculators profited by the premature report,—the gamblers in Texas scrip and Texas land.

Van Buren's steady growth in popularity made the intriguers alter their plans respecting the use of the Jackson letter. After the signing of the treaty, Brown went to the office of the Washington *Globe*, which had been the official organ of both Jackson and Van Buren during their administrations, and asked as "a friend of Van Buren," that Jackson's letter favoring immediate annexation be published. Blair instantly saw through the scheme, but asked time to think it over. He held the letter long enough to copy it, and on March 18, forwarded a transcript to Van Buren. Blair went as far as he could, without leaving himself open to the charge of dictation, to suggest that Van Buren not oppose the powerful slave-States on the eve of the convention. Four days later Jackson's letter—now a year old—was printed in the Richmond *Enquirer*, another loyal organ of Van Buren. The date had been changed to March 12, 1844, to give it the appearance of having been recently written. On March 26 another member of the conspiracy, William H. Hammett, a Representative from Mississippi, wrote to Van Buren, professed friendship, said he was an uninstructed delegate to the Baltimore Convention, and urged him to say if he was for or against immediate annexation.

Van Buren began work at once on a reply to Hammett, and

dispatched Butler to the Hermitage to apprise Jackson how their enemies had made use of him. The Old Hero wrung his hands futilely as he protested that his letter to Brown should not have been used to serve any partisan purpose. This he would say in seeking to undo the harm; he would also say—as he did—that his confidence in Van Buren's love of country was so strengthened by years of intimacy, and his regard for Van Buren so great, that no difference over Texas would change his opinions. But he would like to see him change his views on annexation; and this he communicated to Van Buren through Butler and by letter; but knowing Van Buren he did not expect to see his wishes realized.

Twenty-five years earlier, or even less, Van Buren would have found a way to please both sides; but he was long past that. His reply to Hammett takes prime rank among public documents stamped with rare courage. He answered categorically, as requested. He was against immediate annexation of Texas. He went beyond this and said that annexation, without Mexico's consent, meant war,—an unjust war. He was for annexation when it could be done honorably and with justice to Mexico. He reviewed his own record of fair dealing on the subject. He reminded the people that the Texas which the Jackson administration had sought to acquire only extended as far west as the Rio del Norte, and did not include the larger domain extending to the Rio Grande, now claimed by the Texans. After a lengthy discussion of the law in the case, and of the belligerent relations between Texas and Mexico, he said:

> We must look at this matter as it really stands. We shall act under the eye of an intelligent, observing world; and the affair cannot be made to wear a different aspect from what it deserves if even we had the disposition (which we have not) to throw over it disguises of any kind . . . if, as sensible men, we cannot avoid the conclusion that the immediate annexation of Texas would, in all human probability, draw after it a war with Mexico, can it be expedient to attempt it? Of the consequences of such a war, the character it might be made to assume, the entanglements with other nations which the position of a belligerent almost unavoidably draws after it, and the undoubted injuries which might be inflicted upon each— notwithstanding the great disparity of their respective forces, I will not say a word. God forbid that an American citizen should ever

count the cost of any appeal to what is appropriately denominated the last resort of nations, whenever that resort becomes necessary either for the safety or to vindicate the honor of his country. There is, I trust, not one so base as not to regard himself and all he has to be forever and at all times subject to such a requisition. But would a war with Mexico, brought on under such circumstances, be a contest of that character? Could we hope to stand justified in the eyes of mankind for entering into it; more especially if its commencement is to be preceded by the appropriation to our own uses of the territory, the sovereignty of which is in dispute between two nations, one of which we are to join in the struggle? This, sir, is a matter of the gravest import, one in respect to which no American statesman or citizen can possibly be indifferent. . . .

Van Buren knew the passions of many were inflamed in favor of annexation by friends and relatives who had settled in Texas. We must not be misled by these, or by the fact that most of the Texans were once American citizens, because "nothing is either more true or more extensively known, than that Texas was wrested from Mexico, and her independence established, through the instrumentality of citizens of the United States." The present proposal of annexation, he stressed, bore no analogy to the efforts of two other administrations to acquire Texas by purchase and peaceful negotiation—the first was during the administration of John Quincy Adams. Even granted that they were, they did not justify the committing of a wrong to accomplish the object desired. His jealousy of the nation's good name was no less than his apprehensions of the dangers lurking to our experiment in democracy: immediate annexation would place a weapon in the hands of those who looked upon our republican institutions with distrustful eyes, and would do us more injury than the new territory, however valuable, could repair.

Duff Green had fabricated a second letter—it was not then known that he was the author, although he was suspected—bolstering up the charge in his Gilmer letter that the British government had designs on Texas. Van Buren scoffed at these charges, which had been officially denied by England, and said it would be time for the United States to interfere when England sought more than the usual commercial favors.

In writing his answer, which equaled in length the longest

of his messages to Congress, he left no phase of the subject untouched; he anticipated everything that the annexationists might bring forward in rejoinder. The question was no longer a subject of underhand intrigue, for on April 12—and he had not yet completed his reply to Hammett—public announcement was made of the signing of the treaty with Texas. It was now a campaign issue, and not merely a question of annexation, but an extension of slave territory. He could be charged with attempting to ride into the Presidency on his popularity and dictating to a Congress elected on the issue. This he precluded by declaring that if after a full discussion of the subject, the people chose representatives favorable to immediate annexation, he would yield to the popular will. Yet this could be translated into truckling for the nomination if permitted to stand alone; so he ended the answer to Hammett with: "Nor can I in any extremity be induced to cast a shade over the motives of my past life, by changes or concealments of opinions maturely formed upon a great national question, for the unworthy purpose of increasing my chances for political promotion."

There were mingled emotions among Van Buren's friends when the letter appeared in the Washington *Globe* on April 23. Few doubted his nomination; but many believed that the slavepower—as Van Buren now began to designate the Southern Democrats to his intimates—with Calhoun at its head, would nominate Tyler on a third ticket and defeat him. Clay made himself equally objectionable to the servilocracy with his declaration against immediate annexation printed in the *National Intelligencer* simultaneously with Van Buren's. John C. Rives, who shared control of the *Globe* with Blair, on May 20, wrote to Van Buren that four-fifths of the Democratic members of Congress were opposed to him. A more careful survey led him to say three days later that Van Buren would be nominated on the first ballot.

The Van Burenites on reaching Baltimore, where both conventions would meet on the 27th, found the trail of Calhoun everywhere. More than three-fourths of the States had instructed their delegates, explicitly, or indirectly, to vote for Van Buren. Some of the Southern delegates rather than carry out their instructions to vote for Van Buren resigned. Delegates from Calhoun's own State declined to enter their names in their official capacity, but continued to remain in the convention as spectators. This was Calhoun's way of saying that, officially, he would have no voice in the convention while it considered Van Buren. Unofficially he was ably represented on the floor. Before the convention was called to order, it was known that the strategy of the slaveholders would be to adopt the two-thirds rule. After the convention organized, Romulus M. Saunders, of North Carolina, moved the adoption of the rules of the convention of 1832, which nominated Van Buren for Vice President—Jackson had been nominated by the States and the convention merely indorsed their actions. These included the two-thirds rule by which the slavepower aimed to crush Van Buren. Butler, knowing how the Van Buren ranks had been thinned by the Calhoun corps, rose to oppose the motion. He was sure of a majority of the delegates on the first vote; but many of these had told him that they would vote for the adoption of the two-thirds rule. All day long the Van Buren men and the slavery representatives debated the proposal. Butler deliberately prolonged the argument. He was fighting to delay decision until the next day, and succeeded. After adjournment Butler and his aides visited their followers favoring the two-thirds rule to persuade them to vote for a majority rule. That night Butler posted a brief note to Van Buren at Kinderhook saying that if the two-thirds rule was not adopted his nomination was certain.

The following morning the free territory and slave territory advocates resumed the contest. Not a delegate among the 325 who had answered the roll call on the first day was missing from his seat. Some of these had only split votes. Virginia, with fifty-three delegates, had only seventeen votes. The total number of votes in the body was 266. Every one of these was cast when the angry debate ended at noon, and the undemocratic two-thirds rule, originally adopted to lend a greater appearance of strength to Van Buren's nomination for Vice President, was carried 148 to 118. More than fifty of the delegates instructed to vote for Van Buren had gone over to the slave-power on this test vote.

There was no applause from the victors. The occasion was too solemn. Butler held back the welling tears. He had not lost hope. Pencil in hand, he kept tally as the first ballot was being taken, and when the result was announced the Van Burenites cheered. He had a total of 146 votes, thirteen more than all the others combined. Had these voted against the two-thirds rule, Van Buren would have been nominated on this ballot. Cass was second with 83; Johnson, who had publicly announced that if he could not get first place he would take second, was a poor third with 24; Calhoun trailed behind with 6; Buchanan had 4; a lone complimentary vote was given to another Pennsylvanian, and Levi Woodbury, United States Senator from New Hampshire, received 2. All of Van Buren's strength, save twelve votes, came from the North.

On the second ballot, while Van Buren again headed the list, he no longer had a majority. Cass was gaining on him. The clerk announced: Van Buren, 127; Cass, 94; Johnson, 33; Buchanan, 9; scattering, 3. The third ballot saw Van Buren still losing. Now he mustered only 121; Cass still held second place, but with only 92; Johnson with 38, had gained 5; Buchanan made a similar gain, reaching 11; scattering, 4. On the fourth ballot ten more abandoned Van Buren. Now he stood only six ahead of Cass, the result being: Van Buren, 111; Cass, 105; Johnson, 32; Buchanan, 17. Van Buren lost first place on the fifth ballot, which stood: Cass, 107; Van Buren, 103; Johnson, 29; Buchanan, 26. Cass climbed still higher on the sixth ballot with 116 to 101 for Van Buren. Johnson and Buchanan were also sliding; Buchanan had but 25; Johnson, 23. Van Buren also fell behind on the seventh vote, Cass adding seven, making his total 123 to 99 for Van Buren. Buchanan and Johnson continued to fall, being reduced to 22 and 21 respectively.

By this time the day was ending. Nerves were frayed. The Van Burenites were bitter. They murmured and muttered against the slave-power. Van Buren had more than two-thirds of the delegates, and they had robbed him of several before the balloting began. Then they forced the adoption of the two-thirds rule, designed as a piece of theatrical claptrap for Van Buren's benefit while he was in England. As John L. O'Sullivan, then engaged with Wright and Samuel J. Tilden in forming a new daily, the *Morning News*, wrote to Van Buren, the atmosphere was laden with corruption. Some of the Van Burenites found consolation in the knowledge that the unjust rule could work both ways, for they had arrived at their irreducible minimum when the ninety and nine voted for the ex-President on this ballot. But others who followed his fortunes, remembering the arguments advanced by Butler, that a President should have a second term who had faithfully served the people, and that a majority rule was acceptable to Jefferson, let their anger get the better of them. Butler had emphasized this last by reminding the Convention that the true democratic rule called upon the minority to submit to the majority. These angry ones recalled the point Butler made in opposing the adoption of the two-thirds rule, that at the last convention, which Van Buren's followers controlled, and which had renominated him unanimously, the majority rule had been adopted.

Above the angry murmur a voice rose clear and piercing, and in tones reflecting the temper of his associates, moved that Martin Van Buren, having received a majority of the votes on the first ballot, be declared the convention's choice for President. The Calhoun men instantly became a shouting, maddened, gesticulating mob. They had not anticipated this. Delegates were tired and anxious to go home. It would not do to let this motion go to a vote. After order had been restored, the chair ruled that the motion would require a two-thirds vote for adoption. From the Ohio delegation, whence originated the motion, came the cry: "I appeal from the ruling of the chair!" This was reëchoed throughout the hall. Several were on the floor speaking at once. A confused and violent debate followed, and at the request of the Van Buren leaders, the appeal from the decision of the chair was withdrawn, and the convention proceeded with the eighth ballot. When the roll call was completed a new candidate was in the race, Polk, of Tennessee. He received the solid delegations of his own State and Alabama, seven from New Hampshire, a like number from Massachusetts, whose representation was headed by George Bancroft. Polk had a total of 44 votes. But Van Buren had gained five votes, his total being 104. Cass, with 114, had lost eleven votes. Johnson had been eliminated. Buchanan's followers had shrunk to 2; and Calhoun, who had not received a single vote in the seventh ballot, now reappeared with 2.

A motion to adjourn to the morrow was put and carried. That night Baltimore and Washington talked of the new entrant. Congress was in session, and the members who remained at their tasks had been kept informed of every important action by "the new invention of the electro-magnetic telegraph of Professor [Samuel F. B.] Morse . . . in manuscript bulletins suspended in the rotunda [of the Capitol]" as Adams noted. Three days before the convention met, the first public message had been sent over the line, which extended from Washington to Baltimore. Congress, two years earlier, had appropriated $30,000 to aid the penniless inventor.

That night the Van Buren and the slave-power leaders reached an agreement; and when the convention met in the morning, Butler withdrew Van Buren's name. Immediately the South Carolina delegates, who had been sitting as mere spectators, had their names enrolled as the representatives of their State. Then the ninth ballot was started, and 232 of the 264 votes cast —some did not vote—were for Polk. Before the clerk announced the result there was a scramble by the delegates who had voted for losers to change their votes. While the convention was noisily cheering the winner, some of Van Buren's old friends were disconsolate. In a letter to Van Buren Bancroft wrote:

. . . Butler wept like a child; . . . the delegation of Ohio was distinguished for gallantry, though rather precipitate & fiery. It remained in the power of your friends to have dissolved the convention without any nomination; but such an issue I deprecated as wrong in itself, and as injurious to your Fame. . . .

I have many personal causes for regretting the result; but do not include among them the week I gave to the more particular study of your political career. The present ceases to be the fittest moment for the publication of the little sketch I had prepared. . . .

After Polk's nomination, a recess was taken until the afternoon. Wright was named Vice President, Georgia's six delegates alone voting against him. He was in the rotunda of the Capitol, reading the bulletins, and within a few minutes after his nomination the clerk read his telegram declining. The nomination of Wright was a gesture by the servilocracy toward his defeated friend; they knew Wright would decline. A week before the convention opened Van Buren had instructed Butler by confidential letter to fight for Wright for first place if the slave-power would not accept him. Wright was as opposed to the extension of slave territory and the annexation of Texas as his leader. The insincerity of Wright's nomination was demonstrated on the second ballot for Vice President. Governor John Fairfield, of Maine, received the highest number of votes in a field of five, but he lacked the required two-thirds. The convention, anxious to adjourn, was willing to make Fairfield's vote unanimous if his friends could say definitely that he was for immediate annexation—and war, if necessary. In Fairfield's absence no one could give definite word, so the slave-States chose George M. Dallas, of Pennsylvania, for whose warped principles Buchanan could vouch.

The platform adopted was a confession by the servilocracy that they had sacrificed the ablest leader and statesman since Jefferson. Everything that Van Buren had advocated, save his opposition to immediate annexation and the extension of slavery, was incorporated into the appeal on which Polk and Dallas were submitted to the people. The document opened with this denunciation of the log cabin, hard cider, and coonskin campaign of four years ago:

Resolved, That the American Democracy place their trust, not in fictitious symbols, not in displays and appeals insulting to the judgments and subversive of the intellect of the people; but in a clear reliance upon the intelligence, the patriotism, and the discriminating justice of the American masses.

There was an attack on the bigotry of the newly formed Native American Party which had elected a Mayor in New York City in the preceding month in this:

That the liberal principles embodied by Jefferson in the Declaration of Independence, and sanctioned in the constitution, which makes ours the land of liberty, and the asylum of the oppressed of every nation, have ever been cardinal principles in the Democratic faith; and every attempt to abridge the present privilege of becoming citizens and owners of soil among us, ought to be resisted with the same spirit which swept the alien and sedition laws from our statute books.

The platform closed with this tribute to Van Buren:

Resolved, That this convention hold in the highest estimation and regard their illustrious fellow citizen, Martin Van Buren, of New

York; that we cherish the most grateful and abiding sense of the ability, integrity, and firmness with which he discharged the duties of the high office of president of the United States, and especially of the inflexible fidelity with which he maintained the true doctrines of the constitution, and the measures of the Democratic party during his trying and nobly arduous administration; that in the memorable struggle of 1840, he fell a martyr to the great principles of which he was the worthy representative, and that we revere him as such; and that we hereby tender to him in his honorable retirement, the assurance of the deeply seated confidence, affection, and respect of the American Democracy.

Polk's nomination astonished the country. The jargon of the race track was drawn on to describe his unanticipated victory; he was the added starter, the winning black pony, the dark horse. The last became part of the argot of politics. Many believed that Butler had made a premature surrender in withdrawing Van Buren's name. This thought was embodied in a letter to Van Buren from James S. Wadsworth, a New York delegate. The fault did not lie with Van Buren's managers. Bancroft and others who were loyal to him, perceived at the end of the first day that he could not be nominated. The South said: "Let the North name the candidate, provided he is for immediate annexation." Bancroft was the first Van Buren leader to advocate the switch to Polk, the best of the mediocrities available. The failure of the Democracy of Tennessee to instruct its delegates for a candidate for first place, while declaring for Polk for Vice President, raised suspicion that Polk was a party to the Calhoun intrigue. Before many months had passed, Van Buren had evidence of its truth.

Van Buren received the news with philosophic calm. He made good his promise to support the nominees of the convention. But his friends in New York, led by William Cullen Bryant and David Dudley Field, instituted a secret campaign against the election of Democratic candidates for Congress who favored immediate annexation. Within ten days after the convention adjourned, Van Buren had the satisfaction of seeing Congress reject the war-making treaty for the immediate annexation of Texas.

Had Clay not truckled for Southern votes, he would have triumphed over Polk. The movement initiated by Bryant and others against immediate annexation was the sentiment of the

North, and especially so in New York. Wright had been drafted
as candidate for Governor by Van Buren. He, too, labored for
Polk and Dallas. Twice during the campaign Clay declared he
had no personal objections to the immediate annexation of Texas.
At once the leading Whigs of the North, who had pledged
their reputations for Clay's adherence to the resolves of the
Whig Convention, ceased their labors. Clay now rushed to
explain. "In my second letter, assuming that the annexation
of Texas might be accomplished without war, and with the
general consent of the States and upon fair and reasonable
terms, I stated that I should be glad to see it," said Clay. "I did
not suppose it was possible I could be misunderstood." He carried
but one Southern State, and that was Polk's own State. He lost
Maine's nine votes and New York's twenty-six in the Electoral
College, where he lacked only twenty-three votes to win. Nearly
ten thousand voters remained away from the polls in Maine. These
were moderate anti-slavery men who could not square their con-
sciences with a vote for either Polk or Clay, or for Birney, the
Abolitionist, who again had been nominated for President by the
Liberty party. The Maine vote for Clay was 34,378, being
12,234 less than Harrison received. Polk's vote fell 500 below Van
Buren's. Birney polled 4,836 in Maine. Here a switch of 5,576
would have given Clay the State.

The result in New York must have made Clay spout brim-
stone. Here Birney received 15,812, more than twice as many as
the Abolitionists polled in the entire nation in 1836. The number
of New York votes for Birney, which would have gone to Clay
but for his change of front, has been placed at 10,000. The
moderate anti-slavery men of New York who remained from
the polls because they could not bring themselves to vote
with the Abolitionists, also reached high in the thousands. The
vote in New York was: Polk, 237,588; Clay, 232,482. Polk's
small majority of 5,106, in a total of nearly 276,000 votes, was
due solely to Clay's vain bid for Southern votes. A switch of 2,554
ballots would have given Clay the election. The result in the
Electoral College stood: Polk, 170; Clay, 105. Had Clay carried
New York the count would have been: Clay, 141; Polk, 134.

Not a vote was cast, or counted, in the slave-States, for

Birney. His vote in the thirteen free-States had increased nine-fold in four years, the total counted—there were many that were not—being 62,300. Some regarded the increase as a fungous growth. The excesses of slavery were to metamorphose the mush-room into an oak.

CHAPTER XL

Polk owed his victory to the faithful performance of Van Buren's pre-convention promise. He offered the post of Secretary of the Treasury to Silas Wright, although Van Buren had written him that Wright would be inaugurated Governor of New York on January 1 and could not abandon his elective office. Moreover, Polk also knew that New York, by virtue of the election returns, was entitled to the first place in the Cabinet, the Secretary of State. Nor was he left in ignorance of Van Buren's sentiments on this. Wright was against immediate annexation and the extension of slave territory. Polk wanted no one in his Cabinet opposed to the aims of the servilocracy. In furtherance of his crafty design, Polk then asked Van Buren to suggest a fit man for the Cabinet. Van Buren named Butler, Cambreleng, and Azariah Cutting Flagg.

But Polk had no intention of naming any Van Burenite to the first place in the Cabinet. He offered Butler the Secretaryship of War, and appealed to Van Buren to induce him to accept, knowing, of course, that Van Buren would disapprove. Van Buren continued the amicable correspondence with Polk until he heard that Marcy had been invited to head the War Department. Marcy and Van Buren had broken on annexation, and his former lieutenant was now the leader of the pro-slavery Democrats of New York. Polk's design was no longer a subject of conjecture: the slave-power sought Van Buren's political annihilation. It was now time to act. He sent his son Smith to Washington to protest against the naming of Marcy. Polk listened politely but stood by his selection. That evening he wrote to Van Buren that any error he had made was unintentional and disavowed any hostile intentions. Van Buren would have been satisfied with matters as they stood; but Polk besought Butler to accept the highly remunerative fee office he had held under Van Buren after he resigned from the Cabinet—the United States Attorneyship for New York. Cambreleng, as loyal to Van Buren as Butler, wrote a spirited defense of Butler's course, saying that it would have been impolitic to appear too independent.

Van Buren would have preferred nothing more than peaceful retirement. But it was again too late to retire—he must kick or be kicked. Often did Burr's cynical advice recur to him. They left him no choice save fight. He had everything he could wish for, but peace. His family was grown up; all save Martin, Jr., were married; Smith had espoused the daughter of William James, a rich merchant of Albany, some months before.

On January 18 his enemies saw indisputable evidence of his control of the State when the Legislature reëlected Dickinson to the United States Senate, and John A. Dix was chosen to succeed Wright. The next month, on February 17, would be the thirtieth anniversary of Van Buren's first big step toward the Presidency, his appointment as Attorney General of the State. A fortnight before that day arrived, his son John was named to the same office. There was too much similarity in this retracing of his father's footsteps for the Whigs to let the opportunity pass. Both started as lawyers; Van Buren's first political office was Surrogate; Prince John, as the Whigs always called him, started as a Law Examiner; Van Buren was then elected to the State Senate; the electors sent his son to Congress; and then the next step in the career of each was appointment to the highest law office in the State. The Whigs lampooned father and son anew. A State's choice for the Presidency is called the favorite son. Prince John was derisively named the favorite grandson, and the Magician's son. A Whig who had not plucked his lyre since the Harrison-Van Buren campaign, sang from the slopes of the political Parnassus:

> O, "favorite grandson of the Empire State!"
> O, son of magic, wherefore not be great!
> What! canst thou pause, and shall it then be told
> Thou are not worthy of thy father's fold?
> Forbid it, tall John, prove thyself thy sire's,
> The world a braggart, and her children liars;
> Show that the wand the great Magician sways,
> Thee being good, still lengthens out thy days,
> Feeds thee with pap, and gives thee every good,
> Clothes thy long back, and to thy fire adds wood:

Nor stop thou here, but emulate the man
Who scorns to lie, or touch the flowing can.
These are thy faults: and must I add, that play
Takes up thy time, and leads thee much astray?

There was a lack of sportsmanship in the reference to Prince
John's personal habits. He had been temperate until three months
before his appointment, when he sought forgetfulness of the loss
of his wife in the gaming table and the flowing bowl. But the
example set by his father soon rewon Prince John to a saner way
of living. There was a well-stocked cellar at Lindenwald, but the
modest meal at Kinderhook, or wherever else Van Buren chanced
to be, was washed down with a single small wine-glass of Madeira.
John Bigelow, on his visit to Lindenwald with Samuel J. Tilden,
noted this. It was Bigelow's first meeting with the ex-President,
but he was made to feel so much at home, that he commented
on his host's avoidance of the sweets upon the table. Van Buren
replied that he never took puddings or pastries, preferring a little
fruit. On this occasion he ate an apple. His simple life was reflected in his well-being, for he mounted his horse with the agility
of a youth of twenty, and rode every morning before breakfast.

The first shoots had appeared in Van Buren's farm when
he received a letter from Bancroft, now Polk's Secretary of the
Navy, offering him his old post at the Court of St. James's, which
had just been declined by Calhoun. The South Carolinian regarded himself as in line for the Presidential succession, and did
not wish to be too far removed from his political lieutenants.
Calhoun, too, was annoyed that Polk made Buchanan Secretary
of State. The offer was put on the loftiest grounds; the dispute
over the Oregon boundary had reached a delicate stage; there
were distinguished precedents: "In Europe the prime ministers
are always selected on such occasions. Witness Metternich to
Napoleon; Guizot lately to England; and Talleyrand, Marshal
Soult, and others. On great occasions the highest men are to be
taken; where war is to be averted, none but the highest. I must
quote your own avowed opinion also. Mr. Butler told me, that
you had expressed to him that in your view an Ex-President could
be honorably employed in a foreign mission. . . ."
Van Buren answered that he did not recollect having voiced

this opinion, and added: "I have, however, no hesitation in saying that . . . there would be no incompatibility with his former position in the councils of the Nation, for an Ex-President to accept, under suitable circumstances, an important Foreign Mission; and farther, that an emergency in the affairs of the country might arise . . . which would make it his imperative duty to overlook minor considerations, and devote himself to the public service in the form proposed, at almost any expense of personal feeling or preference for retirement." But the Northwestern Boundary dispute was not a crisis; and moreover, he did not find "the circumstances by which [the] offer is surrounded, agreeable." Polk would now see in this unelaborated phrase that Van Buren viewed the tender as a sentence of exile—such as he had contemplated for Clinton.

There was a Machiavellian cunning in Polk's offer. If Van Buren had accepted, it would have given color to the false cry that England was preparing to war upon us, a stratagem designed to becloud the Administration's evil intentions toward Mexico. A messenger dispatched by Tyler on the last day of his term was now in Texas, offering, on authority Congress assumed to itself, immediate annexation as a State of the Union. Van Buren's acceptance would also have placed the stamp of his personal approval on the Administration's wholesale extension of slave territory, as the resolutions of annexation provided that four additional States might be carved out of pro-slavery Texas. There was a condition in the measure that nothing should be attempted in violation of the Missouri Compromise. But this was an empty gesture to make annexation less obnoxious to the opponents of slavery extension.

After answering Bancroft, Van Buren whipped the streams and ponds of Kinderhook with new rods Tilden had sent him from New York. On the eve of the anniversary of the Battle of Waterloo he draped a small Stars and Stripes over one corner of the portrait of Jackson; on the opposite side he placed a bit of crape. The Old Hero had died ten days before while the sun was sinking behind the trees of the Hermitage.

In the first week in September, Prince John was sentenced to serve a day in jail. His father was distressed at the first reports, but when he heard all, he, too, joined in the laughter and applause. The Dutch counties, where the ancient manorial grants were still in possession of the heirs of the original owners, had been in a turmoil—as they had been on and off for more than a century—during most of the five years following the death of The Patroon in 1839. Armed bands of men, disguised as Indians on the war-path, made incendiary speeches in the manor towns, crying: "Down with rent!" This tenant uprising had been precipitated by the unjust exactions of The Patroon's heir. In Albany County a Sheriff's posse sent to accompany the rent collectors had been driven back by an armed body of farmers who claimed possession in fee simple. In Columbia County the violence ended in December, 1844, when the Anti-renters shot and killed a citizen named W. H. Rifenburg.

Two leaders of the Anti-renters, Dr. Smith A. Boughton, and Mortimer C. Benton, were immediately thereafter captured in the back room of a tavern, and locked in the county jail at Hudson charged with the assassination. Threats to rescue the prisoners brought out a detachment of infantry, a troop of cavalry, and a company of artillery. Four months later Boughton went on trial for his life. Public sentiment being wholly with the prisoner, the jury disagreed. He was again put on trial at the opening of the September term of court. Prince John was in charge of the prosecution. During the selection of the jury, he objected to the manner in which Ambrose L. Jordan, chief counsel for the defense, was examining the talesmen. A dispute ensued; Jordan called Prince John a liar, and was answered with a blow. Presently they were pummeling each other, wholly oblivious of the sitting court. Judge John W. Edmonds ordered the Sheriff to stop the fight and arrest Jordan and Prince John. This done, he committed them to jail for twenty-four hours. The trial was resumed the following day. The story took Van Buren back thirty-four years, when Prince John was only a babe in arms, and he had posted John Sudam as a coward after Sudam had challenged him to a duel and then refused to fight. Fists were an improvement on pistols. This time Boughton was convicted and sentenced to life imprisonment. He was pardoned two years later.

Under the leadership of Marcy, by grace of Van Buren thrice Governor and six years in the United States Senate, opposition candidates for the Legislature were entered against the Van

Buren nominees in many districts. Van Buren had seen the same thing when the Virginia Dynasty ruled the Nation: the Virginia Presidents, from Jefferson to Monroe, had muted New York's voice in the councils of the party by recognizing the minority faction. Yet the Barnburners—the term of opprobrium fastened upon the Van Burenites—won sweeping victories at the polls. The issue was the extension of slave territory. The opposition conceded that the followers of the ex-President might have grounds for their differences, but the inflexibility of the Van Burenites was likened to the farmer who burned his granary to destroy the rats. Van Buren followers retaliated with "Hunkers," an epithet which stuck to the followers of Marcy. Our lexicographers have erred in deriving Hunker from the Dutch *honk*,—a stake marking the terminus of a racetrack; a goal, or home, as used in the children's game of tag. If they would visit, even to-day, any of the old Dutch counties, they would find an occasional scholar who would inform them that Hunker is a corruption of *hunkerer*,—one who desires, a selfish person. *Hunkerer*, in turn, is derived from *hunkeren*, the infinitive of "desire"; *ik hunker* is "I desire." The opponents of Van Buren—they had long been called Conservative Democrats—were led by office holders whose motto, in the language of the Van Burenites, was "to get all they can and keep all they can get." It was to designate this type that "Hunker," with its roots in *hunkeren*, was coined. To the accepted derivations we prefer the humorous suggestion of Bryant in an editorial of October 7, 1847, that "Hunker" was derived from *Henker*, German for "hangman." The poet thought the appellation appropriate, observing that the Hunkers, if given enough rope, would hang themselves.

A week or so after the campaign all relations were broken off between Polk and Van Buren when it was publicly revealed, as Van Buren had long suspected, that the President was responsible for the savage attacks on him in a pamphlet which appeared in September. The booklet bore the title: "The Lives and Opinions of Benj'n Franklin Butler, United States Attorney for the Southern District of New York; and Jesse Hoyt, Counsellor at Law, formerly Collector of Customs for the Port of New York; with anecdotes or biographical sketches of Stephen Allen; . . . John Van Buren; Martin Van Buren; . . . Silas Wright; . . .

and their friends and political associates." The author was William L. Mackenzie, the quondam Canadian leader, now an American citizen. Intimate letters of the Van Burens and their friends which had been written to Jesse Hoyt were sprinkled throughout the 145 pages of text. Mackenzie was employed in the New York Custom House when appointees of Polk forced a locked trunk labeled: "J[esse] and L[orenzo] Hoyt's Law Papers." In May, Mackenzie, having copied many of the letters with the consent of Polk's appointees, sent the transcripts to Polk by a common friend. On May 30, under a government frank, Mackenzie received a note from one of Polk's subordinates from which we cull: "The discovery of these letters seems to be providential, and is duly appreciated in the right quarter. All will go well. . . . on any occasion, in which I can serve you, write me without reserve. You will find me ready to render you any aid in my power." With this equivalent for a royal warrant in his possession, Mackenzie prepared to feed his ancient grudge against Van Buren.

Van Buren could understand Mackenzie's deep hatred for him; for he had, among his papers at Lindenwald, a twelve-page memorial dated: "Rochester Prison, 23rd October, 1839," wherein Mackenzie made a pitiful plea for less rigorous confinement. He wrote of his ill-health and the refusal of the authorities to permit him to exercise in the open air; of his mother of ninety, a wife in delicate health, and six small children. "We are contented with our lot if let alone," he continued, "but that I should be singled out for official proscription, as it seems to me simply because I am an object of dislike to the Canada authorities, and my family left to struggle thro' the world, may be worldly policy, but it is not doing as you would wish to be done by were our places reversed."

Polk, of course, could not afford to place himself before the nation as indorsing the unjust attacks on Van Buren which Mackenzie worked into his pamphlet; so Mackenzie was removed from his Custom House berth. A new volume was issued in the spring. It was more venomous than the first, and bore the misleading title: "The Life and Times of Martin Van Buren." The casual reader, skipping through this book, would close it with the impression that Van Buren was unscrupulous in money matters to the point of corruption. This false atmosphere was created by a most adroit use of references to the corruption of men who had betrayed Van Buren's confidence and robbed the people.

Polk was now offering places right and left to the key men of the Barnburners. Those who were worth while remained steadfast. Tilden, a member of the Assembly, and poor as a churchmouse, spurned the place of Naval Officer with fees of twenty thousand dollars annually. Tilden described the Hunkers as "the venal gathered from all former parties." Dickinson, the senior Senator from New York, had become a Hunker. On July 10, 1846, Polk tried to seduce Dix with the post of Minister to the Court of St. James's. On this same occasion Polk requested Dix to advise Wright that "he had no schemes of conquest in view in respect to Mexico." This was two months less a day after war was declared against Mexico, "not in terms, but by circumlocution," as Adams phrased it. On August 6, the bill carrying out the platform pledge to restore the Sub-Treasury became law. Van Buren's great reform was back on the statute books to stay.

Before this session of Congress adjourned, David Wilmot, of Pennsylvania, a follower of Van Buren in the House, introduced a rider to a bill appropriating $2,000,000 for the purchase of New Mexico, which Texas unjustly claimed as part of her territory. This clause, known as the Wilmot Proviso, provided that "neither slavery nor involuntary servitude shall ever exist in any part of said territory." The House, reacting to the growing sentiment against the slave-power, passed the measure as amended. Every member of the New York delegation voted for the famous proviso. But it was rejected by the Senate. The Whigs, too, were divided on the question. There were Commercial Whigs—also called Cotton Whigs—and Conscience Whigs. The latter were akin to the Barnburners.

The war of conquest was bringing the Barnburners and Conscience Whigs into a common fold. The issues raised by the annexation of Texas had ceased to be abstract questions with those who daily scanned the casualty list. Van Buren's eldest had rejoined the colors. In September, at the battle of Monterey, he was again under fire. During the height of the three days' conflict, while the Mexican cannon balls were falling near where General Zachary Taylor and his staff stood, Colonel Balie Peyton rode up with a message from General William J. Worth. Van

Buren was standing beside Taylor while Peyton was making his communication. Peyton did not recognize him. As Peyton was about to return, he remarked that a letter from Santa Anna had been found in the pocket of a slain cavalry officer. For days the American troops had been asking: "What are Santa Anna's plans?" Taylor, in the hope that the letter revealed the Mexican General's future movements, asked: "Which way is he moving?" Enemy shot and shell were dropping all around the little group. Peyton, as violent a Whig as Taylor—he had served in Congress during Van Buren's Vice Presidency—drew upon the political argot to emphasize his answer. "Upon that point," replied Peyton, "his letter is quite Van Burenish and leaves us altogether in the dark." Taylor forgot that an army was under his command. Bowing to Peyton he said: "Colonel Peyton, allow me to introduce my aide, Major Van Buren." Men were falling on both sides while Peyton in his Louisiana drawl, protested that the discourtesy was unintentional; that while he differed politically with the ex-President, he always entertained toward him the kindest and most respectful feeling. A smile wreathed Van Buren's face as he said Peyton could obtain forgiveness only on condition that he would permit him, on his return to Kinderhook, to give his father a hearty laugh by recounting the incident. And laughter mingled with the thunder of the enemy's guns.

Again the slave-power through Marcy directed an attack against Van Buren. This time their treachery defeated Wright for reëlection. On the following August 27, Wright died at his farm in St. Lawrence County. Toward the close of the short session of Congress of 1846-7, the appropriation for the purchase of New Mexico was increased to $3,000,000. Again the Wilmot Proviso was added to the measure, which was once more passed by the House. The Senate once more rejected the proviso, and passed a measure from which the free soil clause was omitted. The House finally accepted the slave-power's dictation. During the acrimonious debate there were many threats of disunion and civil war. Dix, voicing the sentiments of the Barnburners, answered Calhoun and the slave-power with: "It is virtually declaring that unless we will consent to bring free territory into the Union, and leave it open for the extension of slavery, the Union shall be dissolved. Our Southern friends have heretofore stood upon the ground of defense; of maintaining slavery within their own limits against interference from without. The ground of extension is now taken, and of extending slavery upon free territory. . . . I say for the State of New York—I believe I do not misunderstand her resolutions *—that she can never consent to become a party to the extension of slavery to free territory on this continent."

In the month following Wright's death, the New York Democrats met in State convention to nominate State candidates for State office below the rank of Governor. In 1846 the people had decreed that the Secretary of State, State Treasurer, Comptroller, and Attorney General were to be elected by them, instead of being appointed by the Governor with the consent of the Senate.

No local convention ever assembled fraught with greater consequences. The Hunkers controlled the machinery of organizing the convention; but the Barnburners had a bare majority of the delegates. The Hunkers threw out nearly a dozen Barnburners and seated Hunkers in their stead. Among the delegates unseated was John Van Buren. But there were still 63 followers of Van Buren in the Convention. A few of these were elected to empty honors, which they promptly declined. Among them were Cambreleng, Preston King, James S. Wadsworth, and David Dudley Field. These four led the Hunkers a merry dance; and on the fourth day an obscure Van Burenite introduced a resolution indorsing the principles of the Wilmot Proviso, from which we quote: ". . . we declare uncompromising hostility to the extension of slavery by any act of the National Government, in free territory hereafter to be acquired."

It was now Saturday. The convention had been in session since Wednesday. The adoption of this resolution would be binding on the delegates sent to the next national convention. The Barnburners, to the last man, were for the resolves. And there were many Hunkers, who, if the motion were put, would vote for it, as they would not dare vote against a proposition which had received the unanimous approval of the State Legislature. Robert H. Morris, of New York, was in the chair. His strategy was to

---

* The resolutions adopted unanimously by the New York Legislature directed its representatives in Congress to oppose the extension of slavery. Similar resolves had been voted by the Legislature of Pennsylvania.

prevent a roll call on the motion. Accordingly he entertained a motion to table the resolution. The debate lasted through the day and night, and after midnight, Morris declared the motion carried by a viva voce vote. The Barnburners remained until Morris vacated his chair; they did not secede from the convention as some historians have it.*

After the ruling, Field moved the adoption of another resolution of similar purport. Morris ruled that Field's motion was not in order. The Hunkers cried previous question as the Barnburners appealed from the chair's ruling. "Why this cowardice and recreancy?" exclaimed Wadsworth. "Are the gentlemen too craven to meet this question?"

"Here a scene of indescribable tumult arose," chronicled the *Evening Post*. "Every member of the Convention and the lobby gathering in the center of the room, and gestures, threats, denunciation, and discordant noise, for fifteen minutes, drowned all attempts of discussion of the question."

Many Hunkers, fearful that a roll call might be had on the Barnburners' resolution, and not anxious to commit political suicide by voting against free soil, made a hasty exit, leaving less than a quorum. Morris now refused to heed the angry demands of the Barnburners that he determine if a quorum existed, and declaring that he heard a motion to adjourn, adjourned the convention *sine die*.

A more shameless fraud could not have been perpetrated. The Barnburners, representing the vast majority of the Democratic electors of the State, denounced the fraudulent Syracuse convention, and issued a call for a convention to be held at Herkimer on October 26. In the interim the Hunker press denounced them as traitors; the Whigs held their State convention, nominated a ticket, and adopted the Barnburners' resolution which the Hunker convention tabled. Bryant called this document The White Man's Resolution.

For months local and State conventions were held in the South at which the Southerners formally resolved not to attend a national convention unless opposition to slavery extension was abandoned. The Legislature of Virginia solemnly proclaimed this doctrine as an article of Democratic faith.

* *Vide* Shepard 358 *et seq.*

This new challenge of the slave-power, whose presses re-echoed the local cry of "traitors" hurled at the Van Burenites for calling the Herkimer convention, was answered on Tuesday, October 26, when the delegates assembled. Cambreleng, for many years Van Buren's spokesman on the floor of the House of Representatives, was elected President. Several Democrats from other States attended, including the author of the Wilmot Proviso. The principal speech was made by Prince John. As the ex-President's son took the platform the delegates shouted a noisy welcome. "Fellow Democrats," he began. There was defiance in his tone, and the delegates responded to it with cheers. Quiet restored, he added dramatically: "and fellow traitors." At this assumption of the opprobrious epithet as a badge of honor, the Barnburners, who had heretofore winced at the very sight of the word in the Hunker journals, applauded and laughed by turns. For more than an hour the delegates sat and listened to Prince John, who held their hearts in his hand, and made them beat fast or slow, as the humor seized him. They rose to cheer when he denounced the slave-power's demand that it be permitted "to plant black slavery on foreign free soil." He ended his speech with: "I am aware that a fierce political storm is raging, and that the political sea is rolling mountain high; but I have an undoubting conviction of the correctness of my course, and I think I see the spirit of justice and liberty walking upon the waters, reaching out its arms to my support, saying, 'Be of good cheer, it is I—be not afraid.'" Had this last been declaimed from an ancient pulpit in an Old World cathedral, the effect could not have been more solemn. Silence took possession of all for what seemed an age. But the tall figure of Prince John was presently bowing to the cheers of frenzied delegates whose doubtings were transmuted into an unshakable faith. The resolution proposed at Syracuse was adopted. A second resolve, after reciting that the slave-owners had pledged themselves not to attend a convention which countenanced the principle of free soil, set forth that the Democrats of New York "will be obliged to adopt a counter declaration and proclaim their determination to vote for no man, under any circumstances, who does not subscribe to the preceding resolution." This, too, was adopted unanimously.

The Herkimer Convention did not nominate a State ticket.

As Prince John declared in his speech, the nominees of the Syracuse Convention would have an opportunity to subscribe to the free soil resolution. Only a week remained before New York would go to the polls. The Whig candidates subscribed unanimously to the free soil principle of the Barnburners. The Hunker candidates trusted to luck. They lost, the vote being ten to one against them in several normally Democratic counties. The Whigs carried both branches of the Legislature, outnumbering the Democrats three to one in both houses. The Democratic majority of the New York Congressional delegation was also swept away.

All through the election the *Wilkes-Barre Farmer* had carried Van Buren's name as its choice for President in 1848. Copies of the *Farmer* of October 30, containing a letter from Van Buren, reached the New York newspapers after Election Day. Van Buren said that he was sincerely and heartily desirous to partake of the honors and enjoyments of private life uninterruptedly to the end; his aspirations were of the past; he was conscious of having performed his duty to the people, and had neither heart burnings to allay, nor resentments to gratify by a restoration of power. But being only sixty-five, and with the mind and body of a far younger man, he did not close the door to a unanimous call of his party. This last, Van Buren well knew, was highly improbable.

Van Buren spent New Year's at Lindenwald. All day long he played host to Kinderhook. New Year's calling among New York's Dutch was a ceremony of obligation; its impress has not been wholly effaced. It still flourishes in the cities on the Hudson, and in the interior, where the skyline is still steeple-dotted; and even where the spires of the churches have been overtopped by cloud-piercing creations of steel and stone, the custom is not quite forgotten. Lindenwald this particular January 1 was no different from others that the old pile had seen. On a sideboard in the dining room stood rows of bottles and decanters of brandy and Schiedam and other potent beverages for the grown-ups. On a mahogany console in the great hall was the familiar punchbowl, filled with lemonade, and sparkling red from a generous dash of Burgundy; flanking the bowl were dishes of raisins and figs and the cookies of Van Buren's childhood. While the servants poured for the men and women, the ex-President waited upon the children. Some of the little girls, like their mothers, clung to the ancient custom of wearing two or more warm dresses, one at least being of quilted lamb's fleece. But it was a rare one who gave him the greeting in the tongue they all had spoken not so many years ago.

At nightfall the visits ended. He was now alone save for the servants. Abraham was still at the war. Mat was in Washington making confidential reports to him. Smith was in Albany with his family. Prince John had moved to New York. The house was very lonely; he must go to the city. This wish he gratified before the end of the month. He took lodgings at Julien's, on Washington place, just off the Square. Shortly after his arrival he read the glad news of the signing of the treaty of peace: Abraham would soon be home, wearing a Colonel's epaulettes.

The hostelry of Monsieur Julien was noted for its *"bon dîners à la Paris."* But after Van Buren's arrival it became a center of political activity. Prince John and Tilden invariably attended the conferences in Van Buren's chambers. The most important of these occurred after the Hunkers met in Albany on January 26 and appointed thirty-six delegates to the national convention in Baltimore. Every one was looking forward to a gathering of Barnburners on Washington's Birthday; for the two factions at their respective State conventions in the fall had made similar provisions for selecting delegates to Baltimore. Van Buren recalled that the time-honored way was for the Democratic members of the Senate and Assembly to caucus and issue a call for a convention. The Barnburners outnumbered the Hunkers in the Legislature. Accordingly a caucus was held, and a convention called to meet in Utica on February 16.

At noon on the day appointed, the delegates assembled in the Oneida County Court House. The inns and lodging houses of Utica were overflowing with hundreds of enthusiastic Democrats from all parts of the State. Within half an hour after the temporary chairman's gavel fell, the convention was adjourned to the Methodist Church, to accommodate the unexpected throng.

Save for a speech by Prince John, nothing of moment transpired beyond the formal selection of thirty-six delegates, headed by Cambreleng. The purpose of this speech was to stress that the convention had been convoked by a call of a caucus of the Democratic members of the Senate and Assembly. This, said Prince John, was the only legal way in which a State convention could be summoned.

Early in April, during a visit to Julien's, Van Buren handed a mass of manuscript to Tilden, saying: "If you wish to be immortal, take this home with you, complete it, revise it, put it into proper shape, and give it to the public." Tilden, whose law practice kept him toiling day and night, answered that if Prince John would aid him, he would gladly undertake the task. This, of course, was intended, and Prince John and Sammy—as Van Buren affectionately called Tilden—worked over the document. Save for a brief preamble by Prince John, and a still briefer insert by Tilden, the manuscript was, in all essentials, as it had left Van Buren's hands.

This historic document—longer than his reply to Hammett —was the first real assault on slavery. The Abolitionists, with their extremes of phraseology and program, had appealed only to the emotionalists. But here, in the restrained language of statesmanship, was a pitiless indictment of the trade in human flesh, and the arrogant society built upon it. When this arraignment of the servilocracy was published in the second week of April it was received with silence from the high places in Washington; for interwoven with the presentment was an ultimatum to the managers of the Democratic National Convention which would meet within six weeks. The thirty-six delegates chosen at the Convention of Barnburners at Utica must be seated. Equally masterful was the manner of bringing it before the public: Van Buren—whose hand never openly was shown—had it put forth as the traditional address made to the people of the State at the close of each legislative session by the Democratic members.

The Barnburner delegates to the Democratic National Convention "will but illy reflect the spirit of the Convention which nominated them, and the sentiment of their mass constituency, if they do not unyieldingly claim to represent them without co-rival in that body, and fully assert and firmly maintain, under any and all circumstances the principles, the rights, and the honor of the Democracy of New York." This is outlawing the Hunker delegates. In a review of the decline of the party strength in New York, the Polk administration is assailed because of its recognition of the Hunkers—a "meager list of hirelings" who enjoy "the whole patronage of the Federal Government."

The address then takes up slavery. Here the genius of Van Buren is apparent. He opens the tombs of the hallowed great and calls them forth to bear true witness against the system. Washington is first called upon. His words to Robert Morris are reuttered: "I can only say that there is not a man living who wishes more sincerely than I do to see a plan adopted for the abolition of it." Patrick Henry's stricture on slave-holding is next heard: "I believe a time will come when an opportunity will be offered to abolish this lamentable evil." Jefferson is again thundering against George III for the encouragement he had given the slave trade, in having "waged a cruel war against human nature itself . . . to keep up a market where men could be bought and sold; he has prostituted his negative for suppressing any legislative attempt to restrain this traffic." Then Monroe's testimony is adduced: "We have found that this evil has preyed upon the very vitals of the Union, and has been prejudicial to all the States in which it has existed."

In bringing this dramatic phase of his case to a close Van Buren observes that Madison and other Virginians had displayed an "aversion to slavery of the deepest character." He next assails the slave-owners for denying the constitutional power in Congress to legislative control over slavery in the territories, citing acts of Congress, during every administration from Washington to his own, in which the right was acknowledged. Van Buren does not ascribe this sentiment to the people of the South, but to "the struggles of party leaders at the South for local ascendancy." The cupidity of politicians, and not the avarice of cotton growers, is Van Buren's concept of the root of the evil. This theory, which the student of history cannot reject, Van Buren supports by instancing the hordes of Southern planters who sold their slaves and emigrated to Indiana and to Iowa when they were admitted to statehood as "abodes of free labor."

The vast region ceded by Mexico—all of New Mexico and California—for which we paid $15,000,000 and assumed the claims of American citizens against the Mexican Government, had given added impetus to the cause of the slavery extensionists. To these Van Buren said: ". . . the principle of extending slavery into territories now free from it can never be made acceptable to the freemen of the North."

He closed the address in the key he began it: the thirty-six delegates chosen by the Utica Convention were the sole representatives of the Democratic party of New York. There was talk even now of seating both Barnburners and Hunkers as the easiest way out. This proposed injustice Van Buren rejected in advance with: "If a question is made of their right [to sit as delegates], it must be decided, not compromised. . . ."

Cambreleng, Wadsworth, Prince John and the rest of the delegates went to Baltimore. The convention organized on the morning of the second day. Then ensued two days of wrangling over the rival New York delegations. South Carolina was not represented; yet a lone delegate cast the State's nine votes on all motions. Dickinson of New York asked that the Barnburners be excluded on the sole ground that they had adopted a free soil resolution at Utica. On the evening of the 24th of May the convention seated the Hunkers and Barnburners, giving each delegate half a vote. Immediately the Barnburners withdrew. On the fourth ballot Cass was nominated by the slave-power, with W. O. Butler of Kentucky for Vice President.

On June 6 the Barnburners met in New York City. There was not an unoccupied square foot of the Park when Cambreleng read: "Resolved, That the nominations made at Baltimore by the persons who remained there after the convention was dismembered, and by the aid of nine votes from South Carolina, which were never sent there, are of no validity or force whatever . . . and as invalid as an Act of Congress passed after arbitrary expulsion of the members from any State. . . ."

Throughout Cambreleng's reading the vast crowd interrupted with cries of: "John Van Buren!" A motion to adopt the resolutions was carried unanimously. Prince John was then introduced, and the crowd howled its satisfaction, which he answered with smiles and bows that prolonged the applause.

"The war," he said, "was not fought by us at the North to extend slavery into free territory; it was not for that purpose that the blood and treasure of the North was poured out like water."

When the hand clappings and shouts of approval ceased, he

told of the experiences of himself and his fellow delegates in a manner which made his hearers indignant and amused in turn. He knew the value of a laugh. He reviewed the organization of the convention lasting more than a day. Not a single vote was cast by a New York delegate, Hunker or Barnburner, because the committee on credentials had refused to act. He waxed humorous as he recounted the nine votes cast by one purporting to represent South Carolina.

"I am unwilling," he continued, "that one man should count nine when seventy-two of our people count nothing, considering the vast obligations of the Democratic party to the Democracy of New York. What have they done that they should be made to suffer stripes from such a cat-o'-nine-tails as this from South Carolina?"

He had given them the looked-for hearty laugh. He grew serious again, as he was sounding the call to arms of all the opponents of slavery. And his speech ended, as most of his speeches did, with a bit to stir the soul. "You who hear me may not live to see the end of this contest, but your children will reap its benefits," he said. "You may rely on it that the future historian will look back to the present time to confirm those noble words of the poet—

"Freedom's battle once begun,
Bequeathed from bleeding sire to son,
Though baffled oft, is ever won."

The Barnburners adjourned to meet in convention on June 22 at Utica.

The day after the meeting in the Park, the Whigs met in Philadelphia and nominated General Taylor, of Louisiana, whom we left on the battlefield of Monterey, and Millard Fillmore of New York. This was a hybrid ticket: Taylor owned one hundred slaves; Fillmore was from a State which had abolished slavery in 1827, and whose people, outside of New York City, were anti-slavery. The selection of the colorless Fillmore was dictated solely by the hope of appealing to the disaffected Democrats of his State. The surrender of the traditional party of the North to the slave-power was made complete when the platform was written: there was not a reference to slavery.

Slavery was the only note sounded by the Barnburners in their two-day convention at Utica. Cambreleng, Wadsworth, Field, Tilden, Preston King, and Prince John were there. A letter from Van Buren characterized the demand made by the Baltimore Convention that the Barnburner delegates pledge themselves to support the choice of the convention before their claims to seats had been decided as an indignity of the rankest character. New York had not been given fair representation and the acts of the convention were not binding upon them. He repeated the arguments he had made in the April address of the Barnburner legislators against the abandonment of the right of Congress to impose freedom as a condition of Statehood. As the Baltimore Convention had rejected this doctrine, which had been recognized by Jefferson, Madison, Monroe, and Jackson, all undoubted Democrats—Van Buren, too, had signed a bill imposing freedom on an application for Statehood—he would not vote for its candidates; and if there were no other candidate but Taylor, he would not vote for President. His stand against Northern attacks on slavery in the District of Columbia and in the slave-States was dictated by "convictions that slavery was the only subject that could endanger our blessed Union." He was aware that he had gone further in this than many of his best friends approved; but he would go no further. Anticipating the intentions of the delegates, he protested that it was his "unchangeable determination never again to be a candidate." In spite of this he was nominated for President by the Free Soil Democrats, as his adherents styled themselves. Henry Dodge, United States Senator from Wisconsin, was named for Vice President.

As this was little more than a State convention, a national convention of the new party was summoned to meet in Buffalo on August 9. Free Soil Democrats and Conscience Whigs from most of the States signified their intention to attend. A platform must be adopted and Van Buren and Dodge renominated by the national body. The newspapers supporting Van Buren—he had fifty in New York State alone—carried his and Dodge's names in a box as the paper's choice for President and Vice President. Beneath the names, following the example set by Bryant, the Free Soil press carried this excerpt from Jackson's letter to Butler, written June 24, 1844, a few days after he learned that the Baltimore Convention of that year had rejected Van Buren:

> I cannot hope to be alive to witness the acclamation with which the people of the United States will call Mr. Van Buren to the Presidency at the end of Mr. Polk's term; but you will, and I know you will rejoice at it as a consummation of an act of justice, due alike to him and the honor and fame of the country.

The well-informed knew that Van Buren was a reluctant candidate. It was known also that he would be far from displeased if the Buffalo Convention should select another nominee for President. On June 29 Dodge declined in a letter beginning: "I have long been the friend personally and politically of Mr. Van Buren and under other circumstances would be glad to have my name associated with his." But Dodge's State had been represented at Baltimore, had concurred in the nominations, and he felt obligated to support them. Not long after Dodge declined, Salmon P. Chase, who became Secretary of the Treasury under Lincoln, and later rose to be Chief Justice of the United States Supreme Court, discussed the forthcoming gathering of Free Soilers with another Ohioan, Edwin M. Stanton, who was also to serve in Lincoln's Cabinet. That night Chase wrote to Prince John:

> . . . One of the best and ablest Democrats in the State, I mean Edwin M. Stanton, said to me to-day that if John Van Buren should be the nominee of the Buffalo convention he would roll up his sleeves and go to work till election for the ticket; and I am sure that to all the young Democrats and all the young Whigs in the State your name would be more acceptable than your father's. . . . Our contest is with the slave power, and it will break us down unless we break it down. . . .

Many shared Stanton's views that Prince John would make the most popular nominee; no one in the movement had a greater hold on the hearts of the multitude.

The Buffalo conventions—two were held simultaneously— were held in the Brick Church, and in a circus tent erected in the park opposite the court house. The canvas sheltered 5,000, and was believed adequate to accommodate all. Here was held the popular, or mass convention, whose opening session was attended by 30,000, five-sixths of whom sat under the broiling rays of the midsummer sun. In the church, Charles Francis Adams, son of John Quincy Adams, presided. Every New England State was represented. Delegations also attended from New Jersey, Pennsylvania, Ohio, Michigan, Wisconsin, Iowa, Indiana, Delaware, Maryland, Kentucky, Virginia. Illinois, who numbered Abraham Lincoln among her representatives in Congress—his only term was nearing its end—had her proportionate share in the deliberations.

Adams was not a tyro in politics; he had served six years in the Massachusetts Legislature, and the death of his father made him the leader of the Conscience Whigs of New England. Moderate Abolitionists such as Chase were there as delegates, as well as the other extreme, typified by Joshua Leavitt, a member of Adams's delegation.

A letter from Van Buren informed the delegates that "the convention of which you will form a part, may, if wisely conducted, be productive of more important consequences than any which have gone before it, save only, that which framed the Federal Constitution." He told them also to abandon his nomination if the great end of their proceedings "can be better promoted." On the evening of the second day the convention balloted. Leavitt presented Van Buren's name. John P. Hale, of New Hampshire, who was proscribed by the Democratic party of his State because he refused to follow its instructions and vote in Congress for Texas annexation, received 129 of the 288 ballots cast. This was a complimentary vote to Hale, and a bid for the support of the Abolitionists whose nomination for the Presidency Hale had declined. Van Buren was nominated by acclamation.

There was only one nominee for Vice President—John Quincy Adams's son. The platform was next adopted; and at ten o'clock the delegates adjourned to the mass convention in the park where nearly fifty thousand—their numbers had increased hourly—roared a welcome as Adams, Chase, Prince John, Tilden, Dix, Butler, and other leaders ascended the wooden platform. The nominations were ratified with a thundering aye. Adams was forced to his feet by the repeated huzzas which greeted the mention of his name. Scattered among the multitude, dispelling the darkness, were hundreds of oil torches affixed to saplings and trees, or tied to poles stuck in the ground. The night, the torches, and the trees, added to the religious fervor of the assemblage. The first plank of the platform was a prayer as well as a declaration of political principles: ". . . we, the people here assembled, remembering the example of our fathers in the days of the first Declaration of Independence, putting our trust in God for the triumph of our cause, and invoking His guidance in our endeavors to advance it, do now plant ourselves upon the national platform of freedom, in opposition to the sectional platform of slavery."

There was nothing in the platform to appeal to the Abolitionists of the Garrison school. The next plank read: "Resolved, That slavery in the several States of this Union which recognize its existence, depends upon the State laws alone, which can not be repealed or modified by the Federal government, and for which laws that government is not responsible. We therefore propose no interference by Congress with slavery within the limits of any State."

The platform was replete with ringing phrases leveled at the slave-power, such as: "Congress has no more power to make a slave than to make a king; no more power to institute or establish slavery than to institute or establish a monarch . . . we accept the issue which the slave power has forced upon us; and to their demand for more slave territory, our calm but final answer is, no more slave States and no more slave territory. . . . the only safe means of preventing the extension of slavery into territory now free, is to prohibit its extension in all such territory by an Act of Congress."

The sixteenth and last plank read: "Resolved, That we inscribe on our banner, 'Free Soil, Free Speech, Free Labor, and Free Men,' and under it we will fight on, and fight ever, until a triumphant victory shall reward our exertions."

A little before midnight the mass convention adjourned, after paying a signal tribute to Prince John by unanimously adopting a resolution directing him to make a nation-wide speech-making tour on behalf of his father and Charles Francis Adams.

A holy zeal possessed the Free Soilers, and many of the younger leaders believed that Van Buren and Adams would be swept into office. But Van Buren had no illusions; there was not a Federal office holder among his followers. If he but had the political machine, manned by office holders, Federal and State, which supported Cass! It was he who had introduced this creation of New York politics into the life of the nation. The two-thirds rule, invented to lend an appearance of greater strength to his nomination for Vice President in 1832, had destroyed him in 1844. This, he knew, could not be undone in his lifetime, as to do so would be an acknowledgment by the slave-power that it had robbed him of the nomination in 1844 by this undemocratic device. Nor did he expect an abatement of the evil he had wrought by organizing office holders, high and low, into a well-drilled corps to sway conventions and elections. He had fought against it in his retirement, and the Free Soil platform called for "the election by the people of all civil officers in the service of the government, so far as the same may be practicable." The civil service was as yet an amorphous concept.

In New York, Dix was nominated for Governor on the Free Soil ticket. Elsewhere in the North, men of substance, following the example set by Van Buren and Dix, lent their names to the movement; they ran for the lowliest offices, and gave their time and labor in awakening the country to the menace of slavery.

It did not matter to the slave-States whether Cass or Taylor was elected. The Whig candidate had two qualities that made him preferable to the Democratic South; he was a slave-owner and a Southerner. He had a greater popular appeal because of the glamour of his military achievements. Bigotry was also aiding him. The Native American party at its first national convention, held in Philadelphia, nominated Henry A. S. Dearborn, of Massachusetts, for Vice President, and recommended Taylor for President, although not formally nominating him. This organization was a logical outcome of the Anti-Masonic party, for the sword of intolerance is two-edged. There was a refinement and improvement in methods in the Know-Nothing movement; its members were oath-bound, and held together by a secret ritual. While primarily aimed at all foreign-born, the party was essentially anti-Catholic.

Election Day blasted the hopes of the more sanguine Free Soilers. The returns from the South demonstrated to the country

that the slave-owners had used the Democratic party solely for
its own perpetuation; that the teachings of Jefferson and all else
associated with the party were subordinate to their interests.
With the exception of Virginia, Alabama, South Carolina, and
Mississippi, Cass lost every Southern State; and these he carried
by the slimmest of majorities. But the treachery of the South
alone would not have defeated Cass. Taylor's victory would not
have been possible without the votes polled by Van Buren and
Adams in New York, Pennsylvania, Vermont, Massachusetts,
and Connecticut. In each of these five States the combined vote of
the Free Soilers and the Democrats exceeded Taylor's pluralities.
The thirty-six Electoral votes in these States would have elected
Cass by a majority of thirty-nine. The vote in the Electoral
College stood: Taylor, 163; Cass, 127. Had Cass carried the
other four Northern States where Taylor won by pluralities less
than the aggregate polled by the Democrats and the Free Soilers,
he would have received 194 Electoral votes to 96 for Taylor.

The popular vote was: Taylor, 1,360,099; Cass, 1,220,544;
Van Buren, 291,263. Van Buren polled more votes than Cass in
Massachusetts, Vermont, and New York. In his own State the
vote was: Van Buren, 120,510; Cass, 114,318. Here Taylor's
vote was 218,603, some 16,000 less than the number cast for
Van Buren and Cass. The Whig candidate for Governor, Hamilton Fish, also carried New York because of the split. Delaware,
Maryland, and Virginia were the only States in the South where
any votes were counted for Van Buren. In Virginia he was credited
with the ridiculously low poll of nine votes. "Fraud!" exclaimed
the Van Burenites, pointing to the nine votes in Virginia. A wag
of Virginia conceded the fraud, and solemnly explained that the
prosecuting authorities of the entire State were seeking the Van
Burenite who had fraudulently cast eight ballots in addition to
his own. The country laughed as it marched onward to its Great
Tragedy.

CHAPTER XLI

THE slave-owners' support of a slave-owning Whig demonstrated to the Democrats of the North that they were slave-owners before they were Democrats. Democratic Congressmen from Northern commonwealths reflected the temper of their constituencies in uniting with Northern Whigs against the extension of slavery into the land that had been Mexico's. When the session of 1848-1849 adjourned, Van Buren knew that he had not falsely prophesied to the delegates to the Buffalo Convention when he wrote: "The convention . . . may . . . be productive of more important consequences than any which have gone before it, save only, that which framed the Federal Constitution." Evidence was not lacking that the ideal for which he had fought was a living thing.

Seven months before the Buffalo Convention met, men were opening a trench for a mill race near what is now the city of Sacramento. Their overseer was named James Wilson Marshall. As the ditch diggers turned up the earth Marshall noticed a nugget of gold. Back in 1771, Rudolf Ingulf, in his *Lehrbuch der Geographie von Californien*, had proclaimed to the world that California was a vast gold field. No one paid any heed to the scientific observations of the German sculptor and explorer. But the ring of Marshall's few ounces of gold was heard by adventurous spirits in every corner of the earth. A dauntless courage was all that most of these modern Argonauts possessed; and those who braved the perils of the mountains, the deserts, and the plains, and the treacherous voyage around the Horn, found the land a Colchis of the day. The few who journeyed from the South were typical pioneers, propertyless, and free spirits all.

When Congress was nearing its end in the sitting of 1848-1849, these intrepid ones had increased the population to the proportions of a commonwealth. Accordingly, a convention to frame a Constitution was summoned by Bennett Riley, the military Governor, to meet in Monterey on September 1. On October 13 the delegates finished their labors. One of the sections prohibited

520

slavery. This clause was unanimously adopted by the Forty-niners. On November 13—more than eighty thousand gold seekers had entered the territory since Marshall's find—the people ratified the document adopted at Monterey by a vote of fifteen to one.

About the time the Forty-niners ratified their Constitution, of California, Prince John echoed the sentiments of his father when he voiced the hope that the Democratic party would be "the great anti-slavery party of the Union." Van Buren himself was silent: he had withdrawn from public life; his ambition of more than a generation was realized at last. In politics, as Burr had said, it was a case of kick or be kicked. Prince John must take and give the kicks henceforward. Van Buren would work the farm.

When the Forty-niners were giving added momentum to the Free Soil movement, Kinderhook was thrilled as it had not been since Van Buren, after more than two years in the White House, revisited the village. Henry Clay was fulfilling his promise to call on his old friend. Clay addressed the villagers from the veranda of Stranahan's Hotel, with Van Buren at his side. Clay stayed overnight at Lindenwald. The two compared notes on Calhoun and Webster, and talked pleasantly of their friends. Clay, who came from the West by way of the Great Lakes, then went on to New York, where he remained until it was time to leave for the convening of Congress.

As Van Buren pored over the accounts of the debates in the Capitol during the early part of 1850, he could not have helped wishing at times that he was back in the thick of it and looking forward to his fifty-seventh, instead of his sixty-seventh, birthday. All the great leaders in Congress were now old: Clay, Webster, Benton, and Calhoun. The great nullifier was at the portal of the tomb, and on March 4, when he rose to discuss the dominant issue, he was so weak that another member of the Senate read his speech on Clay's compromise scheme. Clay proposed to admit California as a free State; organize the territories of New Mexico and Utah without reference to slavery; purchase the land Texas claimed in New Mexico; abolish trading of slaves in the District of Columbia, while permitting slavery therein; affirm that Congress had no power over inter-State slave trade; enact a workable fugitive slave law. Calhoun, who had no plan, uttered defiance in his last speech: the Forty-niners had been guilty of a piece of gross impertinence, and the admission of California would be equivalent to notice that the North sought to overwhelm the South. One of the Senators from Mississippi active in the discussion was Jefferson Davis, who had married a daughter of President Taylor. Webster astonished the North on March 7 when he approved Clay's compromise and denounced the Wilmot Proviso as a taunt and a reproach to the South.

Taylor did not live to tarnish his name by signing the oppressive and provocative fugitive slave law: Fillmore, who succeeded to the Presidency on July 9, bears this odium. The act denied a jury trial to a reclaimed slave. Charles Sumner, in Faneuil Hall, said the public conscience would not allow one who had trodden the streets of Boston as a free man to be dragged away as a slave. With only slight variations from its original scope, the Clay Compromise was enacted into law.

During the discussion on the Clay Compromise, Van Buren, through Prince John, told a Free Soil convention in Connecticut that there never was a time when the opponents of slavery extension were called upon to act with more energy or decision to prevent their representatives in Congress from faltering or betraying their trusts.

The nation accepted the Clay Compromise as the lesser of two evils. The Northerners, with few exceptions, believed that the legislation would end all talk of disunion and remove slavery from politics. It did for a while.

On August 27, at the dedication of the monument to Silas Wright, at Weybridge, Vermont, Van Buren made his first public address in years. Here Wright's father farmed while his son studied at Middlebury College. This speech was a simple tribute to his old friend.

While the politicians were scheming for place in the next Presidential campaign, Van Buren was paying court to Margaret Silvester, the spinster daughter of his first preceptor. She had turned forty on January 24, 1851; Van Buren had celebrated his sixty-eighth birthday the month before. She graced the round table at Lindenwald on many festive occasions, and Van Buren's saddle-horse was frequently hitched outside the Silvester home in the village. Her father had died in 1845.

Margaret's mother, who had been Lydia Van Vleck Van Schaack, looked with approval on the ex-President's suit. Her charming daughter was also flattered, but truthfully replied that she would never marry. He had hoped that she would say "Yes," that he might have her companionship on his European trip; but her "No" did not end their friendship. His son Martin was living with him, and while his trip to Europe was still indefinite, Smith, now a widower, also quartered at Lindenwald. Prince John was an irregular visitor; and Abraham and his family lived there only during the summer. One winter day, while Van Buren and his grandchildren, Singleton and Martin III, were walking along the banks of the creek near where he and Billy Van Ness had discussed what should be done in the event of Billy's arrest for his part in the Burr-Hamilton duel, the children slipped and fell headlong into the icy stream. Van Buren plunged in after them. Presently he wrapped the shivering lads in the folds of his blue Spanish cloak, which he had discarded as he leaped into the water, and carried them to the house. This was a feat for a man of Van Buren's size and years; but to the three of them it was only a grand lark.

Most of Van Buren's correspondence now is with his old friend, Francis Preston Blair, who has retired from active journalism and President-making, as he tells Van Buren in one of his letters. Blair has a farm at Silver Spring, Maryland. They talk of fishing and farming. Samuel Houston is dazzling Washington with his leopard skin vest, and there is a movement on foot to nominate him for President and Marcy for Vice President. Van Buren enjoys this intelligence hugely. A gift of seed potatoes from Lindenwald is reciprocated with enough wheat for the fall planting on the old Van Ness place. Blair has "borrowed" the grain from General Harman, who is as proud of his wheat as Van Buren is of his tubers. And Mrs. Blair, knowing that Van Buren always has fruit for dessert, sends some of their peaches which she has preserved in brandy.

The Clay Compromise had not satisfied the extremists in the servilocracy now known as Disunionists. Had the entire problem been left to the people of the South and their moderate leaders, short shrift would have been made of the talk of disunion. Howell Cobb, a slave-holder, of Georgia, who from the floor of the House of Representatives demanded the extension of slavery into California and New Mexico by Act of Congress, was typical of the moderates. When the extremists in his State openly made Disunion an issue in their local campaign of 1851, Cobb ran for Governor on the Union ticket and was overwhelmingly elected. But "the struggles of party leaders at the South for local ascendancy"—to use Van Buren's phrase—kept the slavery issue to the fore.

Fears for the safety of the Union were expressed by many who had followed Van Buren in 1848. Bradford R. Wood, of Albany, wrote to Prince John voicing these apprehensions. He suggested Benton for President and Prince John for Vice President to avoid disunion. Wood, with the Van Burens and most of their followers in New York, had returned to the Democratic fold after the passage of the Clay Compromise.

At their convention in Baltimore, on June 6, 1852, the Democrats nominated Franklin Pierce, of New Hampshire, for President, and William R. King, of Alabama, for second place. The hopelessly divided Whigs convened in the same hall ten days after the Democrats had adjourned. The contest lay between Webster, Fillmore, and Scott. Webster and Fillmore were alike objectionable to their Northern partisans because of their stand on the Clay Compromise. The South stood by Fillmore until the fiftieth ballot, and on the fifty-third, Scott, whose views on the Compromise were concealed from the public, was chosen. William A. Graham, of North Carolina, was named for Vice President. On August 11 the Free Soilers met in Pittsburgh and nominated John P. Hale, of New Hampshire, and George W. Julian, of Indiana.

Six weeks before the Free Soil delegates met, Van Buren indorsed Pierce and King. This pronouncement was embraced in a letter declining an invitation to Tammany's annual celebration of Independence Day. This had been anticipated, as the Tammany broadside for the occasion revealed: it was headed:

Union! Strength!! Victory!!!
Past Grievances to be Buried in Exertions for the Future.

Chase, who had been chosen a member of the United States Senate following the reunion of the Free Soil Democrats and old line Democrats in 1849, was now the heart of the Free Soil movement. In 1850 he had again broken, this time irrevocably, with the Democratic party because it had accepted the Clay Compromise. His vision was neither dimmed by age nor by the conservatism of the East. Three days before Van Buren penned his Tammany letter, Chase wrote to him in the vain hope that his influence would remain with the Free Soil party. But Van Buren had drunk too deeply of the lethal cup Clay had offered the nation.

Various attempts were made to draw Van Buren into the canvass. But beyond a letter to Henry G. Miller and G. H. Pierson, of the Democratic Union Club of Chicago, thanking them for resolutions praising his indorsement of Pierce, he took no active part in the campaign. His views on slavery were voiced by Prince John in his speech at Albany, who said that the Free Soil movement of 1848 had scored two triumphs: the admission of California as a free state, and the abolition of the slave mart in the District of Columbia.

Both parties had declared for the Clay Compromise. The framers of the Whig platform made the error of singling out the fugitive slave act in its indorsement of the Kentuckian's plan. This irritated the Conscience Whigs, who voted for either Hale or Pierce. Scott lost his own State of New Jersey; he carried only Massachusetts, Vermont, Tennessee, and Kentucky. He would have lost Kentucky but for the loyalty of its citizens to the memory of Henry Clay, who died at the beginning of the campaign. Hale polled little more in the country than Van Buren received in New York in 1848. The popular vote was: Pierce, 1,601,274; Scott, 1,386,580; Hale, 155,825. The result for the Electoral College stood: Pierce, 254; Scott, 42.

After the election, Blair, with Van Buren's sanction, sought the post of Secretary of State for Dix. But the appointment of Marcy to the first place in the Cabinet taught the Free Soil Democrats not to expect a voice in the new Administration.

A few weeks after Pierce was inaugurated, Van Buren and his son Martin sailed for Europe. The father was hopeful that the sea voyage and the spas of the Continent would restore young Mat to health. Beyond assembling data for a history of political parties and the *Political Memoirs* which his father contemplated, he had done little for nearly two years. As Van Buren was the first ex-President to leave the United States, court circles were in a quandary as to how to receive him. He solved the problem by requesting that his reception differ in no wise from that accorded other civilians. He visited most of the noted statesmen, calling on Count Camillo Benso di Cavour at his villa in Turin in October.

After his visit to Cavour he heard of his appointment as umpire of the British-American Commission for the adjustment of claims against the two countries for all losses since 1812. On the twenty-second of the month he wrote from Florence to the commissioners, who were sitting in London, declining the honor.

The following month he was received by Pope Pius IX. During his prolonged stay in Rome he was frequently entertained by prelates of the church. A waggish correspondent of a Dublin journal said that hopes were entertained of the ex-President's conversion. In like strain Van Buren wrote to Augustus Wynkoop, a neighbor in Kinderhook. He told of a visit to the monastery of St. Silvester, where he heard the story of the miracle of the turnips; and in the simple tale told by the monks Van Buren saw a great truth: Mother Earth heals all who work in her garden.

. . . If a letter from here which I saw in a Dublin paper, expressing hopes of my conversion, founded on my social intercourse with some of the High Church Dignitaries, should find its way into the American papers, I must beg you to say to my friend, Mrs. Silvester, that there is no danger of any such thing. Thank her and Miss Silvester at the same time for their kind messages which I appreciate very highly. I could not forget them here if 1 would, for the name is as familiar here as in Kinderhook. About forty miles from Rome stands Soracte. . . . Like the dome of St. Peter's, it is seen from everywhere and stands in that regard as its rival. On the highest point is the convent of St. Silvestro, built by the Uncle of Charlemagne, on the site of a church built by St. Silvester before he became pope. His garden where he planted turnips in the afternoon for his next day dinner is still shown by the monks. Although I can hardly believe the turnip story, I have no doubt he was a good man. . . . By the bye do we not find in the turnip story the secret of the old Lady's healing of us all in gardening? . . .

From Blair he hears that all is not going well with the Pierce Administration; the old struggle between the slavery and the anti-slavery forces is renewed; the Know-Nothings are playing havoc with political lines; and he inquires of young Mat's health.

In the spring of 1854 he settled down, as he thought, at the Villa Falangola, Sorrento, overlooking the bay which has stirred the soul of every Latin poet. On June 21 he began work on his *Political Memoirs*.* His opening sentence reads: "At the age of seventy-one, and in a foreign land, I commence a sketch of the principal events of my life." That same day he wrote: "What I may write will not . . . proceed, as is so often the case with those whose public career has been abruptly closed, from a wounded spirit, seeking self-vindication, but will, on the contrary, be under the control of a judgment which satisfies me that I ought to be, as my feelings lead me, at peace with all the world." Although he labored long, and produced an interesting tome, he did not complete his task. On page eight of the *Memoirs*, after a fleeting allusion to his defeat for the nomination at Baltimore in 1844, he promised to discuss the intrigue which led to this dramatic event. But save for three other bare references on pages 227, 393, and 513, he is silent on the subject. And he has not written a word on the Free Soil movement. There are many other gaps in the book.

In the month of October he heard of the engagement of Smith to Henrietta Irving, a niece of Washington Irving. On the twenty-eighth of the month he wrote to Martin that his brother was going to make this pleasing alliance. The letter, written from Nice, shows his concealed concern over the state of the health of Martin, who was in London hoping that the English physicians would succeed where the French at Aix-les-Bains had failed.

In December Van Buren received a letter from his old law partner telling of the political confusion resulting from the repeal of the Missouri Compromise during the last sitting of Congress. The mischief-making law, which Pierce signed without scruple, made slavery the outstanding issue before the nation, as the repeal permitted the extension of slavery into the territory north of the line of thirty-six degrees thirty minutes latitude wherein slavery was "for ever forbidden" by the Act of 1820.

* Van Buren so calls the work which the Government published in 1920.

Van Buren was indignant at the passage of the repeal, and wondered how any but half-baked politicians could have voted for it.

In the first week of January, a measure, popularly known as the Kansas-Nebraska Bill, was introduced by Stephen Arnold Douglas of Illinois. As drafted, it did not contain the provision permitting the States formed out of the vast territory in the Louisiana Purchase not yet admitted to Statehood, to be free or slave soil "as their constitution may prescribe at the time"; nor did it include the declaration that the Act of 1820 prohibiting slavery north of the Missouri Compromise line was inoperative, being contrary to, and superseded by, the Clay Compromise of 1850.

The day following its appearance in its amended form Chase and other objectors described the measure as "a gross violation of a sacred pledge . . . a criminal betrayal of precious rights . . . an atrocious plot to exclude from a vast unoccupied region immigrants from the Old World and free laborers from our own States, and convert it into a dreary region of despotism inhabited by masters and slaves." And this document, known as the "Appeal of the Independent Democrats," characterized the assertion that the Clay Compromise had suspended and rendered the Missouri Compromise inoperative as "a manifest falsification of the truth of history." Sumner said that the bill raised an issue which said to every man in the land: "Are you for freedom or are you for slavery?"

Butler did not overdraw the picture of confusion resulting from the enactment of this bill. Of the forty-two Northern Democrats who voted for the measure, only seven were reëlected. The whole North was at last aroused to the gravity of the issue. Until 1854 Free-Soilism appealed only to analytical and idealistic minds. It had lacked that emotion-evoking ingredient necessary to the popular success of any radical political movement. But the repeal of the Missouri Compromise not only outraged the moral sensibilities of the people, but stirred their souls. The invasion of Kansas in March of this year by bands of pro-slavery Missourians, armed with bowie knives, pistols, rifles, and cannon, who forced the election inspectors to accept their votes for candidates for the Kansas Territorial Legislature, intensified the resentment of the North.

The repeal of the Missouri Compromise originated in the

cunning mind of Seward, then a member of the Senate, and like every other New Yorker of consequence, a vigorous opponent of slavery extension. Only the purblind failed to see that the complete domination of the Democratic party by the servilocracy, and its death grip on the Whig party, would lead to the formation of a third party to give the advocates of Free-Soilism a vehicle of expression. After Douglas introduced his Kansas-Nebraska bill Seward went to Archibald Dixon, Clay's successor in the Senate, and secretly put him up to move the repeal of the Act of 1820. No one suspected Seward at the time; but he later boasted of his unscrupulous act to Montgomery Blair, son of Van Buren's friend and correspondent, and Postmaster General under Lincoln. Blair repeated Seward's boast in a letter to Gideon Welles, Secretary of the Navy when Blair, Seward and he were members of Lincoln's Cabinet. Seward, artful in the ways of machine politics, was aware that this would solidify the anti-slavery elements as naught else. But he did not see beyond the Whig party; nor did he, or any one else, dream that the climax would be an unleashing of passions unparalleled in history's gory annals.

While the Kansas-Nebraska legislation was pending in Congress, a handful of Whigs, Free Soil Democrats, and old line Democrats, met in the Congregational church at Ripon, Wisconsin. This was on the last day of February. Forty-eight hours before the meeting, Alvan E. Bovay, its sponsor, wrote to Horace Greeley: ". . . Advocate calling together in every church and schoolhouse in the free states all the opponents of the Kansas-Nebraska Bill, no matter what their party affiliations. Urge them to forget previous political names and organizations, and to band together under the name I suggested to you at Lovejoy's Hotel in 1852 . . . 'Republican.' . . ." On March 20, seventeen days after the inflammatory measure passed the Senate, a second meeting was held in the little schoolhouse at Ripon; and to quote Bovay: ". . . We went into the little meeting . . . Whigs, Free Soilers, and Democrats. We came out of it Republicans. . . ." The glamour of the name worn by Jefferson and other Virginians, whose faith the Democrats professed and profaned, was not recognized by Greeley until June. On the twenty-fourth of the month he published the second half of Bovay's suggestion in *The Tribune.*

Greeley's tardiness was dictated by caution and a belief, prevalent in the East, that it would be impossible to form a third party. Tilden, and other New Yorkers who followed Van Buren in 1848, held this view. On the August 26 following Greeley's "Republican Party" editorial, Tilden wrote to a friend: ". . . A third party organization, if attempted, would not in my judgment, embody a quarter of the force or numbers our movement did in 1848. I do not know a man who bore any considerable share of the heat and burden of that day, who would enter *actively* into a similar campaign now. . . ."

In September Greeley was a delegate to the Republican State Convention at Syracuse, which indorsed Myron Holley Clark, the Whig nominee, for Governor. Greeley was read out of the Whig party by Thurlow Weed and Seward. The prohibitionists, flushed with their recent success in Maine, indorsed Clark at their convention. Never was the phrase used by Marcy in a letter to Van Buren—"the tangled skein of New York politics"—more applicable than now. Voters of the two old parties were divided into three parts: slavery, Free Soil, and Know-Nothings. The last, under the name of the American party, nominated Daniel Ullmann for Governor. Many Democratic and Whig leaders were, clandestinely, members of this secret, oath-bound solidarity. Among the Democrats were Soft Shell and Hard Shell Hunkers; the Barnburners, or Free Soilers, were dubbed Soft Shells. The Soft Shells, or anti-slavery Democrats, outnumbered the Hard Shells five to one. The combination of temperance voters, anti-slavery Whigs and Republicans, outvoted their rivals. The Know-Nothing candidate for Governor polled only thirty-four thousand less than Clark; but the American party nominee for the state-wide office of Canal Commissioner was elected.

Three months and eighteen days after Clark took office, Van Buren's trip abroad was cut short by the death of Martin. And in the summer, at the head of a newly made barrow, beside the resting place of his wife, Van Buren raised a Parian shaft on which was graven: "Martin Van Buren, Jr." He reserved the place on her right for his own last sleep. Smith acted as his amanuensis when Van Buren resumed his literary labors. He divided his time between his desk and his farm. He still rode to the village every day on his favorite mount. A greeting from a neighbor would cause him to rein up; and in the first few weeks of his return he heard from half the village the story of last December 5 when all Kinderhook celebrated his seventy-second birthday.

On Sundays he was to be seen in his high-backed pew in the little Dutch Reformed church, invariably accompanied by his son Smith and family. Occasionally Prince John accompanied him. Weather permitting, he drove in his famed English coach; and when snow covered the countryside he came in a high-fronted sleigh, horse and vehicle jangling with brass bells that shone like gold, and himself muffled up in a buffalo robe. As he entered the pew on wintry Sundays he would set a small foot stove in a convenient spot, then shake the snow from one of his huge bear-skin gloves, and carefully place it on his head for warmth. His shock of yellow locks was only a memory. When he rose to join in the congregational singing, he would hold his hand on the furry gauntlet to prevent it from falling. And crowded though the church might be, and every voice raised in song, Van Buren's rendering of the hymn could be heard above the rest.

The Presidential campaign of 1856 began on Washington's Birthday when the American party held its national convention at Philadelphia. Fillmore was nominated for President, and Andrew J. Donelson, of Tennessee, for Vice President. The former President was driven into the Know-Nothing movement by Seward and Weed: they never liked him. The Whig party existed only in name. The Republican party had supplanted it. Seward and Weed joined it only when they saw their own party disintegrating. Fillmore's nomination was unsatisfactory to some of the Know-Nothing delegates, who seceded and nominated for President the picturesque soldier, John C. Frémont, of California, surnamed the Pathfinder. William F. Johnston, former Governor of Pennsylvania, was chosen for Vice President by the bolting Know-Nothings.

The Democrats met in Cincinnati in the first week of June. They indorsed the repeal of the Missouri Compromise Act of 1820 and the enactment of the Clay Compromise of 1850. The old doctrine of State rights was reasserted, and an appeal made to Van Buren's followers by pronouncements against a Bank, and against internal improvements by the Federal Government. They denounced the Republicans as a sectional party and the Americans for their proscription of citizens of the Roman Catholic faith or of alien birth. Buchanan, of Pennsylvania, was named for President. Pierce, who—in the language of Blair—"had sold himself to the South," was discarded when Northern delegates threatened to bolt if he was renominated.

The first Republican National Convention was held in Philadelphia on July 17. The choice for President had been prearranged; the leaders had cast aside Chase and other abler men to nominate Frémont in return for the Know-Nothing vote. Supporters of John McLean, Justice of the United States Supreme Court, insisted on a ballot, which resulted: Frémont, 359; McLean, 196; Charles Sumner, 2; Seward, 1. William L. Dayton, of New Jersey, was nominated for Vice President. His vote on the first ballot was 259. Lincoln was second, with 110, Johnston, Frémont's running mate on the Know-Nothing ticket, received only two votes.

With the exception of the border States of Maryland, Delaware, and Kentucky, only Northern commonwealths sent delegates to the Republican convention. Many of Van Buren's intimates had joined the new party. His faithful correspondent, Blair, had presided at the preliminary convention held in Pittsburgh during the winter. Robert Emmet, son of Thomas Addis Emmet, was elected temporary chairman of the national convention. His Irish birth was an answer to the charge that the new party in accepting Frémont had accepted Know-Nothingism. The author of the Wilmot Proviso was a delegate. Charles Francis Adams was also prominent in its deliberations.

The platform contained "a clear-cut statement of the Free Soil doctrines as enunciated by the followers of Van Buren in 1848," to borrow a phrase from Professor Myers's *The Republican Party: A History*. The repeal of the Missouri Compromise was condemned; Federal aid for building a railroad to the Pacific Ocean was favored; and the immediate admission of Kansas as a free State was demanded. Responsibility for the invasion of Kansas by armed bands of pro-slavery men, who for months past had burned, pillaged and slaughtered, was properly laid at the door of the Pierce Administration.

The acts of terrorism, instituted by the pro-slavery Missourians, were more than outmatched by an atrocity committed a fortnight before the Democrats convened. On the night of May 24, a party of eight or nine led by a crack-brained Abolitionist named John Brown, invaded the sleeping settlement built up around Dutch Henry's Crossing on the Pottawatomie, and dragged five men from their cabins. These unfortunates were innocent of wrong-doing. All save two of the raiding party were members of Brown's family. Armed with old cutlasses, they slashed and hacked their helpless prisoners to death. After perpetrating this barbarous massacre, Brown and his band of assassins committed the lesser crime of robbery. Brown escaped before he could be apprehended.

The Whigs met in Baltimore on September 17. It was a national convention in name only. They indorsed the candidacies of Fillmore and Donelson. They adopted a platform criticizing the Democratic and Republican parties as sectional, and declared that the success of either "must add fuel to the flame which now threatens to wrap our dearest interests in a common ruin." The outlawry in Kansas was dignified with the name of civil war; and the platform added: "we proclaim that the restoration of Mr. Fillmore to the Presidency will furnish the best if not the only means of restoring peace."

After the Democrats had nominated, the Tammany Society invited Van Buren to its annual Fourth of July celebration. In a long response declining to attend because of his age, he announces his intention to support Buchanan. This letter breathes despondency. There is an indirect plea to the party to return to the ancient traditions of Jefferson. He speaks in praise of the destruction of the Bank and the establishment of the Sub-Treasury. He laments for his party's departure from its historic attitude toward slavery by the repeal of the Missouri Compromise. He relates that no one was more sincerely opposed to the repeal than himself; but the Kansas-Nebraska Act has become less obnoxious to him. This, he frankly adds, may be due to the unanimous acceptance of it by the party in which he had been reared. He knows that Kansas will be admitted as a free State if the people of the territory are not molested by the armed bands of pro-slavery men. This thought is in his mind when he declares that Buchanan's promise to use his power as President to restore harmony among the sister States can be redeemed only by securing to the settlers a "full, free, and practical enjoyment" of the privilege of suffrage. Slavery is now the living issue; he believes that in Buchanan's election there will be "good grounds for hope" that the Union will be saved.

Van Buren said that this would be his first and his last letter during the campaign. He kept this promise, save for a confidential communication to Moses Tilden, the elder brother of Samuel J. Tilden. Moses, who had been wavering between Frémont and Buchanan, wrote Van Buren he had at last decided to support Buchanan. In his sad and prophetic reply, Van Buren spoke freely of Buchanan and the great issue.

I am happy to find that the "sober second thought" has brought you to the right conclusion. . . .

. . . the crisis is, in my judgment, the most imminent and critical of any we have ever experienced. That union should so long have been preserved in a confederacy which contains an element of discord of such magnitude and so disturbing a nature as that of slavery, is a wonder—more surprising than its dissolution would be. This has been owing to . . . the single fact that there have always been neutralizing considerations of sufficient force to maintain party cohesions between men of the free and slave States. Slavery questions . . . have never before had the effect of dissolving old party connections and sympathies, and the balance wheel has thus been preserved. Now, for the first time in our history, one side, and that the one in which we reside, has undertaken to carry an election . . . against the united wishes of the other. It has placed itself in a position which, for the first time cuts itself loose from all hope, if not desire, of assistance to the slave States. It not only admits that this is its position, but avows that it is a desirable one. It wishes to accomplish its mastery by its own unaided arm. Now, it needs no ghost to tell us that one successful effort of this description will be followed by another, for men have too much the quality of wild beasts in them to stop the pursuit when they have once tasted blood, and it would be against reason and experience to expect a Union, in which political mastery is so plainly exhibited and organized, to continue. . . .

Slavery agitation must be eradicated in some way or another, or institutions cannot continue in their present form. . . . if Mr. Pierce had from the beginning taken the stand he now seems to be taking, . . . the country would have been saved from the disgrace to which our institutions have been exposed in the estimation of the world

Kansas would have been a Territory so decidedly free as to put an end to attempts to make it a slave State, the country would have been quiet, the party united, and he renominated. All that is wanted now tc secure many of the most important of these results is a rigid and effectual execution of the Kansas Organic Act. Although I am not a particular friend of Mr. Buchanan, I have reasons that satisfy my mind that he will, if elected, secure to the country this great advantage. . . . I do have a favorable opinion of Col. Frémont personally, but cannot for a moment doubt, from his utter want of experience in the affairs of government, and his inexperience in everything that belongs to it, that he would, if elected, inevitably be thrown into the hands of Seward, Greeley, and Weed . . . there is the greatest reason to fear that to commit the power of the government into such hands, at a moment so critical as the present, would be but "the beginning of the end" in regard to the confederacy . . .

Weed and Seward were out of one matrix. Greeley, as he knew from bitter experience, was easily swayed, like a feather in the wind, by every passing emotion; he was clay in the hands of the cunning or unscrupulous. Greeley had been crying freedom and Free Soil early in 1848; but on the eve of the election he cast his influence with the slave-owning Taylor. Seward and Weed had taken him to the top of the mountain.

The Republicans paraphrased Van Buren's slogan of 1848 with: "Free Speech, Free Soil, and Frémont." It took in the North where more than 1,300,000 voted for Frémont, Free Soil, and Free Speech. Fewer than a thousand Republican ballots were cast in the border States of Delaware, Maryland, and Kentucky. Virginia, with 291 Republican votes, recorded the only Southern support. Buchanan was elected by a minority vote. His total of 1,838,169 was 377,629 less than the combined totals of Frémont and Fillmore. In two of the three Northern States which Buchanan carried, New Jersey and Illinois, the Republicans and Know-Nothings heavily outvoted the Democrats. The division of his opponents also gave California to Buchanan. Frémont's total was 1,341,264; Fillmore, 874,534. Fillmore ran a close second in the South. He carried Maryland, whose eight votes were cast for him in the Electoral College, where Buchanan received 174. and Frémont 114.

Van Buren is writing for posterity, he informs his old law partner on December 3. Butler and Smith Thompson Van Buren are to be his literary executors. At Christmas he receives a letter from Blair, who fears that Buchanan will truckle to the South. Blair's son, Montgomery, writes of his argument in behalf of Dred Scott before the United States Court. Within a month Van Buren clipped from a newspaper Buchanan's inaugural address wherein he said that whether slaves could be carried into free territory and maintained there as slaves, would be decided in the Dred Scott decision soon to be pronounced.

This was the one point not covered by the Kansas-Nebraska Act, and the prediction of Buchanan was fulfilled within a few days. Dred Scott was a slave. His master took him from Missouri to Illinois, permitted him to marry in the free State, and in 1838 brought him back to Missouri. After the death of his master, Dred was hired out to various persons in Missouri. Disliking this, he sued for his freedom. A lower court in Missouri found in favor of Dred, but an appellate bench, with two of the three judges concurring, held that the condition of slavery reattached to the negro on his return to Missouri. Before this decision was made, the widow of Dred's master deeded over the negro, his wife, and their child, to a relative in New York. Dred, with the aid of white friends, now brought suit in the United States Circuit Court. Losing here, he took an appeal to the United States Supreme Court.

A majority decision written by Chief Justice Taney held that the Missouri Compromise was unconstitutional; that slave-owners could carry their slaves, as property, into any territory; that negroes born of slave parents in the United States were not only not citizens of any of the States when the Constitution was formed in 1787, but could not be made citizens by the States or by Congress. In a dissenting opinion, concurred in by Justice McLean, Benjamin Robbins Curtis held that Congress had the right to pass the Missouri Compromise, and also refuted Taney's contention that negroes born of slave parents could not be citizens by citing the record to show that many such were citizens, and enjoyed even the privilege of suffrage, at the time of the formation of the Constitution. McLean further held that slavery was contrary to right and had its origin in power; and in this country was maintained only by local laws.

The majority decision, instead of allaying the North, as the legalistic believed, inflamed the people the more. The opinions of McLean and Curtis were printed in pamphlets and extensively distributed by the Free Soilers; and like use was made of Taney's decision by the servilocracy. Seward, without revealing any basis for the charge, accused Taney of having divulged the decision of the court to Buchanan so that he could avoid taking a stand on the issue in his inaugural address. Thousands believed the charge, and Lincoln, in one of his speeches, hinted at it.

The Blairs maintain a regular correspondence with Van Buren. In the fall there is another gift of brandied peaches from Silver Spring. The times are hard. A financial panic has seized the country. The Sub-Treasury and the hard money system that Van Buren fought for no longer require defenders. But the new financial structure is not perfect. A relative, John Dash Van Buren, is working on an improvement. It will call for legislative enactment. He proposes that Van Buren run for member of Assembly next fall and introduce his currency reform. This Newburgh Van Buren is very serious; and the ex-President, in declining to return to the State Legislature in his seventy-seventh year, discusses currency reform as though he were writing to an economist.

Blair, evidently chidden for not writing oftener, pleaded on February 6, 1859, that he did not want to distress Van Buren with a recountal of political conditions in Washington. A month later he receives a pamphlet containing the speech of another talented son of Blair, Francis Preston Blair, Jr., whose journalistic pen was at the service of Van Buren in 1848. Young Blair is now representing his adopted State of Missouri in the House of Representatives, where he advocates colonizing the negro population of the United States in Central America. He and all the Blairs are Republicans. Blair senior, on April 3, talks of the possibility of secession and civil war.

A few days later another of those who had striven wisely to keep the balance between the North and South passes on. Benton was the last of Van Buren's able contemporaries in the Senate. Van Buren settles down with renewed efforts to his literary work: he would like to write *Finis* to these two volumes before his own last page is reached.

Blair grows gossipy in his next: all Washington is again

discussing Peggy Eaton. La Bellona is twenty-seven years older now; but she, after the manner of beautiful women, has forgotten the passage of years. Eaton had died in 1856, leaving her a large estate. Along came a poor Italian, young enough to be her son. He raved over her charms. His words took her back many years. He made her young again; she forgot she was a grandmother. And so they were married. Then he robbed her of a large part of her estate before she awakened from her dream of love. Poor Peggy!

Shortly after Peggy has separated from her third husband, Van Buren receives a printed invitation to a dinner of the Order of the Cincinnati. He uses the reverse side to make notes on Jackson's dissolution of his Cabinet over Peggy. In the spring of 1859 Blair invites Van Buren to Silver Spring. The trip will do him good, and after a little rest he can go on to Washington to do research for his *Memoirs*. And Blair will be happy to aid him in the work of revision. The tempting offer is declined. A New York book publisher, Sheldon Smith, appeals to Van Buren to let his house bring out anything he writes.

It was in October that John Brown and eighteen men seized the United States Arsenal at Harpers Ferry. When a detachment of marines from Washington under Colonel Robert E. Lee arrived at the little Virginia village, only six of Brown's band were left. Brown's two sons were killed by the bullets of the townspeople, and he was thought to be dying. After his capture Brown sent word to the zealots who had supplied him with funds and ammunition for the enterprise not to attempt his rescue. The ill-starred curtain-raiser ended December 2 when this descendant of Peter Brown, passenger on the *Mayflower*, died on the scaffold.

In the winter of 1859-1860 John Brown meetings are held throughout the country. They are attended almost wholly by extremists and the curious. In January Van Buren declines to attend one in Albany. In the second week of the month he writes to Tilden. He is concerned over the future of Prince John. He incidentally mentions his hope to see Prince John and Tilden partners. Tilden has one of the largest and most remunerative practices in the city. The financial returns are not the dominating thought in Van Buren's mind: he wants his brilliant son kept occupied. Prince John is more conservative and circumspect in his gaming, and he has become temperate in his drinking. In the latter he has had no choice, as drink has affected his liver. On Februɑ ɻy 21 Tilden replies to Van Buren that the partnership would not be either to his own or to Prince John's interest, as the nature of his practice would furnish "few occasions which would give scope to his powers."

There was one matter that he had been putting off for some time. But it must not be delayed. He must not be taken unaware. So he sits down and writes: "I, Mártin Van Buren, of the town of Kinderhook, County of Columbia and State of New York, heretofore Governor of the State, and more recently President of the United States, but for the last and happiest years of my life a Farmer in my native town . . ." The will finished, he resumes his literary labors.

Before the Democrats met in national convention at Charleston, South Carolina, on April 23, it was apparent that they were hopelessly divided on sectional lines. The servilocracy, which had forced Buchanan to pattern his political conduct on the Dred Scott decision—a course which evoked criticism from Van Buren —demanded that the principles of Taney's opinion be incorporated in the party's platform. When the Northern delegates refused to agree to this, most of the Southern delegates seceded. They were followed by a few from the North.

Both factions postponed making nominations until June. The bolters assembled at Richmond on June 11, and nominated John C. Breckenridge, of Kentucky, for President, and Joseph Lane, of Oregon, for Vice President. The following week the regular Democrats reconvened at Baltimore and named Douglas, of Illinois, for President. Benjamin Fitzpatrick, of Alabama, was given second place, but declined. Herschel V. Johnson, of Georgia, was substituted. Meanwhile the Republicans had nominated Lincoln at Chicago on the third ballot after Seward had led him on two. Hannibal Hamlin, of Maine, was named for Vice President on the second trial. A fourth ticket was placed in the canvass by the Constitutional Union party which had convened in Baltimore on May 9—a week before the Republican Convention. John Bell, of Tennessee, and Edward Everett, of Massachusetts, were the choice of the new party, which carried Virginia and the border States of Tennessee and Kentucky. The result in the Electoral College was: Lincoln, 180; Breckenridge, 72; Douglas, 12; Bell, 39. Lincoln, who swept every State in the North save New Jersey, had a minority of the popular vote, which stood: Lincoln, 1,866,452; Breckenridge, 847,953; Douglas, 1,375,157; Bell, 590,631.

Bennett, whose snobbishness increased with the years, assailed Lincoln before and after the election. He was a "roughspun, disputatious village politician . . . without education or refinement . . . an illiterate Western boor . . . a satyr." He had said almost the same of Van Buren. Bennett was wealthy now: he was no longer a blackmailer.

The secession of South Carolina on December 20 was not unexpected. During the canvass William L. Yancey, who represented Georgia in the United States Senate, speaking in several cities in the North, said that the South would regard the election of the Republican ticket as a notice that it could not expect justice from the Government. Van Buren was aghast at the timidity of the machine politician in the White House, who let things drift while he talked of his conscientious scruples against coercing a sovereign State.

The New Year found Van Buren afflicted with a severe attack of asthma, from which he had been suffering for many months. By the time he was convalescent, Mississippi, Florida, Alabama, Georgia, Louisiana, and Texas had followed the example of Calhoun's State. Lincoln's declaration in his inaugural address that "the Union is unbroken" speeded Van Buren's restoration to health. There was a man again in Washington. Lincoln's proclamation calling for seventy-five thousand volunteers to suppress the "combination, and to cause the laws to be duly executed," gave Van Buren a complete renewal of his strength. He again mounted his horse and galloped to the village. And as he rode, his mind could not have helped galloping back to the end of Jackson's first term. At that time South Carolina had authorized the raising of 12,000 troops to support Calhoun's scheme of nullification. And he thought of Jackson's plan, confided to him by letter, to raise a *posse comitatus* in Virginia and Tennessee, while en route to the seat of trouble, and seize Calhoun, Hayne, and the rest of them and deliver them to the judicial power of the United States. Only a Buchanan or a Pierce would have let things drift into the deplorable condition that confronted Lincoln. And then there was that first Jefferson Day Dinner which Calhoun had planned to make his own. But he and Jackson had spoiled this plan with the toasts they had prepared at the White House the day preceding that memorable April 2. Calhoun was Vice President then, and Van Buren was Secretary of State. Jackson's toast that night—"Our Union—it must be preserved" —was Lincoln's policy now. The servilocracy had also been deaf to his own toast that evening: "Mutual forbearance and reciprocal concessions; thro' their agency the Union was established— the patriotic spirit from which they emanated will forever sustain it." And the warning of John Quincy Adams to the nullifiers, although spoken on a later occasion, was complementary to his: "From the instant that your slave-holding States become the theater of war, from that instant the war-powers of the Constitution extend to interference with the institution of slavery in every way." But the generation of inflammable speeches of slave-holding politicians, big and little, had envenomed almost the whole South.

At this time there was a letter on its way to Lindenwald from Concord, New Hampshire, the home of Buchanan's predecessor. It was written on April 16, the day after Lincoln's proclamation for volunteers. Besides Pierce and himself, there were three other ex-Presidents living: Tyler, Fillmore, and Buchanan. Pierce suggested that Van Buren, as the senior of the five, summon the ex-Presidents to meet in Philadelphia. Van Buren knew that the time for parleying was past. It was now the moment to put down the "combination and to cause the laws to be duly executed." Van Buren's reply to Pierce is dated April 20, and reads:

I have received your friendly letter suggesting for my consideration the propriety of summoning a meeting of the Ex Presidents, at Philadelphia, to consult on the present alarming condition of public affairs, & adopt such action in the premises as they may think, might be useful, & have given the subject all the consideration to which it is entitled. . . . I regret however, to be obliged to say, that after the most careful consideration of the subject in all its bearings, I have not been able to repress the serious doubts I entertain in regard to the practicability of making a volunteer movement of that description, on our part, with such action in the matter as we might think allowable.

. . . But it does not follow . . . that views of the subject imbibed by one, who, like myself, have been longest out of public life, & more completely excluded from all connection with public affairs than any of his associates, will also prove to be those of the rest of the Ex Presidents . . . The belief that such is the case [the suggestion that Van Buren assume the duties of a chairman] can only have arisen from the erroneous supposition that I was entitled to precedence in such matters, on account of my being the Senior Ex President—while in truth, that distinction, as far as it goes, is, according to the opinions of those most conversant in such matters, accorded to the individual of the class, who was the latest incumbent of the principal office. But this is a matter which may, I think, had better, be entirely laid out of view, & all the Ex Presidents regarded, in that respect, as standing on the same footing. If then you, who entertain more hopeful expectations upon the point, continue to think the proposed call, free from the embarrassment under which I labor, or either of our associates, who entertain similar views to your own, shall deem such a call expedient, & ask my attendance, I will accept the invitation without hesitation, & comply with the request it contains, if it be in my power to do so. . . .

Pierce is sufficiently schooled in the language of diplomacy to know that the qualification, "if it be in my power to do so," signifies that Van Buren will plead his inability to attend if Buchanan or another issues the call. When a Philadelphia correspondent urges him to reconsider, Van Buren replies that his mind is unchanged, and that there is a growing disposition in New York—the stronghold of pro-slavery sentiment in the North —to support the Administration. Three weeks later Van Buren makes the same response to a friend in the West. The issue is not to be decided by diplomats, but by grim warriors amidst

". . . blood
And darkness and the barrows of the slain."

To circumvent the work of the Hard Shells, Prince John and other War Democrats address meetings nightly throughout the State. To a war meeting at Kinderhook, Van Buren, unable to attend because of a sudden recurrence of his malady, sends a message to support the Administration. In obedience to the counsel of his physicians he avoids all strenuous exercise. He misses the daily canter to the village and around the farm. The war is entering into its ninth month when he celebrates his seventy ninth birthday. In spite of his illness, he manages to put in a little time occasionally on his manuscript.

In the early part of 1862 he is well enough to go to New York. There, the most noted physician of his day, Dr. Alonzo Clark, treats him from early in March to late in May. Many of his old friends visit him. One is a Clintonian, Azariah Cutting Flagg, who served as Secretary of State under De Witt Clinton. Flagg is led into Van Buren's room. Flagg has been sightless for two years, but this does not prevent his philanthropic work from continuing, nor dim the ardor of his support of the war.

When Van Buren returns to Kinderhook, his plowed fields are green with young life. After resting from the journey he writes to Flagg:

May 28/62

My Dear Sir,

I had hoped to be able to return in person, before I left the City, the visit with which you honored me notwithstanding your unhappy condition; but the state of my health continues to render that gratification impracticable.

Thus driven to the necessity of taking leave in this way, probably for ever, of yourself and your amiable & excellent family and of expressing my earnest wish for the happiness of you all, I must notwithstanding the trespass I fear I will commit on that modest bearing and personal reserve by which your whole political and official career has been so signally characterized, avail myself of the not unfitting occasion to express the opinion with which the latter has impressed one under whose observation so much of it has been exhibited.

With those to any considerable extent acquainted with my own public life, I need not I think fear being thought assuming in making the declaration that there are few still amongst us who have enjoyed a wider and closer intercourse with public functionaries, State & National, during the last half century, or possessed better opportunity to witness their action than myself. With an experience thus enlarged I feel that I can repeat here an opinion which I have often conscientiously expressed elsewhere, that I never met in any branch of the

Public Service a single man who more invariably entered upon the
discharge of the duties entrusted to his management with views more
exclusively devoted to the promotion of the public interest or who
labored with a purer or more disinterested zeal for their advancement
than yourself.

As ever your friend
M. Van Buren

A. C. Flagg, Esquire.

All through June he remains in his room on the second floor.
This was the sleeping chamber of Billy Van Ness's father. Two
windows face the south; and two others catch the rays of the
rising sun. On days when he is not too weak he sits in an easy
chair covered with chintz. Against the southern wall, between the
valanced windows, stands a large wardrobe with a mirror door.
The sleigh-bed, of the same warm-toned mahogany from which
the rest of the furniture is fashioned, is flanked on either side by
a plain chest of drawers. On one of these is an unframed portrait of Silas Wright. It is small; and of the type our early
artists called a cabinet. On top of the other is a Bible. In the
center of the windowless west wall hangs an illuminated tribute
to Jackson. On either side of this memento of his friend is a sil-
houette of Van Buren. These, too, are simply framed. A shaving
stand occupies a corner. Small rugs, woven of vari-colored rags,
and three fiddle-back chairs, with seats of gray horse-hair, complete the furnishings.

About the middle of July Smith wrote to Prince John and
Abraham to hasten to Lindenwald. When they arrived Van
Buren bade his three sons farewell. Shortly after he lost consciousness; and on Thursday morning, July 24, at nine o'clock, he
became one of the nation's glorious dead.

For three days his neighbors and friends from various parts
of the State entered the big hall where Van Buren lay in a simple
rosewood coffin, his feet to the opened half-door. A small silver
plate had graven upon it: "Martin Van Buren. Died July 24,
1862, aged 79 years, 7 months, 19 days." On the third day the
Reverend J. Romeyn Berry offered prayer beside the bier. Then
some of Van Buren's townsmen lifted the coffin on their shoulders
and carried it to the village hearse which was drawn up to the
porch. In one of the first of the eighty-one carriages rode Edwin

MARTIN VAN BUREN

From a photograph owned by
Ellen Van Buren Pell

(The last photograph,
taken in 1862)

Morgan, Governor of the State; the Tildens were close behind. In some of the others were members of the Common Council of the cities of Troy, Albany, Hudson, and New York, and a deputation from Tammany. Hundreds followed on foot.

In accordance with Van Buren's wishes, there was no ringing of bells, and no music, save the hymn, "O God Our Help in Ages Past." His old friend, Dr. Alonzo Potter, now the Episcopal Bishop of Pennsylvania, and the Reverend Benjamin Van Zandt, the former pastor of the church, occupied the pulpit. The Stars and Stripes was draped on the altar. After Dominie Van Zandt said the closing prayer, the coffin was borne past the only empty pew: this was draped with black crape. From the church the procession to the cemetery was led by the red-shirted members of the Kinderhook Fire Engine Company. Most of the firemen were old: these had taken the places of those who had joined the colors. Bishop Potter read the Burial Office of the Episcopal Church. When the casket was being lowered into the grave, cannon thundered throughout the land. Some of these became silent, in accordance with Lincoln's proclamation, after they had fired a Presidential salute to the memory of Martin Van Buren. Others thundered on until the ideal for which he had unselfishly striven was a reality.

FINIS

BIBLIOGRAPHY

Adams, Charles Francis (Edited by). *Memoirs of John Quincy Adams, Comprising Portions of His Diary from 1795 to 1848*. 12 volumes. Philadelphia: J. B. Lippincott & Co. 1875.

Barnes, Thurlow Weed. *Memoir of Thurlow Weed*. Boston: Houghton-Mifflin & Co. 1884.

Beardsley, Levi, Late of the New York Senate and President Thereof. *Reminiscences, Personal and Other Incidents, etc*. New York: Charles Vinten, 1852.

[Benton, Thomas Hart.] *Thirty Years' View, etc*. 2 volumes. New York: Appleton and Company, 1856.

Bigelow, John. *Letters and Literary Memorials of Samuel J. Tilden*. 2 volumes. New York and London: Harper & Brothers, 1908.

Bigelow, John. *Retrospections of an Active Life*. 3 volumes. The Baker & Taylor Co., 1909.

Bigelow, John (Edited by). *The Writings and Speeches of Samuel J. Tilden*. 2 volumes. New York: Harper & Brothers, 1885.

Bonney, Mrs. Catharine V[an] R[ensselaer] (Compiled by). *A Legacy of Historical Gleanings*. 2 volumes. Albany: J. Munsell, 1875.

Bowers, Claude G. *The Party Battles of the Jackson Period*. Chautauqua, New York: The Chautauqua Press, 1923.

Bradbury, Mrs. Anna R. *History of the City of Hudson, New York, etc*. Hudson, New York: Record Printing and Publishing Company, 1908.

Bradford, Alden. *History of the Federal Government, etc*. Boston: Samuel G. Simpkins, 1840.

Byrdsall, F. *The History of the Loco Foco or Equal Rights Party, etc*. New York: Clement & Packard, 1842.

Carlyle, Thomas. *Chartism*. Boston: C. C. Little & J. Brown, 1840.

Carter, Nathaniel H., and William L. Stone, Reporters; and Marcus T. C. Gould, Stenographer. *Reports of the Proceedings and Debates of the Convention of 1821, Assembled for the Purpose of Amending the Constitution of the State of New York, etc*. Albany: E. and E. Hosford, 1821.

[Clinton, De Witt.] *Letters on the Natural History and Internal Resources of the State of New York*. By *Hibernicus*. New York: E. Bliss & E. White, 1822.

Colton, Calvin (Edited by). *The Private Correspondence of Henry Clay*. New York: A. S. Barnes & Co., 1855.

Columbia County at the End of the Century—A Historical Record of Its Foundation, etc. 2 volumes. Hudson, New York: The Record Printing and Publishing Company, 1900.

Columbia County, New York, History of, With Illustrations and Biographical Sketches, etc. Philadelphia: Everts & Ensign, 1878.

Collier, Edward A., D.D. *A History of Old Kinderhook, etc*. New York and London: G. P. Putnam's Sons, 1914.

Curtis, George Ticknor. *Life of Daniel Webster*. 2 volumes. New York: D. Appleton and Company, 1870.

[Cutts, L. B.]*Memoirs and Letters of Dolly Madison, etc*. Edited by Her Grand-Niece. Boston: Houghton-Mifflin & Co., 1886.

Dix, Morgan (Compiled by). *Memoirs of John Adams Dix*. 2 volumes. New York: Harper & Brothers, 1883.

Dwight, Theodore (Secretary of the Hartford Convention). *History of the Hartford Convention, etc.* New York: N. & J. White; Boston: Russell, Odiorne & Co., 1883.

Fernow, Berthold (Compiled and Edited by). *Calendar of Wills on File and Records in the Office of the Clerk of the Court of Appeals, of the County Clerk at Albany, and of the Secretary of State: 1626-1836.* New York: Colonial Dames of the State of New York, 1896.

Forney, John W. *Anecdotes of Public Men While He Was Clerk of the House of Representatives, Secretary of the Senate of the United States, etc.* 2 volumes. New York: Harper & Brothers, 1881.

Gallatin, Count (Edited by). *The Diary of James Gallatin, Secretary to Albert Gallatin, a Great Peace Maker: 1813-1827. With an Introduction by Viscount Bryce.* New York: Charles Scribner's Sons, 1916.

Glenn, Thomas Allen, *Some Colonial Mansions and Those Who Lived in Them, With Genealogies, etc.* Philadelphia: Henry Coates & Company, 1898.

Glenn, Thomas Allen. (Same title and publisher as preceding.) Second Series. 1900.

Greeley, Horace. *Recollections of a Busy Life, etc.* New York: J. B. Ford & Co., 1869.

Hall, Benjamin F. *The Republican Party, etc.* New York and Auburn: Miller, Orton and Mulligan, 1856.

Hammond, Jabez D. *The History of Political Parties in the State of New York, etc.* 2 volumes, Albany: C. Van Benthuysen, 1842.

Holloway, Laura C. *The Ladies of the White House, etc.* Philadelphia: Bradley & Company; Boston: R. H. Curran & Company, 1882.

Hopkins, James H. *A History of Political Parties in the United States, etc.* New York and London: G. P. Putnam's Sons, 1900.

Hosack, David. *Memoir of De Witt Clinton: With an Appendix Containing Numerous Documents, etc.* New York: J. Seymour, 1829.

Howe, M. A. De Wolfe. *The Life and Letters of George Bancroft.* 2 volumes. New York: Charles Scribner's Sons, 1908.

Hunt, Charles Havens. *Life of Edward Livingston. With an Introduction by George Bancroft.* New York: D. Appleton and Company, 1864.

Jephson, Henry. *The Platform—Its Rise and\Progress.* 2 volumes. New York: Macmillan and Co., 1892.

Kent, Frank R. *The Democratic Party—A History.* New York: The Century Company, 1928.

Kent, William. *Memoirs and Letters of James Kent, LL.D., Late Chancellor, etc.* Boston: Little Brown, and Company, 1898.

King, Charles R. (Edited by). *The Life and Correspondence of Rufus King, etc.* 6 volumes. New York: G. P. Putnam's Sons, 1900.

Lee, Robert E. *Memoirs of the War in the Southern Department of the United States, by Henry Lee, Lt. Col. of the Partisan Legion During the American War, A New Edition with Revisions and a Biography of the Author by Robert E. Lee.* New York: University Publishing Company, 1869.

McGrane, Reginald C. (Edited by). *The Correspondence of Nicholas Biddle, Dealing With National Affairs, 1807-1844.* Boston: Houghton-Mifflin & Co., 1919.

Martineau, Harriett. *Retrospect of Western Travel.* London: Saunders and Otley, New York: Sold by Harper & Brothers, 1838.

Martineau, Harriett. *Society in America.* 3 volumes. London: Saunders and Otley, 1839.

Morley, John. *The Life of Richard Cobden.* 2 volumes. London: Chapman & Hall, 1881.

Munsell, Joel. *The Annals of Albany.* 10 volumes. Albany: Joel Munsell, 1869.

Myers, Gustavus. *The History of Tammany Hall.* New York: Boni and Liveright, 1917.

Myers, William Starr. *The Republican Party—A History*. New York: The Century Co., 1928.

Ogden, Rollo (Edited by). *Life and Letters of Edwin Lawrence Godkin*. 2 volumes. New York: The Macmillan Company, 1907.

Pearson, Jonathan. *Contributions for the Genealogies of the First Settlers of the Ancient County of Albany from 1630 to 1800*. Albany: Joel Munsell, 1872.

Pearson, Jonathan. *Early Records of the City and County of Albany and Colony of Rensselaerswyck, 1656-1675; Translated from the Original Dutch With Notes*. Albany: Joel Munsell, 1869.

Phillips, William. *The Conquest of Kansas by Missouri and Her Allies, etc.* Boston: Phillips, Sampson and Company, 1856.

Quincy, Josiah. *Memoir of the Life of John Quincy Adams*. Boston: Phillips, Samson and Company, 1859.

Robinson, Sara T. L. *Kansas; Its Interior and Exterior Life, etc.* Boston: Crosby, Nichols and Company, 1856.

Sargent, Epes, and Horace Greeley. *The Life and Public Services of Henry Clay, etc.* New York: C. M. Saxton, Barker & Co., 1859.

[Scott, Winfield.] *Memoirs of Lieut.-General Scott, LL.D. Written by Himself*. New York: Sheldon & Company, 1864.

Stanwood, Edward. *A History of Presidential Elections*. Boston and New York: Houghton-Mifflin and Co., 1892.

Tuckerman, Bayard (Edited by). *The Diary of Philip Hone, 1828-1851*. 2 volumes. New York: Dodd Mead and Company, 1889.

Tyler, Samuel. *Memoir of Roger Brooke Taney*. Baltimore: John Murray & Co., 1872.

[Van Buren, Abraham and Smith Thompson, Editors.] *Inquiry Into the Origin and Course of Political Parties in the United States. By the Late ex-President Martin Van Buren. Edited by his sons* (Prince John had died the preceding year). New York: Published by Hurd and Houghton, 1867.

van Laer, A. J. F. (Translated and edited by). *Van Rensselaer Bowier Manuscripts, Being the Letters of Kiliaen Van Rensselaer, 1630-1643, and Other Documents Relating to the Colony of Rensselaerswyck. With an Introductory Essay by Nicolaas de Roever, late Archivist of the City of Amsterdam*. Albany: University of the State of New York, 1908.

Walsh, Robert, Jr. *An Appeal from the Judgments of Great Britain Respecting the United States of America, etc.* Second Edition. Philadelphia: Mitchell, Ames, and White, 1819.

Watson, John F. *Annals of Philadelphia and Pennsylvania in the Olden Time, etc.* 2 volumes. Philadelphia: Whiting and Thomas, 1856-7.

Weed, Harriet A. (Edited by). *Autobiography of Thurlow Weed*. Boston: Houghton-Mifflin and Co., 1883.

Wise, Henry A. *Seven Decades of The Union. The Humanities and Materialism, Illustrated by a Memoir of John Tyler, etc.* Philadelphia: J. B. Lippincott & Co., 1876.

A COMPLETE LIST OF BOOKS ON VAN BUREN

Bancroft, George. *Van Buren to the End of His Public Career*. New York: Harper & Brothers, 1889. This work, intended as a campaign pamphlet, was written in 1844. It is typical of its kind: it is a distortion and perversion of the record. (*Vide* 221 *et seq.* of *An Epoch and a Man*.) Bancroft's production was not published until 1889, when the author was in his eighty-ninth year. Bancroft's age explains its appearance forty-five years after he had spent a week in compiling it (*vide* his letter to Van Buren of June 14, 1844).

Butler, William Allen. *Martin Van Buren: Lawyer, Statesman and Man.*
New York: D. Appleton and Company, 1862. In this memorial booklet of
forty-seven pages, appropriately bound in black, the son of the law
partner of Van Buren presents a scholarly sketch of his subject.

Crockett, David, *The Life of Martin Van Buren, Heir-Apparent to the "Gov-
ernment," and the Appointed Successor of General Andrew Jackson. Con-
taining Every Authentic Particular by Which His Character Has Been
Formed. With Concise History, etc.* Philadelphia: Robert Wright, 1835.
A scurrilous campaign "life," largely untrue, designed to aid the pre-
convention candidacy of Crockett's friend and fellow Tennesseean, Hugh
L. White, one of Van Buren's rivals for the Presidential nomination.
The book is not without its amusing side.

Emmons, William (Compiled and Edited by). *Biography of Martin Van
Buren, Vice President of the United States. With an appendix containing
selections From His Writings, Including his Speeches in the Senate of
the United States on the Claims of the Soldiers of the Revolution, and
in Favor of Abolishing Imprisonment for Debt—With Other Documents,
Among which Will Be Found the Late Letter of Colonel Thos. Hart
Benton, to the Convention of the State of Mississippi.* Washington: Jacob
Gideon, Jr., 1835. A friendly campaign "life" of Van Buren.

Fitzpatrick, John C. (Edited by). *Annual Report of the American Historical
Association for the Year 1918. Vol. II. The Autobiography of Martin
Van Buren.* Washington: Government Printing Office, 1920. This memoir
of Van Buren's political career was never finished. He recites but one incident of his youth, which was one of hardships. *Vide* 527 of *An Epoch
and a Man.* It describes, at times, with a refreshing frankness, some of
his political struggles. He began to write these memoirs in his seventy-
first year.

Grund, Franz J[osef]. *Martin Van Buren als Staatsmann und Kunstiger
Präsident der Vereinigten Staaten von Nord-Amerika.* Boston: (publisher's name omitted), 1835. This untruthful partisan appeal of twenty-
nine pages is solemnly described as a biography in *Appleton's Cyclopædia
of American Biography.* To win votes of men of German birth or ex-
traction, Grund makes Van Buren "a son of truth-loving people of
German descent;" and elsewhere the irresponsible Grund speaks of Van
Buren as a man "of German ancestry, with a German heart, and of
German thought"—*von deutscher abkunft, mit deutschem herzen und
deutschem sinn.*

Holland, William M. *The Life and Political Opinions of Martin Van Buren,
Vice President of the United States.* Hartford: Belknap & Hammersley,
1835. This is a voluminous campaign document; and while silent on
events which would not add to the political stature of Van Buren, it is
truthful in so far as it goes. Typical of the omissions is Holland's
silence on the tavern at Kinderhook.

Irelan, John Robert, *The Republic; or a History of the United States of
America in the Administrations, from the Monarchic Colonial Days to
the Present Times.* 18 volumes. Chicago: Fairbanks and Palmer, 1887.
Volume III bears the sub-title: *History of the Life, Administration, and
Times of Martin Van Buren, Eighth President of the United States.
Seven Years' Seminole War, and Period of Great Financial Convulsions.*
Save the first eight pages, which deal with Van Buren's ancestry and
youth, and the last chapter, which considers his retirement, the book
treats largely of Van Buren's public career in Washington. The author
is impartial and sympathetic.

M'Elhiney, Thomas. *Life of Martin Van Buren.* Pittsburgh: J. T. Shryock,
1853. An inane pamphlet. The author vainly attempted to enlist Van
Buren's aid in obtaining a place in the Cabinet under Pierce.

Mackenzie, William L[yon]. *The Life and Times of Martin Van Buren: The*

Correspondence of His Friends, Family and Pupils; Together with Brief Notices, Sketches, and Anecdotes Illustrative of the Public Career of (here follow the names of fifty-one politicians and statesmen). Boston: Cooke & Co., 1846. A noxious mixture of truths, half-truths, and scurrilous fictions. This is an elaboration of an earlier pamphlet sponsored by the Polk Administration.

Mackienzie [*sic!*], William L. *The Lives and Opinions of Benjamin Franklin Butler, etc.* Boston: Cooke & Co., 1845. For Mackenzie's motives *vide* 501 *et seq.* of *An Epoch and a Man.*

Peckham, H. C. Waite Van B[uren]. *History of Cornelius Maessen Van Buren.* New York: Tobias Wright, 1913. A genealogy brought down to the present generation.

Shepard, Edward M. *Martin Van Buren.* (American Statesmen Series.) Boston and New York: Houghton-Mifflin and Company, 1888. Shepard deliberately suppresses much that would reflect on "the tangled skein of New York politics" in which he himself put a snarl or two. In an attempt to appear impartial in this self-serving volume, Shepard accepts the ridiculous gold spoon story. This, if true, would reflect on Van Buren. But Shepard systematically suppresses all incidents reflecting on the organization which nominated him for Mayor of New York City in 1901. Shepard was a son of Lorenzo B. Shepard, a Grand Sachem of Tammany Hall.

Stoddard, William O. *Andrew Jackson and Martin Van Buren.* (The Lives of the Presidents Series by Stoddard.) New York: Frederick A. Stokes, 1887. The author makes no pretense to present more than a hurried sketch which is embraced in the last nine chapters.

No attempt has been made to enumerate the numerous pamphlets read in the preparation of this work. Nor is there a complete listing of the memoirs and lives consulted: only those which have been used as sources are mentioned. Newspapers, periodicals and pamphlets which have been productive are indicated in the text: the same is true of public documents and other source material.

INDEX

Adams, Charles Francis, Free Soil nominee for Vice President, 516; Republican Convention, at, 532.

Adams, John, 307, 450.

Adams, John Quincy, first Presidential campaign, 229 *et seq.;* House of Representatives, in, 376 *et seq.;* how a prayer elected him President, 279-281; offers British mission to Clinton, 281; offers Secretaryship of State to Clinton before naming Clay, 281; peace envoy, 139; silent under scurrilous attacks, 312; when the House sought his leadership, 440.

Albany Regency, its leaders hanged and burned in effigy, 266.

Allen, Peter, 146, 147.

Allen, Stephen, 501.

Allen, William, 442, 469.

Ambrister, Robert, 336.

American Party, bolters nominate John C. Frémont for President, 531; splits old parties, 530.

Anti-Clintonians, 142 *et seq.*

Anti-Masonic Party national convention, 347; its genesis, 314, 315; State convention, 320.

Arbuthnot, Alexander, 336.

Aristides (*see* William P. Van Ness.)

Armstrong, John, 52, 56, 110.

Astor, John Jacob, 256, 257.

Astor, William B., valet hired for Van Buren, 329.

Bancroft, George, advice to Van Buren, 483; appoints Nathaniel Hawthorne to office, 416; Baltimore Convention, at, 490; distorts history for politics, 221, 223, 227; Secretary of Navy, 498; tries persuasion on Van Buren, 499.

Bank of America, 126 *et seq.*

Bank of United States, 88; buys Bennett, 370; collapses, 441, 442; corruptly uses money in elections, 359, 360; feeds the multitude, 375; far-reaching powers, 304; Jackson on

Bank of United States (*continued*) its control of the Government, 372; Jefferson on, 262, 263; manufacturing public opinion, 372, 373.

Barker, Jacob, 144, 198.

Barnburners, 501, 505, 506.

Barney, William, Major, 97, 98.

Barry, William T., 325, 331.

Bayard, William, 148.

Beardsley, Levi, 35.

Bellona, La (*see* Mrs. John H. Eaton.)

Bennett, James Gordon, as a blackmailer, 369, 370; assails Lincoln, 540; impudence of, 437.

Benton, Mortimer C., 500.

Benton, Thomas Hart, 254, 294-298, 379.

Berrien, John M., 331.

Berry, Rev. J. Romeyn, 544.

Beverly, Carter, 311.

Biddle, Nicholas, Bryant on, 483; called "Czar Nicholas," 358; indicted for conspiracy to rob, 478; Van Buren's coldness to, 408.

Bidwell, M. S., 417.

Bigelow, John, 447.

Binns, John, rouses fellow Irish, 268.

Birney, James G., nominated for President, 460, 494.

Blair, Francis Preston, Clay to, 277; corresponds with Van Buren, 523 *et seq.;* fears Buchanan will truckle to South, 536; heads Jackson's editorial corps, 357.

Blair, Francis Preston, Jr., 537.

Blair, Mrs. Francis Preston, sends Van Buren brandied peaches, 523.

Bleecker, Harmanus, 238.

Bloemingdael, Maes, 23.

Bogardus, Everardus, Rev., 19.

Boughton, Smith A., 500.

Botts, John Minor, 480.

Bouck, William C., 479.

Bovay, Alvan, 529.

Bradley's Boarding House, 245.

Bradford, Gamaliel, 93.

Branch, John, 331.

Van Ness, William P., author of anti-Livingston pamphlet, 51; Burr's affection for, 48; evades election law, 73; intrigues for Senatorship, 85-88; seeks Van Buren's aid, after Burr-Hamilton duel, 64, 65; law student of Edward Livingston, 39.

Van Ness, William W., 126, 194, 213, 219.

Van Rensselaer, Jacob Rutsen, 79-81, 213.

Van Rensselaer, Rensselaer, commander of revolting Canadians, 416 *et seq.;* his arrest, 419.

Van Rensselaer, Solomon, 161, 205, 208, 211, 229-234, 324, 325, 425, 426.

Van Rensselaer, Stephen, 37, 42, 70, 105 *et seq.,* 215, 275, 279-281.

Van Schaack, Peter, challenges Van Buren's vote, 63; home at Kinderhook, 29; retires in favor of Van Buren, 70; Van Buren's last visit to, 358, 359.

Van Twiller, Wouter, Governor of New Netherlands, 16, 21.

Van Zandt, Rev. Benjamin, 545.

Varian, Isaac L., 430.

Vaughan, Sir Charles R., Van Buren's relations with, 330, 331, 334.

Verbeeck, Jan, 22.

Verplanck, Gulian C., 142, 240.

Virginia Dynasty, 70, 172, 253, 255.

Wadsworth, James S., 493, 506, 514.

Waldo, Daniel, 137.

War of 1812, opposition to, 93 *et seq.*

Warfield, Peregrine, 94, 98, 99.

Washington, George, 33, 511.

Webster, Daniel, 40, 129; Adams on, 482; nominated for President, 381;

Webster, Daniel (*continued*) on civil war, 130.

Weed, Thurlow, 124, 477, 530.

Wellington, Duke of, 421.

West India Company, 16.

Westmorland, Countess of, 448.

Whallon, Ruben, 80.

White, Hugh Lawson, nominated for President, 381; what he did when defeated, 420.

White, Joseph L., 325.

Williams, Elisha, 36, 40, 66, 79, 80, 129, 213; defies government, 115; on *vox populi vox dei,* 220, 221.

Williams, John, 237.

Williams, Lewis, 440.

Wilkins, William, 361.

Willet, Marinus, 72.

Willis, W. P., 400.

Wilmot, David, 503, 505.

Wilmot Proviso, 503 *et seq.*

Wilson, Isaac, 163.

Windisch Gratz, Prince, 421.

Wirt, William, 347.

Wise, Henry A., 439-441; on the Tyler impeachment, 480.

Wolseley, Sir Charles, 189.

Wood, Bradford R., 524.

Woodbury, Levi, 405.

Woodworth, John, 242.

Woodworth, Samuel, 134.

Worth, Graham A., 198, 199.

Worth, William J., 503.

Wright, Silas, 266, 307, 361, 366, 477, 489, 501; declines Vice Presidential nomination, 491, 492.

Wynkoop, Augustus, 526.

Yankee, derivation of, 87.

Yates, Henry, Jr., 163.

Yates, Joseph C., 151, 156, 238.

Young, Samuel, 137, 206, 219.